"This book presents a persuasive case that you don't have to choose between virtue and success: it's possible to be both a good leader and a great leader."

—Adam Grant, *New York Times* bestselling author of
Originals and *Give and Take*, and coauthor of *Option B*

"The noble profession of business has never been under more intense criticism than we face today despite the existence of more laws and regulations. *Exception to the Rule* presents a compelling case for the return to a marketplace inspired by a commitment to virtues rather than rules while recognizing the rule of law can't be ignored. The reader comes away from this book with an inspiring urgency to examine personal leadership styles and practices."

—Steve Reinemund, Retired Chairman and CEO, PepsiCo,
and Former Dean of Business, Wake Forest University

"Rea, Stoller and Kolp offer a compass to leaders like me who strive to create a high performing culture that is also a meaningful and fulfilling place to work without compromising values. Having spent my life in the results driven business of professional sports, Peter and Alan have always inspired me to continue to build cultures founded on values similar to the virtues. This most recent work is comprehensive and provides supportive evidence that sustained success models exist. I highly recommend *Exception to the Rule* for leaders looking for guidance, inspiration or reinforcement in the journey to create a values driven organization that performs at elite levels."

—Mark A. Shapiro, President and CEO,
Toronto Blue Jays Baseball Club

"There's no way to over-emphasize the importance of virtue in daily life and business. *Exception to the Rule* first treats us to stories that inspire us to be virtuous. Then the text backs up those stories with compelling data to prove the business case for virtuous corporate leadership. Finally, and perhaps most provocatively, the authors propose that practicing virtue must apply to self and *all* others. Quite a challenge—but a worthy one! That's virtue. Read the book, then become the exception."

—Jack Hoban, retired Marine Corps Captain who helped create
the Marines Martial Arts Program and author of *Ethical Warrior*

"This book challenges the reader to understand the *limitations of rules*. Focus on virtues, instead, to see the risks of slippery roads and pitfalls. Mistakes are common and acceptable. They are not failures, if they lead to better and stronger leadership. Once more in their new book with Jamie as a new partner, Alan and Peter spoil us with many stories and techniques *to remember*."

—Pierre Jean Everaert,
Chairman Emeritus, Anheuser-Busch InBev

"I was delighted to read this work, which captures the authors' deep experience and many years of teaching of leadership. *Exception to the Rule* offers unique, practical principles of leadership which we have fully embraced in the Instituto Cardiovascular de Buenos Aires. The clarity of the book, nicely captured in the iconic metaphor of the Parthenon and pillars of the supporting virtues, and the emphasis on culture and leadership character recommend it highly. I congratulate the authors!"

—Jorge Belardi, M.D., Chief Executive Officer, Instituto
Cardiovascular de Buenos Aires, Argentina

"At the Cleveland Clinic, we observed a simple and important result when teams practiced ideas detailed in *Exception to the Rule*. Virtue encourages prosocial behavior, which strengthens engagement and teamwork. Rules are designed for a fixed world. Virtue unites caregivers to navigate a rapidly changing health care world."

—Brian Donley, M.D.,
Chief of Staff, Cleveland Clinic

"Parker Hannifin is a Fortune 200 public company. Parker invested in the ideas described in *Exception to the Rule* to preserve our reputation and to protect our financial strength. The virtues provided us with a common language to protect our culture as a competitive advantage. Our evidence revealed a strength-based approach to applying the virtues increased engagement and teamwork. Among the most fascinating insights from this work is that the virtues were universally embraced by our 50,000 people operating in 50 nations. Our people want to practice virtue not because they have to, but because they want to."

—Jon Marten, Chief Financial Officer,
Parker Hannifin, 2010–2017

"Since we have been practicing the seven classical virtues with our team in China, we have noticed improved working relationships and collaborations, which increases our resilience as a team. Trust and compassion are also more pronounced, even as we've had to take on difficult circumstances/challenges over the last couple of years. Clearly, we're journeying on and sincerely hope that as a leadership team, we will continue to positively impact our colleagues, customers and stakeholders by putting these virtues into action."

—Michael Wee, Country Leader, Greater China, Parker Hannifin

EXCEPTION
TO THE
RULE

EXCEPTION
TO THE
RULE

The Surprising Science of
Character-Based Culture,
Engagement, and Performance

PETER J. REA, PhD
JAMES K. STOLLER, MD, MS
ALAN KOLP, PhD

New York   Chicago   San Francisco   Lisbon   Athens   London
Madrid   Mexico City   Milan   New Delhi   San Juan   Seoul
Singapore   Sydney   Toronto

1 2 3 4 5 6 7 8 9 LCR 22 21 20 19 18 17

ISBN 978-1-260-02683-2
MHID 1-260-02683-3

e-ISBN 978-1-260-02684-9
e-MHID 1-260-02684-1

CIP information is on file for this book at the Library of Congress

McGraw-Hill Education books are available at special quantity discounts to use as premiums and sales promotions or for use in corporate training programs. To contact a representative, please visit the Contact Us pages at www.mhprofessional.com.

CONTENTS

Acknowledgments   xi

Introduction   1

CHAPTER 1: Trust   23

CHAPTER 2: Compassion   45

CHAPTER 3: Courage   73

CHAPTER 4: Justice   101

CHAPTER 5: Wisdom   129

CHAPTER 6: Temperance   159

CHAPTER 7: Hope   195

CHAPTER 8: Integrity—A Growth Market   215

CHAPTER 9: Classical Solutions to Contemporary Challenges   235

Epilogue and Takeaways   253

Endnotes   261

Index   281

ACKNOWLEDGMENTS

Parker Hannifin, the global leader in motion and control technologies, strives to preserve its culture as a competitive advantage. Jon Marten, the chief financial officer of a Fortune 500 company with annual sales of $13 billion, envisioned that an investment in practicing virtue comes back, with interest. The presence of virtue helps protect a balance sheet. Imagine that.

We are indebted to Cathy Suever, the Chief Financial Officer; Andy Ross, Group President; and Kevin Ruffer, Group Human Resource Leader, all of whom were instrumental in exporting the virtues to the 50 nations in which Parker operates. Tom Williams, our Chief Executive Officer, and Lee Banks, our President and Chief Operations Officer, have been incredibly supportive. The practical application of virtue was strengthened significantly by the creativity and commitment of Tanya Malone, the Manager of Integrity and Ethics.

The Cleveland Clinic has been an especially thoughtful partner. Clinic leaders Dr. Brian Donley, Chief of Staff, and Ann Huston, Chief Strategy Officer, have been good friends and constructive sounding boards. At the Clinic, "patients first" and "world class care" are not just taglines but truly reflect the way medicine is practiced at this remarkable institution.

President Emeritus Dick Durst and President Robert Helmer supported Alan Kolp's role as NCAA Faculty Athletics Representative at Baldwin Wallace University. We are appreciative of Kris Diaz, Athletic Director, and the entire Baldwin Wallace coaching staff for actively applying our virtue-based leadership model. The coaches' commitment to teaching virtue means hundreds of student athletes learned and now enact character-based leadership on their teams and in their lives. Lacey Kogelnik, Director of Baldwin Wallace's Center for Innovation and Growth, continues to make the seven virtues the heart of the Center's mission to infuse entrepreneurial thinking across campus. Additionally, Lacey supported the writing and editing of this book. We also offer thanks to Carrie Drozdz for helping with edits and footnotes.

We are deeply appreciative of McGraw-Hill's support to manage, edit, and produce the book. Special thanks go to Scott Grillo and to Donya Dickerson, whose editing and support strengthened the content and its clarity.

Peter's wife, Julie, was vital throughout the editing process. No one could be more supportive and more accepting of a husband's imperfections. His sons, Scott and David, and daughters-in-law, Lisa and Hanna, all demonstrate that millennials practice virtue quite well.

Jamie's wife, Terry, offered thoughtful guidance and input as always. Her support and indulgence are bedrock for this and all his work. His son, Jake, provides the "why" for this work. His journey to grow is inspiring for the future. Jamie dedicates the book to the memory of his parents, Alfred and Norma Stoller, who created an appetite for virtue and achievement.

Alan's wife, Letitia, stood behind another long-term book project. His two daughters, Felicity Kolp, International Finance Corporation (World Bank), and Christina Kolp, University Hospitals, continue to be a source of encouragement as daughters, mothers, and professionals. He wrote the book for his daughters' offspring and his grandchildren, Sienna Kolp West, Logan Kolp West, and Eva Zarate Kolp.

We have learned how soldiers, athletes, astronauts, students, leaders, and physicians practice their own version of virtue. We have been the beneficiaries of thousands of leaders, from San Diego to Stuttgart to Shanghai, who practice virtue in ways that add value. We have learned that the difference between who we are today and who we were five years ago is largely a matter of how well we practice virtuous habits. We have learned that it is possible to be both imperfect and good.

Finally, while this book is the product of our learning from many and while we have strived to "aim at the good," we acknowledge that any oversights or errors in these pages are solely ours.

Introduction

Thomas Merton said, "We might spend our whole life climbing the ladder of success, only to find that when we get to the top, our ladder is leaning against the wrong wall."[1] Practicing virtue leans us against the right wall. The seven classical virtues of trust, compassion, courage, justice, wisdom, temperance, and hope are more than just words. Virtue is the key to any positive relationship including a happy marriage, a sense of purpose, and success in every area of life. What's not to like about a wall like that!

Why the Title of This Book?

Exception to the Rule relies on virtues to help the reader take concrete action to better enhance individual and organizational performance. The virtues point us down a well-worn, 25-century-old path toward excellence, as opposed to the latest management fad. In fact, *virtue* means *"arête"* or "excellence." Virtue is about peak performance.

In a way that is down to earth and actionable, we explore ideas that are often considered abstract. It is a practical book that details an evidence-based approach to driving high performance under pressure in an uncertain world. While rules are designed for a fixed world, virtue provides moorings to navigate a volatile world.

We begin by defining these virtues. Then, because experience with this approach has worked in a Fortune 500 company and a large academic medical center, as well as in many other sectors, we offer examples from business and healthcare leaders who, by embracing these virtues, have changed the cultures of their organizations to drive the outcomes we all seek.

Practicing virtue also helps us in our personal life. People can underestimate how leaning against an unethical wall is destructive not only to others but to ourselves as well. Chronic anger, guilt, and fear drive emotions deep into our brain that can create physical problems. When medicine uses the term *psychosomatic*, it means mental distress which leads to physical distress.[2] Without a sturdy virtue wall to lean against, why bother developing self-control, sacrifice, and service to others?

Virtue: Competitive Advantage or Disadvantage?

Virtue "aims at the good." This means to enhance and protect others, all others, even people outside my team, outside my organization, outside my culture, and even people who are disrespectful toward me. Here is how we do this. We enhance and protect others by practicing trust, compassion, justice, courage, and hope. Importantly, it is not a virtue until we act. Virtuous behavior and leadership require action. This is why we practice wisdom and temperance, which helps make virtue habitual.

Except for an occasional sociopath, everyone wants permission and encouragement to practice virtue. But there is a catch. And it is a really big catch. Perhaps we can readily imagine practicing virtue with our teammates, with people where we work, with patients, and with customers. It is not as easy to imagine practicing virtue when we don't have to. When we have power over suppliers and distributors, they have to do what we say. It is harder still to imagine exhibiting virtue toward people who have treated us disrespectfully. When we reflect on a time when someone treated us with contempt, hard feelings quickly boil up all over again. We can more easily imagine wringing the neck of someone who disrespected us.

It is not without reason that I might want to be virtuous, but not if it puts me at the mercy of an unvirtuous competitor. So it is a pretty tough standard to consider how to execute a business plan that considers employees, customers, investors, suppliers, distributors, and the environment and that, when needed, treats unvirtuous people respectfully. It can seem pretty idealistic to imagine being respectful toward someone who cheats, someone who abuses power, or someone who lies about me.

The Case for Respecting Others

Just as is taught to the U.S. Marines, here are four reasons to at least consider respecting others, even those who do not plan to return the favor! First, when we disrespect others, we are the ones who get hurt. The Marines are on a journey to shift their culture from being killers to being protectors. Physicians specializing in post-traumatic stress disorder (PTSD) for soldiers have uncovered interesting brain imaging data. When soldiers abuse their power, they are the ones who get sick.[3] In the commercial sector, when people make money by dehumanizing others, they might get rich, but we will share data in this book that make it clear that they lead a life that is unfulfilled and isolated, and the odds are increased that they will get sick.

Second, we desperately need a moral compass that does not waver during turbulent times. Yet, if the value and meaning of virtue are not articulated, we risk moral confusion during periods when moral clarity is most needed. The default ethic can quickly become treating people with respect unless you have to hurt others to get ahead or gain a profit. The organizational ethic becomes *do what you have to do.*

Third, when virtue shrinks to only "my team" or "my tribe," then we start our walk down the slippery slope. We best mitigate risk when we take into account the widest possible concern. This does not mean that I will never fire someone, lay someone off, or sue someone. It does mean that I will strive to respect everyone to the best of my imperfect ability.

Fourth, virtue is a sustainable way to compete. Who is more dangerous than a mother bear protecting her cubs? People who are protecting

3

others, who enhance the life of others, are on a mission. They are tough to beat. In the marketplace, just as mothers protecting cubs are tough to beat, caring cultures are also tough to beat.

This is why the virtues are not just nice terms that relate to nice people. Character and virtues move us beyond our personal needs. Teams that practice virtue communicate more effectively with each other and are more willing to share ideas and knowledge. These are teams that effectively execute strategies. One of the clearest benefits of developing virtue in organizations is increased engagement. The reason is simple. Engagement is a function of trusting and meaningful relationships, and relationships are more trusting and meaningful when we practice virtue.

A Volatile, Uncertain, Complex, and Ambiguous (VUCA) World

Building a sturdy virtue wall is achieved by focusing on our convictions rather than our circumstances. Often, circumstances cannot be controlled, but the way we respond can always be controlled. Like virtue, high performance also focuses on what can be controlled. This is why there is much to be gained by learning how high performance is taught to soldiers, athletes, and astronauts. Most of us are not involved in the life and death decisions of a soldier. Few of us understand the anxiety of playing in front of thousands of fans in a stadium and millions of fans on TV the way athletes do. We don't know what it feels like to experience weightlessness. Yet we can learn how to focus on what we can control from the same lessons taught to the soldier, the athlete, and the astronaut.

Here is what soldiers, athletes, and astronauts have in common with all of us: they experience a volatile, uncertain, complex, and ambiguous (VUCA) world. Since turbulence is the new normal, the choice to adapt to instability is not really a choice after all. Instability is our future, though adapting to this new norm is anything but easy.

Oliver Wendell Holmes, Jr., who served on the Supreme Court for the first 30 years of the last century, described the challenges we face this way: "I think that, as life is action and passion, it is required of a man that he should share the passion and action of his time at peril of being judged not to have lived."[4] One way to define the "action of our time" is to ensure high performance under pressure in a VUCA world. People do not have to adapt to VUCA, though as W. Edwards Deming cautioned, "It is not necessary to change. Survival is not mandatory."[5] Organizations that employ soldiers, astronauts, and athletes say up front we expect high performance under pressure before contracts are signed and agreed upon.

VUCA rewards excellence and is harsh on mediocrity. Remember the word *virtue* means "excellence." This is why 2,500-year-old virtues are relevant and useful to innovation. Innovation during uncertain times is best navigated from a secure base. A culture of character is key to creating a secure base.

The intersection of high performance and character is this: Focus on what you can control. Live by conviction not circumstances. When we are able to do this, we lower angst and increase performance.

The military is up front to those who enlist that cadets will be put in harm's way when they voluntarily sign up. They make no apology about their intention to take the cadet up on this offer. At their best, the military teaches soldiers to focus on what they can control, despite the VUCA reality of confrontation or combat. Doing so increases performance and reduces the pressure that comes with deescalating conflicts, or when needed, with fighting.

Professional sports teams make it clear to athletes that they intend to win, and they make no apology for expecting individual athletes to help the team win. At their best, athletes learn to focus on teamwork, tactics, and conditioning to increase the odds that the team will win while reducing the anxiety that can result from the pressure to perform.[6]

NASA hires astronauts who are prepared to be separated from their families for months, or even years, to complete dangerous and uncertain missions that will put their life at risk. NASA also accepts responsibility to prepare astronauts and their families to be resilient so the astronaut can focus fully on the mission.[7]

All profit and nonprofit organizations worth their salt expect high performance under pressure in a VUCA world. But they too owe people a way to cope with this pressure and uncertainty so that they can perform at the level that the organization needs to prosper. Despite pressure and uncertainty, organizations still need to reach or exceed key performance indicators (KPIs). Typical KPIs include superior customer or patient experiences, sustainable growth, and financial metrics, such as increased market share, operating margins, and total shareholder returns. In healthcare, KPIs include ensuring outstanding quality, affordability, and patient safety, while also optimizing the patients' and the caregivers' experiences. This is the "quadruple aim."[8]

Responsible leaders can be tough when holding people accountable to meet or exceed KPIs. They are tough for good reason. They desperately want to avoid layoffs that come with poor financial performance, and they want their organizations to thrive so that people have more opportunity. Sadly, some lead more through coercion and cunning than through caring and character. This type of flawed leadership can work—in the short-term. However, the downside is increasing anxiety, which reduces, rather than increases, sustainable high performance.

What if the organization made clear that virtue was the most important KPI? They might even take expectations further by stating the pressure to perform in the service of others is a privilege. When virtue is internalized this way, it begets engagement, which begets profitability. In other words, market share, operating margin, and share price are by-products of a culture that takes care of their team, their customers, or their patients by practicing virtue. In order to be financially successful, organizations must first take care of others—teams, customers, and patients. Character defined by virtue cannot be legislated, although character *can* be cultivated. A virtue-based culture acts as a silent supervisor to mitigate risk without the unintended consequence of squashing creativity and growth. While the value of virtue-based leadership is well documented, unfortunately the actual practice of character defined by virtue remains the exception to the rule. Rather than benefit from practicing ways to internalize virtue, we more often rely on extrinsic carrots-and-sticks and rules.

Discretionary Effort

As Mark Twain cautioned, "It ain't what you don't know that gets you into trouble. It's what you know for sure that just ain't so."[9] The idea that you can lead either with a carrot or with a stick is what too many people "know for sure that just ain't so." In the 1950s and 1960s, Douglas McGregor named this concept "Theory X," which holds the view that workers are "lazy, dislike and shun work, have to be driven and need both carrots and sticks . . . and have to be looked after."[10] McGregor introduced Theory Y, which disputed the view that "carrots and sticks" improved performance. Theory Y asserted that employers recognize that "people have a psychological need to work and want achievement and responsibility."[11] A half century later, the "know for sure that just ain't so" grip that Theory X rules has on many leaders remains stubbornly resistant to McGregor's research.

Gallup has reported each year for about 10 years that only about a third of a typical workforce is highly engaged.[12] So, if carrots and sticks don't motivate 70 percent of employees, what's going on? Perhaps some people are disengaged because life has tossed them a hard blow and shattered their confidence. Others might be part of a toxic culture and can't rise above teams that are dysfunctional. Maybe some just got a bit too comfortable and complacent. Whether people are forced to play a tough hand dealt by a cruel life or whether people shoot themselves in the foot, it is far from obvious why any of us falls short of our potential.

John Gardner concluded that given time and maturity, people can learn to avoid self-destructive behavior: "You learn that self-pity and resentment are among the most toxic of drugs. You find that the world loves talent but pays off on character."[13] Gardner wrote this in the last century. His point that character pays off is hardly new. About 25 centuries ago, Aristotle made the same point.

Yet, Theory X leadership persists today despite McGregor's research, Gardner's insights, and Aristotle's wisdom. This is why "virtue-based leadership" is an exception to rules about carrots and sticks that presumably increase motivation and engagement.

Rewards and Punishments

Here's an old "rule" that you may have heard: people who want more of a behavior reward it, and people who want less of a behavior punish it. Compliance and engagement are two growth industries that often embrace this element of behavioral psychology. To reinforce behavior, compliance relies more on sharp sticks, and engagement relies more on sweet carrots. In naming this book *Exception to the Rule*, we aim to offer a virtue-based approach that challenges the traditional carrot-and-stick paradigm. We'd like to convince you that a virtue-based approach to leadership unleashes the potential of people, rather than herding them with sharp sticks and sweet carrots. In this way, virtue-based leadership is an important "exception to the rule."

Let's start this analysis with the stick. What's wrong with it? For sure we need rules, but they are expensive. The word *ethics* has come to mean compliance with a set of rules rather than excellence. *Compliance* defines the moral bottom or floor, whereas *virtue* defines us at our best. We need rules to set minimum expectations. Virtue without rules would come with plenty of risk. Yet making people comply with rules is expensive. In 2015 and 2016, about two-thirds of companies expected compliance costs to increase, largely driven by demand for qualified staff to manage volumes of regulatory requirements. While the regulatory changes facing companies are significant, the number one concern is conduct of individuals and the culture of firms. We need to understand that when compliance is taken too far, the consequence is more "box ticking" rather than actually creating an ethical culture.[14] This is why concern about conduct of individuals and culture of firms takes us back to the value of virtue-based leaders and cultures.

The compliance industry took off after Enron, WorldCom, and other corporate scandals prompted the passage of Sarbanes Oxley (SOX) legislation in 2002. SOX was designed to prevent fraud—a good thing to be sure. But have SOX and the push for compliance worked? Not always. The global financial system imploded five years after SOX was passed. The worst financial crisis since the Great Depression started when a housing bubble burst and credit evaporated. The housing bubble started and grew as a result of trying to meet the noble goal to increase the number of Americans who own a home. But things got off the rails when lenders knowingly put people into loans they could not afford. In a game of hot potato, the mortgage brokers quickly passed these high-risk loans to investment bankers. The bankers repackaged and sold thousands of these loans, claiming they were safe when they weren't. Credit agencies conspired to misrepresent these toxic assets as safe.

Then bad stuff started to happen. The housing bubble burst, and the radioactive assets defaulted. Millions of people lost their jobs and homes. Businesses couldn't get credit.

Here is the really important point. Smart people knowingly misrepresented what they sold. They lacked virtue. This is why the term "character crunch" might be a better explanation for the financial meltdown than "credit crunch." Keep in mind that in a court of law, the accused are judged as being capable of understanding the difference between right and wrong or not being capable of that understanding because they are insane or suffer from a mental deficit. And yet each day, there is ample evidence that people fail to do what is right not because they do not know the rule but because of habits such as impulsiveness, fear, or indifference. What's been the traditional cure for the "character crunch"? More compliance, meaning more sticks.

In 2010 the Dodd-Frank Wall Street Reform and Consumer Protection Act was passed with the worthy goal to prevent banks from failing. As of 2015, the rules were about 9,000 pages long, and they were still growing.[15] Business isn't the only sector that is doubling down on a rule-based approach to ethics. Special education teachers spend 75 percent of their time on paperwork and meetings in order to comply with well-intended 2004 federal legislation entitled Individuals with Disabilities Education Act (IDEA).[16] Physicians, accountants, and truck drivers all spend more time today complying with rules intended to prevent abuse of medical records, reduce fraud, and keep unqualified and tired truck drivers off the road. All this is to say, the crimes of the few are causing an awful lot of work—a lot of sticks—for the many. When taken too far, rules have the unintended consequence of reducing the most meaningful parts of a job: teaching students to learn, caring for patients, being a business partner and coach, and delivering products safely. Too many rules also reduce creativity and innovation. *Innovation* means "new action," so by its very nature, innovation requires rules to be loose, not tight.

Just so there is no misunderstanding here, we need to be clear that the rule of law is the foundation of a civilized society. There must be consequences to people who break the law in ways that harm others. Put more positively, rules can help make our food safe to eat, our drugs safe to take, and our bridges safe to cross. In the case of following the laws of physics or natural sciences, there is no room for the flexible application of virtue. We need to comply with the rules of the natural world that keep people safe. Rules have their place when the goal is to restrict people's thinking and to conduct critical tasks such as complying with acceptable accounting principles.

What is often missing—and another strong reason to call this book *Exception to the Rule*—is an understanding of the limitations of rules. For example, there is no rule book big enough to manage all the uncertainty that people face. Heavy-handed rules restrict innovation and creativity at the very time that organizations are struggling to grow. Rules certainly don't inspire high performance. In situations that involve human conduct, rules fall short in encouraging people to be good leaders, teammates, engineers, physicians, or, for that matter, friends, parents, or spouses.

Engagement

Let's now switch to carrots. Too often, the stock-in-trade of this cottage industry called "engagement" is a heavy dose of extrinsic reward and recognition strategies. More lunches, more team building, and more time with the boss—it all sounds great. But what if a lunch with the boss results in disengagement? Gallup reports that supervisors account for 70 percent of the variance in engagement, so more time with the boss can demotivate rather than motivate people to increase their discretionary effort.[17]

Just as compliance hasn't reduced ethical breaches, extrinsic rewards and recognition haven't moved the engagement needle. Remember that Gallup reports that only 30 percent of employees are highly engaged. Here is why. Trusting and meaningful relationships are more important than extrinsic rewards and recognition. People are engaged when they are surrounded by meaningful relationships—relationships with their boss, with the people who report to them, with their peers, and with family and friends. It's that simple, and it's that hard.

Here is the really important point. An extrinsic, rule-based approach to ethics (sticks) and extrinsic rewards and recognition (carrots) does not promote excellence. Please read this sentence again. Rules, rewards, and recognition do not promote excellence. At best, sticks prevent failure, and carrots promote mediocrity. It is intrinsic virtue that promotes excellence.

Engagement is a really big deal, so it is worth understanding what it is and its benefits. Engagement is about discretionary effort—what people will do when they don't absolutely have to and when no one is watching or measuring. Discretionary effort is about how people go "above and beyond." Engagement has become the magic elixir that drives business performance. For example, Gallup reported earnings per share were 147 percent higher for organizations with an average of 9.3 engaged employees for every actively disengaged employee.[18] Compelling facts like these make us want more engagement, and they have inspired some leaders to institute engagement mandates that are driven by metrics. This can mean that all managers will have an engagement score of 80 percent. Sounds good, but when this happens, the metric tail wags the engagement dog. Extrinsic motivators do not improve trusting and caring relationships that drive engagement. It is the other way around. Intrinsic motivators to practice virtues that create trusting and caring relationships drive engagement.

So the point of *Exception to the Rule* is that excellent leaders and teams are not governed. They are self-governed. They are governed more by virtue than by rules. Exceptional leadership and teams understand that a virtue-based culture is more powerful than a rule-based culture. In other words, carrots and sticks will only take us so far. While leaders and teams need rules, fewer rules mean that trust is high. Trust is a by-product of leaders and teams practicing virtue. Table I.1 lists the qualities of rule-based leaders and teams compared to the qualities of virtue-based leaders and teams.

RULE-BASED LEADERS AND TEAMS	VIRTUE-BASED LEADERS AND TEAMS
• Rule-based ethics	• Virtue-based ethics
• Compliance	• Character
• Command and control	• Empowerment
• Extrinsic motivation	• Intrinsic motivation
• Pay for performance	• Purpose, mastery, and empowerment
• Metrics	• Meaning
• Recipes	• Resilience

TABLE I.1   The Qualities of Rule-Based Versus Virtue-Based Leaders and Teams

Many organizations are dominated by the column on the left, and might be unaware of the column on the right. The ancient Greeks might have attributed this to being dominated by *logos*, or "logic," rather than *mythos* or "meaning." People need both, though the order matters a lot. Mythos precedes logos, not the other way around. Here is what is interesting. Several decades of scientific evidence (logos) demonstrates that mythos drives performance. Empowered, resilient teams guided by virtue and purpose are tough to beat.

The virtues represent what has always worked. The virtues are a 2,500-year-old approach to leadership, known as Plato's Academy, which is the foundation of higher education. The mission of Plato's Academy was to develop "good" leaders—leaders of character who would create a "good" society. The word *ethics* in Greek means "character." The word *classical* means "universal," so the seven classical virtues apply in any part of the world.

The Global Benefits of Virtue

Having grace and grit under fire is a by-product of having a character defined by virtue. The virtues are time-honored, and they are admired in virtually all cultures. Each virtue may not align perfectly inside every culture. Yet, does it seem plausible that any sustainable culture would not stress courage, trust, compassion, and hope? Does it seem plausible that an American, Chinese, Brazilian, German, or South African parent would be indifferent to whether their children grew up to be cowardly, dishonest, cruel, and frozen by despair?

The standard for virtue is simple: does it lead people to live better lives? If not, virtue has failed. If so, it has succeeded. Our experience shows that just as virtue has taught people to live life well for 25 centuries, it is still doing so. On a professional level, part of living life well involves leading engaged teams. We have extensive experience and evidence that bringing to life the ancient wisdom of virtue does just that.

Virtues are caught more than taught. So the way in which virtues are introduced into a professional setting matters. Virtues are best learned with humility, rather than zealotry or cynicism. Arrogance birthed from being a know-it-all or "knowing nothing will work" isn't just annoying. It shuts down learning. On the other hand, we are opened to learning through humility.

The virtues also need to be introduced in a way that is relevant to dealing with difficult challenges. Let's take a common healthcare challenge. One of the authors is a physician at the Cleveland Clinic, an institution striving to better care for the 50,000 caregivers who work there—doctors, nurses, allied health providers, administrators, and all the folks who make Clinic work. Taking care of caregivers is a noble goal, but it is not the Clinic's only goal. Since healthcare already consumes 18 percent of the U.S. gross domestic product (GDP), costs must be contained or the healthcare system will bankrupt the country and pass on a boatload of debt to the next generation.[19] The Clinic has three difficult goals to juggle: providing the highest-quality care, ensuring access to care, and making care affordable by lowering its cost. Lowering costs is best achieved by appropriately allocating resources and reducing waste of unnecessary spending.

The rub comes in looking out for caregivers, while also demanding that they improve patient care and access. Inevitably, this kind of change demands that caregivers have to let go of familiar practices so that they can embrace unfamiliar practices. Part of the reason that people struggle with change can be explained by behavioral economics research. People tend to fear loss more than they appreciate gain.[20] Despite an obvious need to change, people resist because of the fear of what could be lost. One person might respond to uncertainty by checking out, another by complaining, and a third by micromanaging. If we don't see the need for virtue beneath these behaviors, then dysfunction runs the show.

People resist change even when they see it coming. For years, newspapers understood the business risk of the Internet and declining circulation rates as the young read news from a screen rather than a piece of paper. Plenty of newspapers recognized these trends. It is one thing to spot disruptive forces. It is quite another for newspapers and, for that matter, any organization, to change because cultures are often committed to existing products and the existing business model.

Disruption might be unsettling to some, but it is embraced by innovators and entrepreneurs. Turbulence creates opportunities for those who have better ideas. In fact, every corner of the planet is desperately seeking leaders and teams who improve healthcare for patients, develop products that add value for customers, create jobs and skills for people, generate profits for investors, and provide tax revenue for governments.

The challenge is this: only about 30 percent of a workforce is fully engaged. That means that too few people are courageous and passionate, and too many people are discouraged and dispirited. It is hard to encourage entrepreneurship and innovation when people are sleepwalking, hunkered down, or scared.

Virtue-Based Leadership, Teams, and Cultures

Virtue loosens the grip that fear of change can have on us. Virtue-based leadership increases engagement, enhances teamwork, and develops leaders. When people accept the responsibility to lead change, they become pioneers. The key point is this: a virtue is an excellence that we can develop like any other excellence. Achieving a high level of fitness requires training and practice, and so does virtue. For about five years, we've been practicing virtue at a Fortune 500 company and at a world-class healthcare organization.

One of the authors is an executive at Parker Hannifin, the number one motion and control technologies company in the world. Parker Hannifin is a $13 billion Fortune 500 company employing 50,000 people in 50 nations. Since 2012, Parker Hannifin has intensified its journey to help leaders and teams make character-based decisions. The impact of seminars, coaching, and Internet-based instruction was measured, and here is what was found: pre-seminar assessments versus post-seminar assessments demonstrated a statistically significant self-reported increase in engagement, teamwork, and leadership development.

An especially promising result was the impact that virtue has had on engagement in a $1.3 billion revenue Group with operations in North America, Europe, and Asia. This Group is composed of a dozen divisions with separate profit and loss responsibility located in 65 communities around the planet. In 2013, each division staff started to integrate virtues into its business practices. Prior to undertaking this initiative, the Group had the lowest engagement scores among Parker Hannifin's seven large operating Groups. Over a two-year period, this operating Group's engagement scores went from worst to first.

The Cleveland Clinic has operations throughout the United States and the world, employing approximately 50,000 people. The Clinic has integrated the virtues into its leadership development programs (such as Leading in Health Care and the Chief Residents' Leadership Workshop) that are directed at caregivers inside the Clinic and at caregivers who visit the clinic to learn healthcare leadership at the Samson Global Leadership Academy. The Clinic recently accelerated its commitment to leadership development by forming the Global Leadership and Learning Institute. Physicians, nurses, and administrators who participated in Leading in Health Care were nominated as high-potential emerging leaders. Over more than a decade of offering these programs, post-course evaluations have consistently revealed that healthcare leaders valued the insights they gained on the impact that virtue has had on engagement, teamwork, and leadership development. Post-course evaluations also revealed that leaders wanted to learn more about the practice of virtue in their professional and personal lives.

To be clear about the limits of our evidence, we have pre- and post-intervention data from Parker Hannifin and Cleveland Clinic, although these data are correlational and not causal. That said, our findings are absolutely consistent with those from other organizations that study the relationship between character defined by virtue and performance.

Beyond lessons learned from these two organizations representing a 100,000-person global laboratory in different sectors, we have also accumulated evidence that virtue has a favorable impact on performance from our focused visits to the U.S. Military Academy West Point, the U.S. Air Force Academy, and the U.S. Naval Academy, in addition to the Ethical Protectors program in which former Marines teach New York and New Jersey police officers about character. We have also corroborated evidence through focused visits with academicians from the University of Miami in Florida, Wake Forest University, the University of Pennsylvania, Stony Brook University School of Medicine, and the Institute for Management Development (IMD) in Switzerland. In-depth and frequent discussions explored performing under pressure with senior leaders from the Cleveland Indians professional baseball team and the America's Cup. We collaborated with varsity coaches at a university athletic program to create an extensive character-based leadership program for student athletes that has been in place for years.

All this is to say that the content and tools in *Exception to the Rule:*

The Surprising Science of Character-Based Culture, Engagement, and Performance are evidence-based, drawing on field research and on research in fields such as philosophy, psychology, evolutionary biology, neuroscience, innovation, leadership, and culture. While we rely on evidence, we don't claim that *Exception to the Rule* is perfect or foolproof. Just like the practice of medicine, continuous improvement leads to new insights and new questions.

The Challenge

Mahatma Gandhi said, "We but mirror the world. All the tendencies present in the outer world are to be found in the world of our body. If we could change ourselves, the tendencies in the world would also change. As a man changes his own nature, so does the attitude of the world change toward him. This is the divine mystery supreme. We need not wait to see what others do."[21] Gandhi's tip surely isn't easy, nor does it come with a formula or five easy steps to success.

This might lead you to ask whether virtue can be taught. This is actually the wrong question. Every day, we teach virtue to our colleagues, our families, and our friends more by our actions than by our words. So the question isn't "can" we teach virtue. Rather, the real question is "how" can we teach virtue better.

While "we need not wait to see what others do," you can expect at least three challenges putting into practice the ideas detailed in *Exception to the Rule*. First, expect many to underestimate how malleable we are. Second, expect many to underestimate the power of culture on our conduct. Third, expect examples of hypocrisy to be raised loudly or, more likely, to be muttered in hushed tones out in the hallway.

By *malleable*, we mean our ability to develop character, to change, and to grow. Our ability to develop virtue is far more in our control than many people may have considered. We are not as captive to our genetics, parents, and neighborhoods where we were raised as we might think. We can learn to be more compassionate, just as we can learn to be more ruthless. We can learn to be more just, wise, and hopeful, just as we can learn to be unjust, unwise, and full of despair. So the good news is that we can change. The bad news is that change only comes with intentionality and significant effort.

By *culture*, we mean how people think, feel, and act inside their organization or out in the community or in the country in which they live. It certainly is far easier to develop our character in a culture that actively promotes virtue. In truth, it takes a remarkable person to be courageous and to exhibit self-control in a culture where cowardice and intemperance are the norms. While it is possible to rise above a toxic culture, it certainly isn't easy. This is precisely why a character-based culture is such a powerful competitive advantage.

To understand hypocrisy, we turn to Ralph Waldo Emerson: "What you do speaks so loud that I cannot hear what you say."[22] Or we can post the following sign next to the office coffee pot: "This department requires no physical fitness program. Everyone gets enough exercise jumping to conclusions, flying off the handle, running down the boss, knifing friends in the back, dodging responsibilty, and pushing their luck."[23]

The thing about being part of a culture is that the hypocrite card can be played by any of us between our morning coffee and lunch. We see evidence of leaders who climb over others to get ahead. We even see good leaders fall off the virtue wagon. Predictably, this is why you can expect to hear two clichés when you discuss virtue: "It starts at the top," and "Walk the talk."

For most of us, it is easier to see hypocrisy in others than in ourselves. If we accept that we are all hypocrites, then hypocrisy is just a matter of degree. This is why none of us has earned the right to be self-righteous. In truth, it's more honest to humbly acknowledge our long list of flaws than pretend we are immune to hypocrisy.

Calling out leaders for being hypocrites can be good sport, and it has the added benefit of getting us off the hook for responsible conduct. While cynicism can be entertaining, Aldous Huxley gives us reason to pause: "Cynical realism is the intelligent man's best excuse for doing nothing in an intolerable situation." In 1759, Voltaire wrote *Candide* to make the point that the violence and corruption of kings could not compare to the peaceful and productive life of "cultivating our own garden" and trading surpluses with our neighbors.[24] When we accept the burden to "cultivate our own garden," we strive to live by conviction to act with virtue. We strive to not be defined by circumstances that might include when our peers or bosses misbehave at worst or simply fall short of the best version of themselves. The important word here is "strive." Virtue will always be aspirational, and we can expect to fall short of our ideals. Yet, there is overwhelming evidence that we are all capable of becoming the best version of ourselves. And when we do, we live better lives.

Conclusion

The practice of virtue is a lifelong journey. Plato recognized this by requiring individuals to be 50 years old before graduating from his academy. Given the life expectancy of Greeks 25 centuries ago, the graduation class must have been quite small! The Greeks understood that it takes time to realize that the stories of others matter as much as our own story. It takes time to practice virtue as a way to live. It takes time to become self-aware. Socrates said the principal goal of life was to "know thyself," but the principal barrier to self-knowledge is self-deception.

Since we are all capable of making a mess of things, wise people practice virtue with humility. Saint Augustine's classic *The Confessions* detailed his conversion from a sinful youth to a man of faith. Before he became a priest, he fathered an illegitimate child with his mistress. He was known for the prayer, "Grant me chastity, but not yet." If even saints are flawed, the destiny for the rest of us is clear. Imperfection is part of the human condition.

This isn't to suggest that sainthood is the goal for most mortals. You could pack into a Mini Cooper the number of leaders who are ready to jettison their worldly possessions for the life of a monk. Most leaders want to be virtuous, but they also want to be successful. Remember that there is clear evidence that virtue and success coexist quite well.

The core decision that will shape our lives is whether success or virtue will be our lead dog. When virtue precedes success, it makes our life simpler, though certainly not easier. When done well, we preserve our practice of virtue while we change our business practices to adapt to VUCA situations. When we put the practice of virtue before our business practices, it causes us to think about success differently. While not assured, virtue can contribute to success and net worth. What is assured is that virtue creates a life worth living—a life lived well based as much, if not more, on who we are, rather than on what we have.

A Roadmap for This Book

We start each chapter with a definition of the virtue that is being discussed. To round out the reader's understanding, we also provide a diagram that presents a spectrum of states for that virtue: what things look like when the virtue is being practiced and is present versus what they look like when the virtue is absent. The spectrum illustrates that our behavior is not defined easily as either virtuous or unvirtuous. In a given moment, our conduct falls along a continuum that leans toward virtuous at our best or toward unvirtuous when we are not at our best. When we use and apply the language of moral excellence to our life, it helps call us to be the best version of ourselves.

We start each chapter with pillars and a pediment. To capture the concept that the seven virtues are on the one hand interdependent, but on the other hand individually foundational for a life well lived, we have created the image of the Parthenon. This "pillars and pediment" graphic will be deployed throughout this book to frame the discussion. This image is that of seven pillars—one for each of the seven virtues—supporting the pediment, which is integrity, or a life well lived. Each chapter will highlight one virtue or pillar. For example, the figure looks like Figure I.1 when we discuss justice.

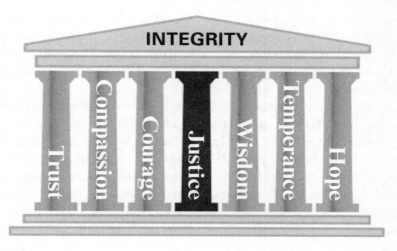

FIGURE I.1

Source: Copyright © Parker Hannifin.

We hope to bring the virtues to life in this book through telling stories that capture what life looks like when the virtues are present and what life looks like when they are less present. Importantly, the Parthenon and the pediment will not stand when none of the pillars is present or even if most are absent. In the unfortunate circumstance that all or most of the pillars are absent, the building "disintegrates"—its integrity is lost.

We also hope to capture the concept that the pediment of the building—a life well lived, with integrity—is best supported when each of the virtues—the pillars—is present and strong. And the stories will provide examples of what life looks like when some of the pillars are especially strong and what life looks like when other pillars (virtues) are thinner.

You could also imagine the pillar and pediment graphic as a self-assessment instrument. As you look at each of the pillars necessary to support your life well lived, you might ask yourself, "Which of my pillars are stronger, and which are not as strong?"

Each of the next seven chapters addresses one of the virtues—what it is, how it works, and how the virtue can be further developed. To emphasize the practical value of the virtues in real life—both for organizations as they live in the marketplace and for all of us as we navigate our lives as individuals—the book closes with three focused chapters: Chapter 8, "Integrity Is a Growth Market," which ties the virtues to creating an innovative culture; Chapter 9, "Classical Solutions to Contemporary Challenges," which provides practical advice on how to thrive in uncertain conditions; and the "Epilogue and Takeaways," which provides a concise synthesis.

Finally, in the context of a book on virtues that were very early discussed by Aristotle in ancient Greece but that have immense relevance for life in the twenty-first century, the pillars and pediment graphic invites a story about the building that inspired the image of the pillars and pediment. In Athens, the Parthenon's east pediment is a sculpture of the birth of Athena. Zeus, Athena's father, had an affliction that gives new meaning to the phrase "splitting headache," which was cured when Hephaestus (God of Fire) split Zeus's head open with a hammer. Every being watching this scene is stunned when Zeus's head miraculously births Athena, who pops out in full armor, ready to go as the goddess of reason, wisdom, arts, literature, and purity. Athena was brave in battle, though she fought only in those wars that defended Athens from outside enemies. She was a terrific engineer, inventing the bridle to tame horses, instruments such as the trumpet and flute, tools such as the rake and plow, and modes of transportation such as the ship and chariot. She was a political leader who won the contest to become the patron goddess of Athens against Poseidon by offering the olive tree, the symbol of peace, to the Athenians.[25]

Athenian virtue is beyond the reach of mere mortals, though her story teaches us what a morally excellent life looks like. She also teaches us that the practice of seven classical virtues is within our reach. Doing so offers us a pediment of a life of integrity, a life well lived.

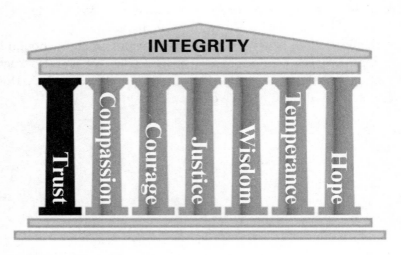

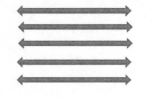

FIGURE 1.1 Pillars and Pediment: Trust

CHAPTER 1

Trust

Giving trust and being trusted can make you fast and save you money.

*They (virtues) are not the stuff of saints and heroes,
but tools for the art of living.*
—KRISTA TIPPETT[1]

Trust is a good place to start when you are trying to build an ethical culture because it is fundamental to any relationship. Trust is the first virtue chapter because trust is foundational. It is the social glue that makes things work. Without trust, no relationship can occur. Unless people trust the people to their left and to their right, they cannot achieve anything great. Economists call this *social capital*. Sociologists call it *reciprocal altruism*.

We are all on a trust quest. People live and perform better when they are part of a trusting culture. People feel safe when they trust others and they know others trust them in return. When people have trust, they take risks. Trust gives people confidence. In fact, the word *confidence* means "with faith."

Trust and *faith* are synonymous. The root word for *faith* is from the Latin word *fiducia*, or the English word *fiduciary*. The word means that effective leaders look out for the interests of others as if their interests were our own. We earn trust by enhancing and protecting the lives of others. Concerns about risk decrease when boards fulfill their "fiduciary" duty to protect and create wealth, auditors conduct independent

23

evaluations, and analysts report accurate and unbiased research. The word *trust* means that people believe the engineer built a safe bridge, the driver will deliver the package on time, and the chef will prepare a delicious meal. Trust is giving former offenders a second chance, as long as they are willing to learn to earn, deepen, and restore the trust of others through honest hard work.

Consider a real-world example of trust.

CASE STUDY:
EDWINS LEADERSHIP AND RESTAURANT INSTITUTE

"Hospitality is the virtue of a great soul that cares for the whole universe through the ties of humanity," said Chevalier Louis de Jaucourt.[2] About 300 years after this French scholar spoke these words, a French restaurant was serving frog legs to its customers while serving fresh starts to its employee-students. The Edwins Leadership and Restaurant Institute students enroll in a rigorous six-month training program to learn about fine dining and extraordinary hospitality. Since the supply of people who possess this expertise is limited, there is no shortage of job opportunities for the Edwins graduates.

Here is the interesting part of the Edwins (short for "education wins") story. If you don't have a criminal record, Edwins won't hire you. If you have been incarcerated, Edwins will give you a fresh start.

This all started when a judge granted Edwins' founder, Brandon Chrostowski, a second chance after he got on the wrong side of the law. The judge offered Chrostowski a mentor rather than a jail cell. While Chrostowski was on probation, Chef George enrolled him in the Culinary Institute of America. After graduation, Chrostowski became a terrifically successful chef at elite restaurants in Chicago, New York, and Paris. A happy ending for sure, but it turns out that it is only the beginning of the story.

Chrostowski realized that his fresh start was achieved more by luck than design. While he was learning about fine dining and hospitality, his family and friends were rotating in and out of courtrooms and jail. He wanted to teach former offenders what Chef George taught him—competence and character. In 2004, Chrostowski returned to the Culinary Institute of America to create Edwins' business plan and curriculum. In 2008, Edwins was incorporated in Cleveland, Ohio, as a nonprofit. There is a perverse reason why a Detroit native started a new restaurant in a city where he knew no one. Chrostowski selected Cleveland because at the time he started his restaurant, the city had one of the lowest high school graduation rates in the United States. Sadly, Chrostowski knew that high school dropout rates predict high incarceration rates

Here's the business case for Edwins. Each year, about 4,000 convicts are released into Cuyahoga County where Edwins is located, but almost a third of those released from prison return in three years.[3] Recidivism goes up when offenders lack goals, structure, skills, jobs, housing, and perhaps most important, a mentor like Chef George. A criminal record means that you are no longer trusted, and many employers screen out applicants convicted of a crime. This makes it difficult for former criminals to turn their lives around.

So what to do with the vast majority of former offenders released from prison coming to a neighborhood near you? The restaurant industry is America's second-largest private sector employer. Since restaurants can't find enough qualified people to run their businesses, Edwins provides a steady supply of talent. Clearly, citizens are safer when former offenders cook rather than commit crimes. It is expensive for taxpayers to pay the equivalent of a Harvard education to incarcerate a prisoner.[4]

Helping people change their lives requires a sophisticated understanding of how former inmates currently live, the importance of social support, and the difficulty of living in disorganized circumstances. To help build the resilience needed to complete the Edwins program, students learn the seven classical virtues. Imagine this scene. After learning how to calculate the cost of food waste and which wine goes with which entree, Edwin students study and apply virtues to their new trade of hospitality.

They discuss what virtue means, why it is important to hospitality, and how they become more virtuous.

When about 30 Edwins students were asked to put their hands up if they had at least one person they trusted completely, only one or two hands went up. Many students told stories in which they were hurt when they trusted other people. Listening to these stories sympathetically, one student reminded his classmates about what is needed to make it: "I don't have anyone to trust either, so that means all we have is each other." Another student said, "Yeah, man, I'm all for trust, but you have to be careful. I lent someone money, went to get paid back, and got shot in my back end!"

While the Edwins program works for many, it does not work for all. About 60 percent of participants complete the program. Some of those who drop out don't like the hospitality business, and some are unable or unwilling to wait for higher pay in the future. They might need or want a job that pays more immediately, even if they will make more later. Some don't want to deal with the long days and demanding expectations. And some can't untangle a complicated web of broken families and neighborhoods. That said, what's most impressive about the program are the results: only 2 of about 160 graduates who completed the program returned to prison after graduating from Edwins Leadership Institute.

The Business Case for Trust

The business case for virtues in general and trust in particular is quite easy to make. Distrust increases expenses and makes teams slow. A trust "deficit" slows decisions and increases risk aversion. The absence of trust makes any attempt to innovate and grow a nonstarter. Since trust is largely unregulated, regulations and metrics are not the keys to more trust and better teamwork. Trust cannot be commanded, though it can be cultivated. What happens when trust is missing?

Consider an all-too-common scenario from healthcare.

CASE STUDY:
KEEPING COMMITTEE DELIBERATIONS CONFIDENTIAL

You are the chairperson of a newly formed committee that is charged with a confidential process: reviewing the clinical competence of another faculty member. Everyone on the committee has expressed awareness of the absolute need to keep the deliberations confidential until the final recommendations are sent to the leadership of the medical center.

You then become aware that some of the committee's deliberations have been leaked. The committee has lost trust with the hospital leadership and with each other. As the chairperson, you meet with each committee member to discuss the leak and learn who broke the confidence. You discover who was responsible for the leak. You ask that committee member to step off the committee, and you carry on with the remainder of the group.

Yet the damage is done. Despite the recommitment to maintain confidentiality, everyone on the committee is now guarded in their comments. There is ill will toward the dismissed committee member, both because the committee's trust was violated and because the remaining members are absorbing the extra work. Though they understand that leadership's displeasure is not directed toward them, they feel their reputation has been unfairly "painted with a broad brush." These unintended, perverse effects of lost trust speak volumes about the importance of integrity. Trust is "gained in drops and lost in buckets."

The benefits of trust are huge in a world full of ambiguity that rewards fast fish over big fish. Teams that trust each other move fast, save money, and demonstrate resilience to overcome inevitable obstacles. Trust doesn't happen by accident. It is earned and practiced. For example, people who cultivate trusting relationships readily express empathy. When people will sacrifice for us, our natural response is to trust them. When we trust others, we feel safe, and we start to cooperate. In this regard, trust and compassion go hand in hand.

Relationships come with risk—some less, some more, and some with lots more. For example, when people face a decision to have surgery, risk and trust is a high-stakes game. Patients must trust the surgeon to split them open, and they place their lives in the physician's hands. Despite the risk to life and limb, few people audit the surgeon's credentials, class rank, board scores, or medical errors or interview former patients. Instead, patients take a leap of faith based on a physician's recommended treatment and a few minutes of pleasant bedside conversation. Some patients might also decide not to have surgery if scheduling the appointment took too long or if they had to wait two hours in the lobby. Perhaps the surgeon is great, but patients don't follow through because of a heartless or hapless receptionist. Despite living in an era of "big data" and metrics, patients still give considerable weight to the surgeon, trusting she will look out for our interests as if our interests were her own.

Preserving a Reputation for Being Trusted

Trust is more than a "feel good" exercise. To function, commercial markets depend on trust. This is why reputation has significant economic value and why financial meltdowns happen when trust is lost. Intangibles, such as good will and reputation, account for 30 to 70 percent of the difference between the *book value* (the total value of the firm's hard assets) and the *market capitalization* (the share price times the number of shares). When more investors trust and buy a firm's bonds, interest rates drop. When more investors trust and buy a firm's stock, share prices appreciate. Trusted brands earn higher margins that increase earnings multiples and market capitalization and lower the cost of capital. Intangibles such as trust are just as real as tangibles such as cash.

A bond was issued by the Cleveland Clinic, where one of the authors serves as a physician. But hospitals issue bonds all the time. What's so special here? The bond was a 100-year bond. Investors had confidence that the Clinic will endure for a century, based on its performance over 95 years to date. That's trust translating into financial benefit in healthcare.

28

On the clinical side of healthcare, compliance with physicians' recommendations is often a good thing. After knee surgery, being conscientious about rehabilitation is critical to a full recovery. After a heart attack, compliance with diet, not smoking, and taking medications can be lifesaving. Lots of data show that it is far more likely that patients will implement rehabilitation consistently and change their lifestyles when they trust their doctors. Without trust, organizations do badly and people die. Trust promotes healthy organizations and healthy people.

How people behave or misbehave leaves a reputation trail that determines how much they can be trusted. In this sense, our reputation is a vital asset built by earning trust over time. For good reason, wise people avoid bad choices because trust is fragile. Although no person or organization is completely virtuous, it is also true that people and organizations do not completely lack virtue. So, what happens when people make a mistake? Now what? Let's answer that question by discussing a story about reputation.

The U.S. Military Academy West Point, having been first occupied by the Continental Army in 1778, is the oldest Army post in the United States. West Point's mission is to develop character-based leaders for the military and the nation.[5] The academy is dedicated to taking the best and making them even better. All West Point cadets are required to comply with the West Point Honor Code: "Don't lie, cheat, steal, or tolerate those who do." West Point, along with the Air Force and Naval Academies, expanded their definition of ethics from compliance to rules to practicing virtue. That's right—virtue. Each of the service academies teaches character education slightly differently, though all define ethical leadership as virtuous leadership.

Overlooking the Hudson River, the entire campus of West Point is a national landmark, including the Thayer Hotel. Each hotel room is dedicated to West Point's most accomplished and distinguished graduates. One of those graduates is David Petraeus, a four-star general who commanded all the Iraq forces and served as the Central Intelligence Agency (CIA) director. He graduated in the top 5 percent of his class and went on to earn a PhD in international affairs from Princeton. When the news broke that Petraeus had had an extramarital affair, he resigned as CIA director immediately. We happened to be at West

Point to learn about the Army's approach to virtue when this scandal broke out.

Our first meeting was at breakfast with the leader of the academy's character education program. As an important aside, keep this thought in mind: West Point, along with the other service academies, has a position entitled "director of character education." And character is defined as virtue. While we were obviously curious about how the academy would respond to the story, we certainly didn't want to offend our host. However, before our waiter had even had a chance to fill our coffee mugs, our host made it clear that the academy wasn't shying away from the Petraeus story because it represented a "teachable moment."

As a practical matter, the academy's professors were well aware that cadets were talking about the news anyway. So they asked the cadets a question: whom did they think Petraeus had let down? Answers included his family, West Point, and the nation. Then cadets were reminded that General Petraeus was arguably the best general of his generation. He was a remarkable person who had served his nation extraordinarily well and had a reputation for mentoring countless individuals, including West Point's director of character education. The cadets were asked an especially penetrating question: if this can happen to our very best, what makes any of us think we are immune from poor judgment?[6]

People can be quick to judge and slow to understand, never mind forgive. Judging others can now be done with lightning speed thanks to social media. However, when we are the one who made the mistake, we certainly hope for plenty of understanding and forgiveness. We leave others to judge whether General Petraeus was treated too leniently or too harshly. What's clear is this: few have achieved more than General Petraeus, and he made a big mistake. Like General Petraeus and the Edwins students, when, and not if, we make a big mistake, then what? The world can be tough on those who fall from grace or on former offenders whose lives often come with little grace. No one wants to be judged forever based on the dumbest mistake we ever made.

CASE STUDY: LOST TRUST

You are leading the search for a new nephrologist to join your faculty. A candidate from the University of New Algiers—Dr. James—has applied and looks good on paper. Your colleague happens to have trained with another nephrologist—Dr. Peter—at the University of New Algiers, and, in keeping with your usual practice, you call Dr. Peter, introduce yourself, and invite Dr. Peter's confidential comments about Dr. James.

The comments are very favorable, and despite explicitly asking about any concerns Dr. Peter has that might lead you to withhold an offer to Dr. James, you receive none. Reassured by this personal endorsement of a colleague, you offer the position to Dr. James, and he joins your group. Within several months, Dr. James has earned the reputation of being disruptive. He has derided colleagues, has alienated nurses (some of whom refuse to work with him), and has created a hostile environment in the dialysis unit. Disruptive behavior undermines a culture of safety and causes harm to patients. Dr. Peter misrepresented Dr. James's character in your vetting call. Dr. James is dismissed from his role and from the hospital.

Dr. James has been hurt by the breach of trust that caused him to move once and, in leaving, to move a second time. Dr. Peter's reputation has taken a hit and so has yours. Your group has been hurt by costs associated with the resulting physician turnover, both in training and on-boarding costs, the lost clinical volume during the practice-building phase for a new colleague, and the extra work borne by the other members of the group as they have collectively absorbed the work of the departed Dr. James. Breaches of trust harm reputations, cost money, and decrease productivity.

Trust and Trade

If you are Chinese, your views about what to trust are influenced by when you were born. If you were born in the 1960s or earlier, then you experienced firsthand the oppression of the Cultural Revolution. If you were born in the 1980s or later, then the only China you have ever known has grown year in and year out. After the Chinese revolution in 1949, competition was limited, and many people led a reasonable and predictable life. In 1966, the Cultural Revolution shifted China's traditional priority of family to the Communist Party.

All this Chinese history comes together in the personal story of Victor, a 60-year-old Chinese engineer with whom we talked. Victor's father started a watch factory that created a modest lifestyle for Victor, his sister, and his mother. But the Cultural Revolution dealt Victor's family a cruel fate. From 1966 to 1976, China's Communist leader Mao Zedong launched the Cultural Revolution to purge the nation of "impure" elements. Mao organized students into paramilitary groups called the Red Guards to attack China's elderly, intellectuals, and business owners. Their mission was to stamp out bourgeois values, including entrepreneurship as symbolized by even modest watch factories.

Even though it had been 50 years since the Red Guards pounded on the family's front door, tears streamed down Victor's face as he relived the horror of watching his father dragged into the street to be beaten in front of their neighbors. His father was punished for being a capitalist rather than a communist. He was sent to one labor camp, his wife to another, and Victor and his sister to a third and fourth camp. For seven years, Victor led a life of hard labor. Regular beatings and torture are the reasons that his neck no longer functions normally. The last day he saw his family was the day his father was beaten by young Red Guards.[7]

The Cultural Revolution destroyed business and imploded China's economy, until Deng Xiaoping started to restore trust when he gained power in 1977. Deng told the Chinese that it was "glorious to get rich," and for nearly four decades, the Chinese have pursued his advice with vengeance! The migration of millions from rural to urban China has driven the cost of housing beyond what most people can afford. "Mega cities" such as Shanghai have exploded in population growth. For perspective, more people live in Shanghai than in Ohio and North

Carolina combined. The generation called "after '80s"—that is, people born after 1980—wonder if they can pay for a home, a car, and a child's education, despite China's rapid growth. If you can afford a home, you need to sign a 70-year mortgage to service the debt. And when you buy a home, it means that you own the house, not the land. The Communist Party owns the land.

While the Chinese economic growth has caused some to prosper, the growth itself has created a threat to trust. This threat and the growing economic inequality in China gets lampooned by Jesse Appell, who claims to be the best macroeconomic Chinese-English bilingual rapper in the world. He performs in Beijing comedy clubs. His parody is called "Mo Money Mo Fazhan" or "Mo Money Mo Problems." *Fazhan* is the Chinese word for "development." According to Appell, more money means more good things to buy, while more problems mean more bad things to endure.

A focus on money minus morality has caused the Chinese to conclude that they suffer from a "morality crisis." Too many are confused about their moral guideposts. Even if you have to cheat, you can live a better life. More money may make you feel empty, but it helps you survive. While morality is getting sorted out, many will quit one job for another that offers a modest raise. This is one reason that attrition rates in China's factories can be 10 percent a month.

Jack inherited leadership of a manufacturing plant with an annual 60 percent turnover rate. A 60 percent attrition rate is actually about half the rate experienced at many factories in China. However, Jack could not build a profitable business based on 60 percent annual attrition. Profits were eroded by tangible costs, such as recruiting and training new workers, and intangible costs, such as the inexperience of employees driving scrap rates up and on-time shipments down. Faced with all this, Jack believed he needed to restore trust in the manufacturing plant.

So Jack met with employees to learn more about their needs. They had excellent insights about workstation design. But one suggestion surprised Jack: people wanted a library, but not just any library. They didn't want books about business and making money. They wanted books about raising children well. China's "one-child policy" means four grandparents and two parents raise one child. If these six adults aren't careful, they end up raising little emperors and empresses! Jack's people wanted help to raise good and happy children. Jack provided the library, and this, along with other changes that were made, reduced attrition from 60 percent a year to 20 percent a year.[8]

Trust earned by leaders who are caring and fair is the virtue that investors cannot see, but it is the virtue that makes possible the wealth that investors can see. A journal entry on an income statement fails to grasp the relationship between profit and the most precious intangible asset of all: trust. Financial statements provide investors with a snapshot of a firm's financial health. What investors cannot see by looking at financial statements are the culture, leadership, and teams that make wealth possible.

It takes imagination to understand how tangible net worth and intangible worthiness can be mutually supportive. Net worth is measured by subtracting what a person owes (liabilities) from what they own (assets). While net worth is critically important, it is a means rather than an end to doing what is worthy. In fact, even people with a negative net worth can be worthy. A Latin word for "worth" is *dignus*, the root of dignity. People who are worthy earn dignity. People can inherit net worth, but they cannot inherit worthiness. Worthiness needs to be learned and earned by ourselves. In a world where consumers are looking for trusted businesses, *dignus* isn't just a better way to live. It is also a way to increase the venture's net worth.

Building Up Trust

How do you get more trust? First, let's answer this question from a culture point of view. Then, let's answer the question from the perspective of how trust is earned, deepened, and restored.

Culture Bulldozing Strategy

Consider the elements of leadership and culture as shown in the diagram in Figure 1.2:

- Team A: Brilliant strategy led by brilliant people who are egomaniacs
- Team B: Acceptable strategy led by reasonably smart people who are a high-trust, character-based team

FIGURE 1.2 Successful Organizations Integrate Strategy, Culture, and Leadership

Who will win in the marketplace? Team A or Team B? An enlightened bet would be that Team B's superior leaders and culture will beat Team A's superior intelligence and strategy. We often experience firsthand how strong cultures act like a tailwind to strategy and how weak cultures act like a headwind even to a strong strategy.

Defining and Protecting the Culture

Boards and senior leaders put plenty of effort into strategy to create a sustainable competitive advantage. Despite the power of culture, little, if any, time is devoted to defining, protecting, and growing the culture. This is a huge missed opportunity because it's the culture that is far harder for competitors to replicate than the strategy.

Leadership and culture are two sides of the same coin. However, it's the leaders who shape the culture, although not always positively. Team A's brilliant egotistical leaders will shape the culture in a way that isn't just annoying. It's risky. An arrogant culture makes teams blind to opportunities and threats. In a world where integrity, innovation, teamwork, and partnerships are competitive advantages, big egos get in the way of candor, and they hurt relationships. In contrast, humble leaders acknowledge and make room for what they do not know—not just because humility is an aspect of virtue but because until this mindset is adopted, breakthrough strategies cannot occur. Big egos become big barriers to growing a culture and, for that matter, the organization. When people are arrogant, they don't learn.

Expect trouble when a big ego is attached to a bureaucrat. Bureaucrats who excel and focus on making rules create more angst than trust. Bureaucrats can't innovate or build teams, but they sure are brilliant rule followers. Bureaucrats do not ask how things can be done better. They simply make sure that others follow the rules. A bureaucrat is also skilled at micromanagement. Micromanagers dictate that a job must be done in a particular way, even if there is a better way. Now, in an era of empowerment, no one wants to be accused of micromanagement. Since micromanagement has become a difficult thing to defend, avoiding it can create the opposite problem: leaders who abdicate responsibility in the name of empowerment. While innovation and growth require that leaders loosen rather than tighten controls, some form of oversight is part of responsible leadership. Leaders need a Goldilocks, "just right," solution that neither micromanages nor abdicates responsibility. We offer the solution called the *leader's intent*.

Leader's Intent

The military resolution to balancing responsible oversight and empowerment is called the "commander's intent." To fit it to our perspective, let's change the language from "commander's intent" to "leader's intent" because the concept is not a solution unique to the military. Intention starts with the basic question: why are we doing this? Leader's intent, then, demands that the "commander" be eminently clear about the purpose of an initiative, project, or mission. With this clarity, the team is then empowered to figure out *what* they will do to achieve the leader's intent and *how* they will achieve it.

This is not to suggest the military has figured out how to implement a culture of trust with complete integrity. Clearly, the military is one of the world's largest bureaucracies. It's the military that coined words like "fubar" and other words far more vulgar. *Fubar* is mangled German for the word *furchtbar*, which means "horrible." *Furcht* means "fear" or the opposite of *wunderbar*, which translates into "wonderful." So our challenge is to reduce *fubar* and share power (empowerment) in a responsible manner.

Leader's intent places the burden of responsibility squarely on the person in charge. This burden is especially difficult when it comes to tough ethical decisions between two (or more) competing "goods" or, even tougher, between a number of bad options. For example, in the business context, a dramatic decline in revenue gives a leader two lousy choices: let people go or put the organization at risk. Virtue-based leaders also wonder if a task is worth doing in the first place. This might mean spending less time filling out reports so that more time can be spent with customers. Of course, virtue-based leaders don't differ from others in having doubts, questions, and difficulties. What makes them different is that they confront their doubts and fears with courage and honesty.

Rules, bureaucracies, and micromanagement cannot anticipate every circumstance. By practicing leader's intent, accountability is clear, and controls are loosened rather than tightened, which builds trust. Inevitably, teams bump up against unknown opportunities and threats. Leader's intent guided by virtue helps provide teams with far more direction than simple bromides, such as "just do the right thing." If the team gets confused, then it can go back to the leader's intent that includes practicing virtue. Once the team is clear about the leader's intent, it is empowered to answer questions of what and how. This means that the burden of leadership is that it must be very clear about intentions. This also means that the burden of teamwork is to make sure that you don't lose sight of the leader's intention, including how the team will work together by practicing virtue.

Culture as Strategy

A virtuous culture is the exception to the rule, precisely why a virtuous culture is a competitive advantage. Virtuous cultures increase trust, and therefore the speed to execute strategies that add value to customers, colleagues, and investors. This idea can be applied just about anywhere, including Klaipeda, Lithuania, off the Baltic coast about 30 miles from the Russian border. Russian and Lithuanian CEOs attended a seminar to learn how virtue is applied to leadership, culture, and strategy.

One of the participants was a Russian CEO who had been a captain in the army of the former Soviet Union. He initially described the impact of virtue on leaders and strategy this way: leaders trust that strategic planning will change the company. However, after spending a week studying and applying the virtues, this Russian CEO concluded that virtues change the leader far more profoundly and quickly than does strategic planning. So if a leader wants to change a company quickly, our Russian CEO friend now recommends trying virtue first and strategy second.

This is why we will make a case for betting on a virtuous culture whenever it competes with strategy. In fact, it won't even be a fair fight. Culture wins in a knockout. While some dismiss culture as "soft," wise leaders view culture as "hard." A price discount might provide a 30-day competitive advantage. Products and services might provide a 2- or 3-year competitive advantage. Culture might provide a 10-year advantage because it is unique and nearly impossible to replicate by competitors.

A healthy culture increases discretionary effort and reduces disengagement. The competitive advantage of discretionary effort and commitment was revealed by a landmark study that has since been supported by other studies. In 1992, Kotter and Heskett researched the impact of culture on the long-term financial performance of 200 companies. The best cultures encouraged everyone, not just those in corner offices, to make changes to meet customer needs. The financial differences, as shown in Table 1.1, between high-performing cultures and firms without performance-enhancing cultures are staggering.[9]

	AVERAGE INCREASE FOR 12 FIRMS *WITH* PERFORMANCE-ENHANCING CULTURES	AVERAGE INCREASE FOR 20 FIRMS *WITHOUT* PERFORMANCE-ENHANCING CULTURES
Revenue growth	682%	166%
Employment growth	282%	36%
Stock price growth	901%	74%
Net income growth	756%	1%

TABLE 1.1 Financial Differences Between Firms With and Without Performance-Enhancing Cultures

Source: Adapted from John P. Kotter and James L. Heskett, *Corporate Culture and Performance,* Simon & Schuster, New York, 2011, 78.

Let that fact sink in. A strong company culture increased the value of a company by 900 percent versus 75 percent for a weak company culture. Let's allow for measurement error and sampling error. The difference is so huge that it is difficult to discount the impact of culture on these results.[10]

Earning and Deepening Trust

The space program offers an interesting example of how to start and deepen trust. Space missions now last six months, and they may last up to three years if there is an attempt to land on Mars. So that's a long time for a team of astronauts, selected independently from the space agencies of the United States, Russia, Japan, or Europe, to spend with each other in a confined space station. The technical progress in areas such as propulsion, shielding, and robotics is nothing short of remarkable. However, the real challenge for deep space travel will have as much to do with improving teamwork as improving technology.

So imagine this. Since the Cold War ended, American and Russian astronauts have worked together to explore space. While their research is typically independent, they must come together as a team during launches, landings, and emergencies. What's fascinating is that for decades, capitalists and communists have learned to trust each other, even though their governments don't trust each other. Their shared commitment to space exploration and their shared training in science and medicine transcends political differences.[11]

American astronauts are selected from nearly 20,000 applicants. About 120 are advanced to a medical review, which eliminates about 60 applicants from consideration. Then, psychological assessments are used to select about 8 astronauts. An important attribute sought by NASA is that those selected can perform at a high level under extreme conditions. Because there is no way to predict what might happen in space, astronauts need resilience.

Through the years, astronauts have reported that while they were prepared to give their life to the mission, they needed confidence that their family would be looked after should something happen to them. To NASA's credit, they not only help astronauts develop resilience to perform in uncertain conditions but they also help the families develop resilience. As a result, NASA's astronauts are more focused because they know their family is supported.[12]

So here is where things get tricky back on planet Earth. When people are betrayed, a deep hurt cuts through them. For good reason, people wonder if the person who betrayed them can ever be trusted again. How do we learn to rebuild trust? While people can restore trust, it will be different than the initial trust. Perhaps the trust will be more rooted in reality and less naïve.

The biggest challenge to repairing a broken relationship is that people may not be prepared to park their pride. If people manage to avoid the age-old problem of failing to watch out for pride before the fall, then they have a chance to restore trust by practicing 3As:

1. *Apologize* for the trouble we created.
2. *Acknowledge* the pain, hurt, and problems we created.
3. *Atone* by taking a step to make things right.

No one can control whether the 3As will work, but practicing the 3As represents the kind of person we want to be—at least when we are at our best.

RESTORING TRUST

It takes a long time to earn trust and moments to lose it. True enough. Though our reality is not if, but when, trust is lost. Then what?

Linda loved being the leader of a $50 million business. However, her one fear was having to tell family members that a loved one was killed on the job on her watch. One day, this very feared event happened. In a rush to keep production moving, one of the employees, Bob, took an unnecessary risk and was electrocuted. Linda was devastated, although her response to restore trust was exceptional. The rest of us can learn from her example that can be remembered by putting the 3As into action:

Apologize: Linda met with Bob's wife and the brother who worked at the plant. Her eyes filled with tears as she apologized that an accident had cost the life of their loved one.

Acknowledge: Linda struggled to acknowledge there was nothing she could do to bring Bob back or to take away the pain that the accident had caused the family. Now everyone was sobbing.

Atone: Later, Linda met with the family to let them know about the safety steps that had been taken to ensure that the accident that took Bob's life would never happen again. Bob had two children in high school. Linda started a fundraiser to pay for their college educations.

TRUST AND ENGAGEMENT TOOL KIT

Simple steps can be followed to earn, deepen, and restore trust. If we want to earn people's trust, we must trust others. This starts with the assumption that most people can be trusted, and so we can presume good will on the part of others. A good start in a relationship can be earned by taking on more of the risk and more of the workload. Trust is earned by being the first to trust. Vulnerability is part of it. If we get burned, then we can sort out how to mitigate future risk in this relationship without being wary in all future relationships.

Start by applying a strength-based approach through making the team's strongest features even stronger. This means focusing first on the 30 percent of people who show discretionary effort. Figure out what you are doing right and how can you do more of it. Odds are that the answer to increasing discretionary effort will be direct supervisors who trust and care about their people and who empower them practicing some version of leader's intent. Next, apply what you are doing right to the 50 percent who will do what you ask and not much more, as well as to the 20 percent who are disengaged.

The importance of engagement needs to be made clear at the top of the organization, though moving the engagement needle will depend on the direct supervisor. A realistic outcome is to stabilize the 30 percent providing discretionary effort and, if all goes well, to move 5 percent from the middle to the top and 5 percent from the bottom to the middle. While having 100 percent engagement is a laudable goal, an organization will have done extremely well to stabilize 30 percent and move 10 percent. And this math is the kind of difference that can increase trust in ways that will make a team faster and save money, as well as make life more pleasant.

According to Gallup, the math of "30/50/20" hasn't changed more than a couple of percentage points in about a decade, so we should be skeptical of quick-fix solutions. This means that in a typical organization, about 30 percent of the workforce are highly engaged; 50 percent will do what's asked, but not much more; and 20 percent are disengaged.[13] Recall a few key facts about engagement:

- *What does engagement mean?*
  Discretionary effort: This means to look around to see what needs to be done, figure out whom you should work with, and make it happen.
- *What drives engagement?*
  Trusting and caring relationships.
- *Who affects engagement?*
  According to Gallup, 70 percent of the variance in engagement is attributed to the direct supervisor.
- *What does it mean to empower people?*
  Leader's intent: The leader answers the question why. The team answers the questions what and how.

That simple roadmap offers a way to increase engagement and trust, though simple doesn't mean easy.

Trust is not an either/or type of situation; there are always levels of trust. Trust is a gift that requires us to consciously decide whom we want to trust and what we are willing to give in return. Trusting relationships are also certainly more pleasant than relationships that are full of distrust.

So how do we do get more trust? There is no attempt here to be exhaustive, though we offer some simple suggestions to put trust into action:

1. Listen more, talk less.
2. Ask more, tell less.
3. Have a trusted friend count your "statement-to-question ratio" because we seldom learn anything when we talk.

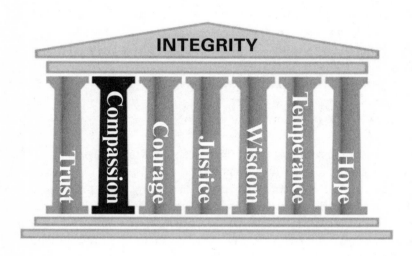

Compassion-to-Ruthlessness Spectrum

Empathy	⟷	Apathy
Giver	⟷	Taker
Engaged	⟷	Disengaged
Selfless	⟷	Selfish
Sacrifice	⟷	Self-absorbed

FIGURE 2.1   Pillars and Pediment: Compassion

Source: Copyright © Parker Hannifin.

CHAPTER 2

Compassion

Build for belonging.

Cure sometimes, treat often, comfort always.
—HIPPOCRATES

Compassion is the concern for the suffering or misfortunes of others. Compassion touches every aspect of our lives. We want compassionate doctors, of course, but compassion in the workplace is also a powerful driver not only of satisfaction with work and engagement but also of enhanced organizational performance.

The word *compassion* comes from the Latin word *compati*, which means "to suffer with." In other words, acting with compassion is about relieving the suffering of another. In its simplest form, compassion is enhancing and protecting life without any thought of being paid back. In this sense, compassion is an unconditional gift. As a virtue, compassion always aims at the good. Machiavellian manipulation and coercion can work in the short term, but virtue is more enduring.

Consider an example of compassion in Mexico.

CASE STUDY: TIJUANA

The movement of people, cars, and trucks between Tijuana, or TJ for short, and San Diego is the human version of the wildebeest migration across the Serengeti. Each year, over 50 million people cross the planet's busiest border—that is, the one connecting San Diego and TJ. South of the U.S. border, Maquiladora factories not only build products and medical devices but also create jobs and living wages. As job opportunities have increased and security has improved in recent years, TJ's population has swelled to about 1.7 million, ranking it among Mexico's fastest-growing metropolitan areas.

The Parker Hannifin culture in TJ is especially impressive, as evidenced by being ranked among the best places to work among all employers in Mexico. Parker Hannifin has about 350 facilities worldwide, and the TJ facility has the highest engagement scores of all the company's locations. Predictably, extraordinary engagement scores translate into excellent financial results.

But the facility's high engagement and superior financial performance haven't always been the case. About 15 years ago, the facility in TJ didn't treat people badly, although people were not at the center of the business the way they are today. People were busy getting their job done, but there was not a particularly strong sense of belonging. While people were paid a fair wage, their ideas were not actively sought to solve operational challenges in the plant. The factory was dirty and not air-conditioned, making working conditions brutally hot during the blistering TJ summers. Today, the factory is air-conditioned, clean, and well lit, and it has the feel of a retail mall that clangs.

What caused the change? The leadership team decided that there was a better way to run a business. As leaders, they felt privileged and responsible to care for their people. Their first step was a simple one: ask their people what they could do to make their lives better. Their teammates appreciated being asked, but they too felt they were in a privileged position. The compensation they earned provided a middle-class life in Mexico. While they lived well, every day they watched neighbors struggle with poverty.

A middle-class life in TJ doesn't insulate you from watching squatters carry everything they own on their back while they look for work on an empty belly. The United States has no shortage of poverty either. However, most members of the middle class in the United States don't watch, feel, and smell poverty every day the way their counterparts do in TJ. For most Americans, poverty is a drive-by experience. We drive from a nice house to a nice place to work and never see poverty. In TJ, a middle-class life means you live and work in a nice place, but each day you drive through, rather than past, poverty. This is why the people who worked in TJ told the leadership team to focus on their neighbors rather than on them.

Helping others in need, especially those who are less fortunate than we are—in other words, being compassionate—is associated with good health, better employment options, and stronger families. Those who offer support generally report that their lives changed for the better afterward. Those who receive support increase their ability to cope and even recover from significant illness more than those who lack support. People who are compassionate receive more favors of support from others. In this sense, it is in our self-interest to be compassionate.

Today, Parker Hannifin leaders in TJ not only want to build a better business but also want to build a better country. Of course, they want to be profitable. And they know that if they take care of their people and their customers, profits will follow. Thus, Parker Hannifin engineers in Mexico tutor local students in math. Parker Hannifin employees buy book bags and school supplies for students and adopt neighborhoods to teach sustainability.

Parker Hannifin's TJ story is an example of what Jody Gittel has called "relational coordination."[1] This term is defined as "the coordination of work through relationships of shared goals, shared knowledge, and mutual respect." Relational coordination clearly depends on trust and caring relationships among workplace colleagues. Gittel has shown that when there is good relational coordination in the workplace, including in complex organizations like hospitals, outcomes are improved. For example, surgical performance (which reflects patient satisfaction, length of stay, postoperative mobility, and freedom from pain) improves when relational coordination among caregivers is high. Gittel has also shown that better airline performance—measured by a decrease in long turnaround times, customer complaints, lost bags, and late arrivals—was also strongly associated with improved relational coordination, so the concept has generalizable impact.[2]

Leaders Who Are Willing to Share, Sacrifice, and Surrender

The caring mission of the Cleveland Clinic was framed by one of its founders, Dr. William E. Lower, who said, "A patient is the most important person in the institution—in person or by mail. A patient is not dependent on us—we are dependent on him or her.[3] A patient is not an interruption of our work—it is the purpose of it. . . . The patient is a person and not a statistic. It is our job to satisfy him or her."[4] As obvious as the role of compassion is in healthcare, compassion also plays a huge role in the success of any organization. When people care about what they are doing and about their colleagues, organizations work better. Compassion is bedrock.

Despite evidence about the business case for compassion, talking this way can seem sappy or stupid! In a world of ruthless competition, some might conclude that compassion makes us soft and turns us into chumps rather than champs. Through a hard-edged business lens, compassion could be viewed as a sign of weakness that sets people up to be roadkill in a "dog eat dog" world.

However, compassion really has to do with leaders who are willing to share, sacrifice, and surrender. There is nothing weak about that. Compassionate doctors are not wimps. They are the doctors we want to take care of us. Passionate people are two times more likely to take on a challenge; there is nothing easy about that. Compassion increases trust and toughness, and compassion tightens the ways teams work together. Caring teams who cooperate well with each other are tough to beat—nothing soft about that.

Compassion might seem like a big, loaded word—reserved for Mother Teresa types of people, far beyond the standards of most of us. However, there are more ordinary levels of compassion. Caring is an easier way to think of compassion, rather than looking at it as some huge heroic sacrifice. In fact, being cared for is the way most of us learn about compassion. And caring is likely the more normal way that compassion shows up in real life. Most of us do not face heroic demands. Rather, we are faced daily with little possibilities and opportunities to care for someone or to care about something. Consider the story of "redcoats" as caring greeters at Cleveland Clinic.

CASE STUDY: PATIENTS FIRST

The Cleveland Clinic holds a "patients first" commitment. You see it everywhere. As part of its attempt to make the hospital more hospitable, a crew of "redcoats" were recruited. Dressed in red coats for visibility, these redcoats are compassion ambassadors. They greet everyone, guide visitors to destinations, share a kind word, and wear beacon-like smiles in an environment in which folks are often dealing with stressful, life-changing events. They look for patients and visitors who seem distressed or lost, and they proactively greet and help them with small gestures—lending them a caring ear, accompanying them to a clinical destination, giving them a handshake, or patting them on the back.

Praise for the redcoats abounds. Patient experience surveys frequently cite the redcoats as contributors to patients' well-being under the trying circumstances of an illness. It seems that compassion lives in the small stuff but can make a huge impact.

Investing in redcoats makes clear virtue is always our choice. But if we choose not to care, our lives are a bit worse and our organizations underperform.

There is good rationale for cultivating passion since it is an especially powerful booster shot to productivity. Passion is the ignition that drives our willingness to forgo comfort now for bigger gains later.

"Only passions, great passions, can elevate the soul to great things."[5] Passion provides the energy and commitment to do the hard work needed to start and grow new ventures. When people don't love what they do, they rarely work hard enough to be great. No passion, no innovation. However, according to Deloitte, only 11 percent of employees of large companies are passionate about their work.[6] Sadly, at a time when organizations need passion as the key to growth, their people are anemic.

People cannot be passionate about something that is mandated. Passion cannot be faked, borrowed, stolen, or bought. Passion is created, cultivated, and contagious, and its benefits are considerable:

- Passionate people are twice as likely to take on challenges as people who are disengaged.
- Passionate people are twice as likely to connect with others as people who are disengaged.
- Self-employed people are twice as likely to be passionate about their work as those employed by large firms.[7]

Oddly enough, both passion and compassion are stabilizing factors in an unstable environment. This is because passionate people are deeply committed to taking care of their customers and taking care of their team. They ask how they can serve others.

The front door of compassion is *empathy*, which can easily be understood as putting ourselves in another person's shoes. Empathy and compassion are at the heart of whatever "put the customer first" slogan any company has. But the challenge with slogans is that they say everything and, by themselves, do nothing. People do things; slogans do not. For slogans to live, the people in organizations must embrace and enact the values that the slogans talk about. For example, for the Cleveland Clinic to be consistently ranked among America's best hospitals, caregivers in the hospital must truly believe that "patients come first."

Empathy and compassion demand action. To have a virtue, we must act. Pity is the opposite. If I have pity for you, it means that I feel badly for you, but I'm not necessarily going to do anything about it. In fact, I'm glad it's you and not me! Pity aims our fear against someone's pain in a way that can be arrogant and condescending. Pity is cheap compassion. It costs us nothing and requires no action.

Research makes it clear that when we choose to care—to be compassionate—our life is better, and we are more productive.[8] And if we amplify our choice by the choices of our colleagues, we begin to imagine how a little bit of caring can change things in a big way.

The Reasons Why Compassion Is Relevant and Useful

The rules that govern left-brained organizations start and finish with metrics and numbers, so it is a struggle to figure out where compassion fits. Many leaders are more comfortable counting, rather than feeling, their way through life. Even when leaders understand that the numbers alone don't inspire us, they are unsure how to articulate a business case for compassion. Yet we all have seen that digits alone do not ensure that a great strategy will be realized. For a strategy to come out of its binder and become a reality, compassion defined by a willingness to sacrifice for a better future must be practiced.

Adam Grant offers an insightful way to measure whether we are more likely to succeed by giving, matching, or taking. *Givers* help people unconditionally by being generous with their time, insights, and connections. *Matchers* balance giving and getting. They take when negotiating a salary, they give when mentoring others, and they match when serving customers. Most people are matchers. *Takers* are just like the word suggests: the purpose of other people is to serve the takers' ends. The only situation in which takers will give is if they get something out of it. They are brilliant at kissing up and kicking down.[9]

So who performs best? The givers are the worst and best performers. They need to learn to not become doormats, especially when they compete with takers. Takers win in a sprint, but they burn bridges by asking for and not giving favors. While people root for givers, they look for ways to knock takers down or at least not help. It takes time for givers to earn good will and trust, but when they do, success is more likely. For example, givers are initially at a disadvantage in traditional medical schools because class rank determines opportunities. As medical school changes from a focus on class rank to clinical rotations and patient care, givers excel when success depends on teamwork and service.[10]

The lesson from Grant's research is that success does not have to come at the expense of others. And when we expect the worst in others, it brings out the worst in us. Givers create environments that help people learn, create, and innovate more. In contrast, takers are unlikely to acknowledge that a team has a problem—and all teams, especially the strongest teams, acknowledge that they have problems.[11]

Baird, an investment firm headquartered in Milwaukee, offers a crude but quite clear example that takers have no place offering financial advice. We will tone down Baird's policy by stating it has a "no jerk policy." Their on-boarding process starts something like this. Let's discuss what a jerk is: a person who is not well liked and who treats people badly. Once we are clear about that, then let's discuss what you do when you come across a jerk. Now here is what will happen if we discover that you are a jerk. Grant's research supports Baird's strategy that the best predictor of financial advisor success isn't expertise. It's putting the client's interest before their own. Apparently, Baird's policy works. According to Fortune, Baird happens to be one of the best places to work in America.[12]

Baird's policy deals directly with a problem that every organization confronts. Takers destroy trust because they escalate, rather than deescalate, fear. Here is a simple test. When an error is discovered, do your people shut down and turn inward instead of coming together? Is the question that people ask, "Whose fault was this?" When organizations hunt for scapegoats, failure's grip on the culture tightens. No organization can drive fear out completely, but we want to loosen its grip. Fear and self-preservation hold teams back.

Our only way to break through fear is with empathy, which creates the trust needed to take risk. It takes a while for any group to develop the level of trust necessary to be truly candid without fear of reprisal. No process overcomes people's refusing to hear criticism without getting defensive. We resist and reject failure because it is a lousy feeling. Yet great teams think about failure differently. They understand that the opposite of failure isn't success. The opposite of failure is growth.

In healthcare, quality of care is an imperative. And yet errors do occur. The huge focus on optimizing quality in healthcare institutions focuses on creating a "just culture," one in which we don't seek to blame, only to understand and improve. Such just cultures allow caregivers to be vigilant for opportunities to improve without the distracting fear of being blamed or punished. Hospitals with just cultures operate at a higher level of quality, and they are safer places to receive care.

If we are going to move the needle on only 30 percent of employees being engaged and only 11 percent being passionate about their work, then people will need to experience empathy and compassion. Caring for teammates communicates three important qualities to your colleagues. It says you belong, you matter, and you make a difference. If you can combine this with a sense of appreciation, some good, important relationship building will take place. And if this can be sustained over time, this will be a culture enhancer that helps the bottom line. The really good news is that compassion is usually cheap or even free!

Let's summarize a business case for compassion. People who care about each other, about their customers, and about their business will reduce risk. We always need to be alert for those who "couldn't care less!" They can be cancer cells in an organization. The best you can hope for is they are benign. But we all know that cancer kills—and so do those who couldn't care less.

The second business case for compassion is that compassion helps focus the business on its reason for being: its customers or patients. Too often, customers and patients are treated merely for what they can do for the organization. They are a means to the organization's end—namely, making money and protecting people's salaries. It is as if customers and patients are necessary evils. However, we are naïve if we think that customers and patients do not have "care antennae" functioning when we are in their midst. They are usually aware when they are being treated as a means to your end. When that happens, what ends is your business with them! Remember Dr. Lower's quote: "A patient is the most important person in this institution. A patient is not dependent on us; we are dependent on him or her."

The third focus is whether people care about the organization and have a sense of belonging. The common mistake here is for leaders and others to assume that this care already is in place—or that it does not matter that much. If folks don't care about their business, mediocrity may be the best you can hope for.

This is where the virtues come in—compassion and the others. If the caring that has been described is in place, then a caring community with its strong culture has been established. While a virtue like compassion is good for its own sake, there are mercenary benefits too.

The rest of this chapter focuses on compassion in two groups of people: customers and patients (the people whom the organizations are designed to serve) and team members and caregivers (the people who deliver services and products). Employers and caregivers need to first create value before they can extract value. The order matters. First create value. Then extract value. First care. Then succeed.

Taking Care of Customers

Customers are not targets to be aimed at. And patients are not statistics to be measured and placed into demographic buckets. Customers and patients simply think about themselves as people, and we are well served to do the same. Compassion enables me to care. If I care, then the other person—not me—is at the center of my attention. That steady focus requires a form of self-control or temperance. Empathy frees me to read another person's emotion. Asking questions allows me to gain a sense of not only *what* they are thinking but *how* they are thinking. All of this opens possibilities that simply don't appear with any other approach.

Earning someone's business isn't about techniques to "build rapport." Plenty of customers and patients suffer under our noses, which creates business opportunities *if* we can relieve their pain—even if they themselves are being a pain.

If we are to grow an organization, then we need to understand the suffering, or *pain points*, of the people we serve. Paying attention to the *voice of the customer* (VoC) can replace denial and delusion with insight about customer suffering. VoC is an innovative skill that is fundamental to creating customer or patient value. When we listen with empathy to the VoC, growth opportunities are uncovered by answering three questions:

1. Who is the customer?
   This can be a very difficult question to answer. Odds are high that different members of your team have different answers to this question. Ask and see.

2. What are your customers' pain points?

A pain point isn't just mildly annoying. A pain point causes us to lose sleep or be frustrated because we can't realize our goals. How do we know the cause of another's pain? We care. We ask. We learn.

3. What are customers' competing alternatives to solve their pain points?

When your customers are experiencing pain that cannot be solved by doing nothing or solving it themselves or through a competing alternative available to them, now you have an opportunity to provide a valuable solution.[13]

Let's start by defining the customer. Who is he or she? Sounds simple, but the answer turns out to be elusive. How do we lessen suffering and create sophisticated marketing strategies when we do not agree on who it is we plan to help? In healthcare, is the customer the patient, employer, physician, or the insurance carrier? You answer this riddle by getting clear about who gets an invoice. In other words, who will pay the bill? In the United States, patients have co-pays, although employers and the government pay most of the bill. For the most part, the patient is the user, but the government or the insurance company is the customer—they get the invoice for services rendered.

Clearly, treating patients is the purpose of healthcare, although purpose is different from payment. Defining our customer based on who pays the bills has another important benefit. It is not an innovation until we have a sale. This metric cuts through a lot of noise and static. A sale makes clear that a customer validated the value that the organization offered. Until a customer is prepared to pay, it's just an idea. The pain point of those who reimburse medical expenses is to prevent, rather than treat, illness. Of course, people will need to be treated for disease and ill health. But the real victory for both the patient and the insurer is to prevent disease, rather than treat it, once it has developed.

The best way to learn what people need is through stories, not through surveys. An effective VoC interaction strives to understand the customer's pain point before we try to fix it. Surveys have their place when you want to know how many people think in a particular way. However, surveys are often limited when it comes to uncovering pain points and competing alternatives.

A skilled VoC interviewer frequently asks questions and prompts, such as, "Tell me more about that." Avoid being a bad date who—as Bette Midler often does—asks, "Enough about me. What do you think about *me*?"[14] You may not know who Bette Midler is, but everyone has met similar self-absorbed people. A story about cup holders in cars illustrates this point.

When Chrysler launched the minivan, its success was historic. People turned in their station wagon keys for brand-new minivan keys. After record sales during the launch year, Chrysler increased van production. However, the following year, minivan sales were flat. Everyone who had wanted a van now owned one. To uncover what would increase customer satisfaction and sales, Chrysler sent surveys to potential customers. From a list of possible improvements, the most overwhelming customer request was more cup holders. Consequently, engineers made sure that cup holders were placed in every conceivable spot to ensure that customers always had a place for their drinks. Cup holder numbers soared, but sales numbers of minivans still remained flat.

The story goes that a recent hire to Chrysler put up her hand in a meeting. During her internship at Honda, she had learned that they didn't rely on surveys. The room gasped, "Oh, my. Don't they care about customers?" She said, "Actually they care so much about customers that they don't rely on surveys." This is how Chrysler applied this insight. First, they needed to find out who was buying minivans. In this case, the answer was easy—soccer moms. So Chrysler headed to soccer fields to give vans to soccer moms to drive free for a week or more. In exchange for the loan of the minivan, Chrysler wanted to place a video camera in the vehicle to observe behavior. Studying consumers the way anthropologists do would provide insights that a survey would never reveal.

The video cameras showed several important behaviors among soccer moms. Mothers walked back and forth outside the car dozens of times to open the single sliding door that was opposite the driver's side. The strength of a professional weight lifter was needed to take out a seat. And short of being shot putters, people didn't have a chance at success in trying to toss groceries into the back storage area because it required getting the groceries over a back seat that was too high.

Consumers knew they wanted cup holders. They did not know they had problems with doors and seats and with packing groceries too. At that moment, engineering aligned its design work with the insights of an anthropologist: to design vans with two sliding doors, seats that folded down easily, and low spaces in which to store groceries. Then, voilà! Sales of minivans went up. The moral of the story is that cup holders do not increase sales, and surveys may mislead. Instead, *real* pain points need to be addressed, the ones that customers may not be able to articulate but that can be understood by careful VoC analysis.

VoC interviews also uncover the customers' competing alternatives. DN and DIY are the ferocious competitors. DN means "do nothing," and DIY means "do it yourself." This is why the right question to ask is this: "What are a customer's competing alternatives?" It's not, "Whom do we compete against?"

In dominating the "burger war," understanding what the customer wants as an alternative to a burger is more important than understanding how McDonald's and Burger King compete against each other.

For example, how often have people you know asked only whether they wanted a Happy Meal or a "burger their way"? Customers who want a fast meal have more than two options. They can miss a meal (DN), or they can cook a meal themselves (DIY). The customer can grab a taco or a pizza, eat a salad rather than fast food, or eat at a friend's house. In other words, McDonald's and Burger King are competing for your stomach against far more alternatives than the other one's burgers, including to do nothing or to do it yourself. We need to understand all of the customer's competing alternatives, not just the easily identified competitors.

The critical insight about VoC interviews versus surveys is this. Make sure to ask open-ended questions designed to uncover pain points and competing alternatives, rather than just counting preconceived ideas, as often happens in a survey. Ultimately, we must answer the following question: for a customer like the one you plan to serve (who has competing alternatives such as DN, DIY, and other options), why is your value proposition superior?[15] A legitimate answer to this question offers an example of how compassion works in the commercial world. You solve a "pain point" for a customer and create a job for an employee.

Taking Care of Our Teammates

An MIT study showed that leadership and teamwork explained about two-thirds of the reasons why new ventures succeed or fail and that strategy explained only about one-third of the reasons for success or failure. Five years later, a second study replicated the first study and came to the same conclusion—that success and failure were defined more by the leadership team than by strategy.[16] Yet, how many organizations focus more on strategy and less on the leadership team? Strategy will and should change based on a marketplace you can't control. What you can control is who is on the team and, even more important, how the team behaves.

So, what does excellent teamwork look like? Our research revealed the same insights uncovered by research conducted by Google. Google is outstanding at uncovering patterns. Interestingly, when it came to uncovering the patterns of great teams, there were few patterns. Good teams were just as likely to be composed of introverts as extraverts. Good teams were just as likely to be made up of people who were friends outside work as they were to be made up of people who limited their relations to work. Good teams had strong leaders just as much as shared leadership.[17]

Google's reliance on analytics merely confirmed what Aristotle taught us 25 centuries ago. Virtues trump everything else, and in the case of teamwork, virtues associated with compassion and trust are preeminent in predicting high performance. Table 2.1 summarizes the characteristics of high-performance teams.

The team size is right ("two-pizza" teams of four to nine members).
There is shared clarity of purpose ("Why does the team exist?").
There is psychological safety (trust and compassion).
Everyone has a sense of belonging (empathy, trust, and compassion).
Everyone has a voice (empathy, trust, and compassion).
Everyone feels accountable to each other and to the team's mission.
There is clarity of roles and tactics to achieve the team's goals.

TABLE 2.1   Characteristics of High-Performance Teams

Source: Adapted from Charles Duhigg, "What Google Learned from Its Quest to Build the Perfect Team," *New York Times Magazine*, February 25, 2015.

Google's data demonstrated that great teams were skilled at empathy. Everyone made sure that everyone else felt a sense of belonging, and they took time to care and support each other. Second, empathy led great teams to be composed of people who spoke in roughly the same proportion. All team members cared enough about each other to ensure that everyone had a voice, which built trust.[18] In other words, compassion was always present.

Google's Project Aristotle research demonstrated that when the right behaviors were present, the collective IQ increased, and when the wrong behaviors were present, the collective IQ decreased. Our research has demonstrated that the right behaviors are exercising the virtues. We have also found, as Google and Gallup have reported, that team performance increases significantly when the group actively takes advantage of each member's strengths.[19]

The critical insight is that good teams are different from dysfunctional teams based on how they treat each other more than who is on the team. Let's repeat that. How people treat each other on a team is a better predictor of performance than who is on the team. Great teams create a psychological safety net of trust. That's it. It is that easy. It is that hard.

This is why teams whose members care for each other and cooperate beat teams whose members don't care for each other, even if those teams are more talented. This conclusion is similar to what Darwin reported about 150 years ago—tribes that survived cared for each other and excelled at cooperation. Tribes that struggled to survive didn't cooperate. There was less sense of belonging. Care cultivates trust, freeing people to focus on important organizational priorities— growth, innovation, and profitability. When trust has been established, hesitancy, doubt, and trepidation are minimized.[20]

Social Capital

Social capital is a fancy phrase to capture whom we know, which happens to be the best predictor of who will innovate.[21] Big surprise that the more people we know, the more ideas come our way. The more people we know, the better we are able to build a team of people who will collaborate well. This is why the critical pathway to shape the future that the organization wants is to have more, different connections than ever before. Like a bank account, people can build social capital through reciprocity; serve the giver, not just the receiver. Social capital is not a fluffy, idealistic concept. It is a real and practical one. The number of levels of reciprocity predict occupational success, social status, and economic rewards even more than education and experience.

Clearly, there is the exceptional solitary genius like Leonardo da Vinci, but which company can routinely count on hiring Renaissance people like him? Someone like da Vinci comes along once every 500 years and offers no option to replicate or scale! While organizations seek superstars, consider the benefit of developing the social capital of ordinary people to perform extraordinary results. Organizations prosper when innovators expand their social capital beyond their silos to include suppliers, regulators, and customers. And even better are innovators who expand their social capital beyond their industry and national borders. This is where compassion comes in and connects with social capital. This is one of the reasons that giving pays off in the marketplace.

Let's use your funeral as the place to center the purpose of building social capital. Consider David Brooks's distinction between "eulogy virtues" and "résumé virtues." There certainly aren't firm and fast rules about what a good funeral looks like. However, have you ever heard a eulogy praise someone for having a spacious home, a sporty car, or safari vacations? Eulogy virtues are about our character and what we hope people will say at our funeral. Résumé virtues are about achievements and what we hope creates opportunity for us in the marketplace. We know résumé virtues are not as important as eulogy virtues because we certainly don't mourn people's wealth, status, power, or fame at their funeral. We mourn people for how they made life better for others. Eulogy virtues may not be enough to defeat cynicism, although they should qualify as evidence that, as humans, our desire to give is stronger than our desire to have.[22]

The Number of Teammates Matters: Two Pizzas' Worth

As we've said, there are important benefits that teams derive from their members' treating each other well, but a team is even stronger when it consists of the right number of people. A team should be no larger than it takes two pizzas to feed. This means the group size should be at least four and no more than nine.

This idea was birthed at Amazon.com, and it is now widely practiced at high-growth companies such as Google, Intuit, and WalmartLabs. At Amazon.com, leaders traditionally recommended that employees increase communication to each other during company retreats. Jeff Bezos, Amazon.com's CEO and founder, had a surprising response: he didn't think more communication was a good idea! In other words, the solution to communication problems wasn't necessarily more communication. Instead, he suggested that as groups got larger, they struggled to communicate. Compare how 6 people communicate when they share two pizzas compared to how 150 people communicate at the company picnic. When conversations work well at the picnic, it is because the number of people involved doesn't exceed the two-pizza rule. As group size increases, the math to communicate effectively gets exponentially high and exceedingly difficulty to make work. For the Navy SEALs, the optimal number on a team is 4. For other teams, it might be 6. To ensure that a team remains agile, the size of the team shouldn't slip into double digits.[23]

While the two-pizza size is a critical component of teams, here is the key point that is often missed: empowerment and accountability are key requirements for team success. In the commercial world, accountability often means profit and loss (P&L) responsibility. However, teams often don't have P&L responsibility. This is why effective two-pizza teams agree on a critical metric or two to ensure that they have clear focus and accountability. The purpose of the team's task is made clear by the leader's intent. This requires the leader to answer the question "Why does the team exist?" When the team is empowered to figure out the *what* and *how*, it will achieve the leader's intent.[24]

Here's another example of how small teams—with 5 to 9 members—are better than bigger teams. Figure 2.2 relates a measure of political instability in a country (on the vertical axis) to the size of the country's ruling cabinet (on the horizontal axis).[25] You'll notice that having a large cabinet, especially one with greater than 20 members, is associated with values of political instability below zero—namely, more political instability. Countries with the greatest stability had two-pizza team cabinets. The notion is that big teams dilute the voice of their members, thus hampering group effectiveness. The lesson is this: when you are assembling a team, shoot for having a team of 5 to 9 members for maximal effectiveness.

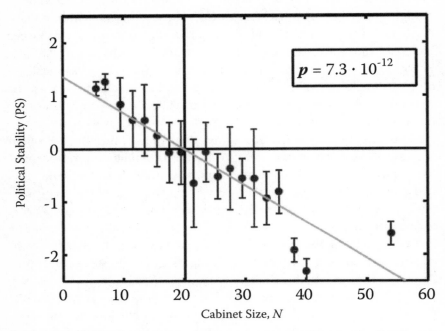

$$p = 7.3 \cdot 10^{-12}$$

Source: Adapted from P. Klimek, et al., *Journal of Statistical Mechanics: Theory and Experiment,* 2009: P03008.

FIGURE 2.2 Political Instability in a Country Related to the Size of That Country's Ruling Cabinet

Speed, efficiency, and productivity are the reasons to stick with small, empowered teams over larger teams. When teams get large, people get lost. They don't know their teammates well, and they don't know who can help them. In a big group, too many are not committed, and too few offer to help. Those who need help are reluctant to ask because doing so might suggest they are incompetent or on the verge of failure. Big teams too often lack empathy, and too few have a voice. In contrast, the members of two-pizza teams can relate to each other effectively.

In healthcare, there is lots of evidence that shows that great teamwork among colleagues—built on trust and compassion—produces better outcomes. For example, when cardiac surgeons are learning a new surgical technique, they perform surgery better and in less time when they emphasize the importance of teamwork and when the surgical team comes together to huddle before the case, communicate during the case, and debrief after the case on how each member can contribute to optimizing performance.[26] In the intensive care unit, better teamwork among the members of the ICU team is associated with enhanced survival.[27] Lung doctors and radiologists make more accurate diagnoses when they work together to interpret CT scans than when they read the films separately.[28] The evidence goes on and on.

It is pretty easy to describe the benefits of compassion. The hard part is that care requires intentionality, commitment, effort, and time. Clearly, we can say we care, but care becomes real only when it is actualized. Up until then, it is just an idea. Great teamwork is the result of deliberate practice. It is not an accident.

In order for care to become characteristic of a culture, caring has to be a habit. If the commitment is not widely shared, you will have only some individuals who care. Sometimes caring is easy. Naturally, caring for our friends and the folks who like us is easy. That takes little effort. But compassion is caring for others regardless of whether we like them or not. Now that's hard.

A caring culture certainly isn't about being perfect. It's a given that people will offend each other or worse. Caring communities aren't without warts. What makes them different is that people with compassion care enough to apologize, to acknowledge that they made mistakes, and to atone to make things right.

So why don't most companies and organizations opt for a caring culture? Perhaps it is precisely because it is an option. It is a choice. It requires effort, and it works only if people put the interests of the company and others ahead of their own interests. This makes creating compassionate cultures more difficult than it sounds.

COMPASSION IS UNIVERSAL

The case for compassion makes itself. Compassion is what we want to do anyway. Acts of compassion lead to a more positive perspective, more positive impact on others, reduced stress, and increased satisfaction. Stress soars when people are out to get each other. Stress declines when people look out for each other and they all feel like they belong. This insight is backed up by neuroscience research. Magnetic resonance images (MRIs) of the brain light up when we give more. Compassion activates the area of the brain that is associated with positive feelings.[29]

Our DNA wires us more for compassion than for self-absorption. To test this point, an interesting experiment relied on puppets with 6- and 10-month-old infants to test their attraction to selflessness or selfishness. One puppet was helpful, another neutral, and the third puppet was hindering. A doll struggled to open a box of toys. The helpful puppet lent a hand to help the doll open the box of toys. The neutral puppet watched the doll struggle and did nothing to help. The hindering puppet slammed the door shut to stop the doll from getting the toys. The infants overwhelmingly preferred the helpful to the neutral and hindering puppet, not just by a slight majority, but nearly every baby.[30]

From infants to adults, there is overwhelming research that compassion is universally appealing. While our research about the impact of compassion and other virtues on engagement is compelling, it is interesting that we still need proof. Would you bet engagement is more likely to go up when people are selfless or self-absorbed? Narcissism defines self-absorption, and over the long haul, narcissists fail more often than others because they take too many risks. Their narcissism blinds them to their weaknesses. Narcissists anger more quickly and are more likely to engage in unethical acts. An indicator of narcissism is the frequency of using the pronouns "I," "me," and "my," which is related to higher blood pressure and increased coronary atherosclerosis. In most cases, these findings hold up, even controlling for risk factors such as smoking, cholesterol, and age.[31] Narcissism contributes to loneliness because who the heck wants to spend time with the self-absorbed? Loneliness is linked to inflammation at the cellular level and to a weakened immune response.[32] Compassion is not something you add to the plate. Compassion is the plate.

COMPASSION TOOL KIT

We know that compassion isn't a simple matter of whether we have it or not. All of us are capable of great care as well as remarkable callousness. When we are compassionate, we take responsibility to care for family, friends, fellow workers, and even strangers. We are as concerned for others as we are about ourselves.

1. Four O'Clock in the Morning Test

Here is a simple compassion test. Is there one or more people you could call at four in the morning, knowing they would want to help you? The length of your 4:00 a.m. list is a pretty good measure of your compassion. Now, most people want to be compassionate and would like a long 4:00 a.m. list. Most of us don't actively seek ways to cause someone grief, and we don't want to be grumpy. Three options we can consider to increase our 4:00 am list include strengthening our appreciative orientation, serving others, and practicing active constructive communication.

2. Pleasure Versus Serving Others

There is nothing wrong with enjoying ourselves. It is simply worth considering that acts of altruism are more enduring than good times. Most opportunities for compassion are found in our ordinary, routine lives, so look there first. This might include simply doing something for a person who is having a tough time. Or it might include getting actively involved in some form of community service. When we help others, we feel better about ourselves.[33]

3. Active and Constructive

The kind of positive statements we make matters. People like us better and share more of the details of their life when we communicate using an active and constructive method. We also feel better about ourselves. When a friend shares good news about a promotion, we can respond in one of four ways:

- *Active and constructive:* Ask questions to learn about the details of your friend's good news. Offer honest and detailed praise for the news about his or her promotion:

"Bob, congratulations on your promotion. The new business you have brought to the company, the way you have built high-performance teams, and your rock solid integrity are the reasons people are happy your efforts were recognized."

- *Passive and constructive:* Say something positive like "That's great" but not much else:
  "Bob, congratulations on your promotion."
- *Active and destructive:* Say something like "Sounds like a lot of responsibility" without recognizing the person's achievement:
  "Bob, why would you want to take a job that requires so much travel and hard work? Sounds like a terrible lifestyle."
- *Passive and destructive:* Completely ignore the good news the person just shared with you:
  "When are we going to eat dinner?"

TEAM TOOL KITS: TOUGH, NOT ROUGH

Practicing compassion requires that we are tough without being rough. Teams need toughness to develop resiliency so they can bounce back from setbacks. What is too often missed is that toughness actually decreases when roughness is added to the mix. When people don't trust each other, resiliency decreases.

In contrast, trusting and caring relationships make us tough enough to take on tasks that are hard and important. Consider the "foxhole" mentality reported by soldiers. In battle, soldiers rarely report fighting hard for the strategic mission. Instead, they fight ferociously to save the life of the person they care about in the foxhole with them.

TEAM TOOL KIT

1. Team Checklist

A pilot who already knows how to fly a plane relies on checklists. A checklist simply helps the pilot make sure that he or she does not forget a key task. Similarly, an accomplished leader knows how to run a meeting. However, the leader benefits by using a checklist to ensure that everyone feels a sense of belonging and that everyone is contributing to team performance.

Since we know that how people treat each other is a better predictor of team performance than who is on the team, here is a team checklist that Google uses to improve team performance. A leader can simply keep this checklist nearby with her to ensure that empathy is demonstrated, that everyone has a voice, and that a psychological safety net exists so people can speak up freely:

- ✔ Listen by summarizing what others said.
- ✔ Admit what we don't know.
- ✔ Make sure everyone speaks.
- ✔ Avoid interrupting teammates.
- ✔ Encourage people to express frustrations.
- ✔ Encourage teammates without judgment.
- ✔ Call out conflicts and resolve openly.[34]

2. Safety and Accountability

Trust earned by teams whose members care about each other and accountability to achieve results are not mutually exclusive. In fact, they can be mutually supportive. People in high-performing teams trust each other and are also motivated to achieve results.

Consider the teams you are on. On a scale from low to high, rate whether team members care about each other and look out for each other. On a scale from low to high, rate whether team members are motivated and accountable to achieve results. Based on your rating, in which of the following four zones would you place your teams (Figure 2.3)?

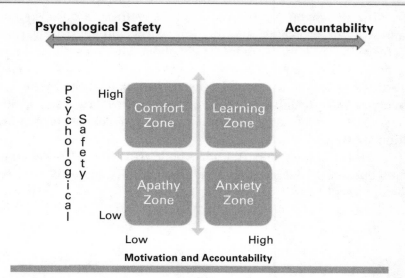

FIGURE 2.3 The Four Motivation and Accountability Zones

Source: Adapted from Amy Edmondson, "The Competitive Imperative of Learning," *Harvard Business Review,* July-August 2013, and Parker Hannifin.

- *Comfort zone:* Team members happily have a latte and muffin with each other, but they don't get much done.
- *Apathy zone:* Team members don't care about each other and don't get much done.
- *Anxiety zone:* Team members don't care about each other, but they achieve results.
- *Learning zone:* Team members care about each other and achieve results.

Our research shows that people take seriously the goal to look out for each other when they adopt the common language of virtue. The use of virtue language helps teams aspire to be the best version of themselves. A vision of moral excellence is clearly aspirational though the use of a common language contributes to a team's operating in the learning zone. This is critical to high performance because cooperating and learning are essential to thrive in VUCA conditions.

Teams can improve learning and reduce apathy and anxiety by

reframing the challenges they confront as learning problems rather than execution problems. A shift from apathy and angst to learning is achieved when leaders are forthright about what they do not know. Confident and secure leaders seek help from their teams. When leaders exhibit vulnerability and take the risk to ask for help, they create a safety zone for team members to also ask for help, to speak up, and to take risks. Leaders can promote learning by modeling curiosity and asking questions.[35]

Here is the important part: leaders build trust when they help their teams operate in the learning zone first. Results come second. The order matters.

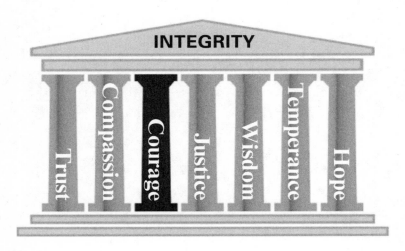

FIGURE 3.1 Pillars and Pediment: Courage

Source: Copyright © Parker Hannifin.

CHAPTER 3

Courage

Choose the hard right over the easy wrong.

*Success is not final; failure is not fatal. It is
the courage to continue that counts.*
—WINSTON CHURCHILL[1]

Courage has many faces and is recognized by its presence and also by its absence. In 2014, a Pakistani woman named Malala Yousafzai was selected as the youngest Nobel Peace Prize laureate. She had survived a shot in the head by terrorists who kill young women seeking an education. Miraculously, after she recovered, Malala said, "The terrorists thought they would change my aims and stop my ambitions; but nothing changed in my life but this: weaknesses, hopelessness, and fear died. Strength, power, and courage were born."[2]

From Pakistan to the United States, all cultures celebrate courage as noble. People are admired for risking their lives for others or for a principle. This is an example of moral courage, which is taught at West Point. The academy tells its cadets to "do the hard right rather than the easy wrong." People with moral courage put self-interest aside and exercise courage in the moment. However, practicing courage when pulled into an emotionally charged, high-stakes situation isn't easy.

A study of 6,000 employees who had witnessed unethical conduct helps us understand why "doing the hard right rather than the easy wrong" is hard. The employees in this study had observed serious unethical acts such as sexual harassment, giving or accepting bribes, falsifying financial records, and discrimination. When employee supervisors or co-workers were rated low on ethical behavior, only 40 percent reported unethical conduct. When employee supervisors or co-workers were rated as highly ethical, 65 percent reported unethical conduct. The culture created by supervisors and colleagues matters a lot. Ultimately, we are social animals who pay attention to what other people do, especially when courage to blow the whistle on unethical behavior is necessary.[3] Let's take a look at the powerful impact that being courageous can have.

BEING FORTHRIGHT IN DELIVERING BAD NEWS

A three-year-old was admitted to the children's hospital with a low platelet count and a bleeding risk. The child was fussy and complained of a headache. The doctor was called. The doctor visited the child, performed a cursory examination, and reassured Mrs. Tom, the mother. No tests were ordered or performed. Less than an hour later, the child had a seizure and developed a fatal brain herniation, the obvious result of bleeding in the brain.

The children's hospital's quality officer, Dr. Ireland, happened to be on call that night and became aware of the tragic events. Dr. Ireland visited the weeping mother and explained that by failing to order a CT scan of the head, the hospital had made a terrible mistake. Though Dr. Ireland was not involved in the child's care, she owned the error, explaining meticulously to Mrs. Tom what should have been done and how it might have caused treatment to change in a way that might have saved the child.

Dr. Ireland courageously risked experiencing the wrath of a parent who had just experienced the inconsolable loss of a child. She risked feeding a lawsuit. She risked making an unpopular decision that could negatively impact her professional relationships with colleagues.

Three months later, the hospital asked the mother to help prevent similar events by inviting her to make a videotape about the event that would emphasize how important it is to be vigilant and to speak up. Mrs. Tom could have understandably been enraged by the invitation and refused. But she didn't! Instead, she embraced the opportunity and made an impassioned videotape about vigilance, about working with the hospital and its doctors so that this would never happen again to any other child. The video was posted on the hospital's website, and it has been viewed by hundreds of thousands of visitors to the site.

All this was the result of Dr. Ireland's courage. By exercising honesty in the face of personal and institutional risk, she doubled down on principled care, practicing courage in service of justice and professionalism. Even in the face of terrible loss, Mrs. Tom recognized these virtues and rallied behind them. No suit was ever filed, and Mrs. Tom has used her personal tragedy to prevent other tragedies. She has experienced the healing that comes with translating tragedy into good for others. Altruism can help heal.

To have moral courage means that we have to know what our moral standard is. Enhance and protect the lives of others. Without the language of moral excellence, we settle for moral mediocrity. Courage is rooted in the French word *coeur*, which means "heart." It derives from the Latin *cor*, which translates as "heart, mind, or soul." To be courageous is to "take heart," to be or to do something "with all your mind or soulfully." Courage is also about strength of character. Think of the word *fort*, which comes from the Latin *fortis*, meaning "strong." A brave person demonstrates "strength and firmness" in the face of mortal danger.

In addition to physical strength, courage can be discussed in terms of overcoming self-pity or feeling like a victim when confronted with a life-threatening illness. The elderly, frail, and ill may demonstrate incredible courage when facing a life-threatening disease. Death is usually thought of as being a medical event, but death is also about relationships—to ourselves and to those we care about and who care about us. Death can be an extraordinary mirror through which we see ourselves.

In his book *Chasing Daylight*, Eugene O'Kelly, CEO of a major American firm, is facing death in several months from a terminal brain tumor. He writes, "The verdict I received the last week of May,

2005—that it was unlikely I'd make my daughter Gina's first day of eighth grade, the opening week of September—turned out to be a gift. Honestly, because I was forced to think seriously about my own death. Which meant I was forced to think more deeply about my life than I'd ever done."[4] This is courage.

From saying something unpopular to coming to grips with death, all levels of courage involve risk. Courage does not eliminate risk. It takes on risk and its associated fears. Courage is not the absence of fear. It is learning to cope with fear. Courage does not guarantee success. It does make success more likely. At any level, courage means a willingness to try and a commitment to hang in there for as long as courage is required.

The Business Case for Courage

While being courageous in and of itself is good, it becomes even more powerful when we understand that there also is a strong business case for courage. The rallying cry to innovate or die has become a cliché for good reason. The number of Fortune 500 firms that have managed to stay on the list between 1955 and 2011 is only 13 percent. The remaining 87 percent went out of business or were acquired.[5] This is why the status quo is a death warrant with only the actual time of death to be determined. As Prime Minister Harold Wilson said in a speech to the Consultative Assembly of the Council of Europe, in Strasbourg, France, on January 23, 1967: "He who rejects change is the architect of decay. The only human institution which rejects progress is the cemetery."[6] About a hundred years before Wilson's speech, Charles Darwin taught that even smart, intelligent species can become extinct if they resist change.

We are built to worry. We pay attention to exceptional events because fear and worry are survival tools. We need not notice or take time to explain normal events that do not threaten us. This is why we more easily remember bad experiences, such as being abandoned, than good experiences, such as gaining friends. We also have a bias toward nostalgia that our past was simpler and better. Parents and grandparents in virtually all cultures believe the current generation is not up to the standards of their generation. This leads adults to push children to up their game so they can survive.[7] So, seeing the status quo as a death warrant might just help even the reluctant see that commitment to the status quo is actually the riskiest thing to do.

While risk makes us vulnerable, the words *vulnerability* and *courage* rarely appear in the same sentence, though we want to make a case why they should. Once we understand that courage is about taking risks, it makes sense to include vulnerability as an element of courage. This is why vulnerability is part of the deal to be courageous. The word *vulnerable* comes from the Latin *vulnerabilis*, which means "to wound." But vulnerability is not a guarantee. It is a possibility. To be vulnerable does not necessarily mean that we will get hurt, but it does mean that we are in a situation where we might get hurt. Vulnerability means it's OK to be exposed. Folks who are unwilling to be vulnerable cover up. At our worst, we may choose to deceive—ourselves or others—rather than be at risk. In fact, this is exactly what *cowardice* means: cover up, turn away, or even back away.

One way to deal with the fear of risk is to realize that not all risks are equal and that some risks can be minimized. Courageous leaders put products out of business before their competitors do. In contrast, risk-averse leaders fail to adapt to market forces and join the list of endangered species. This is why courage is a major component in the character of every leader. It takes fortitude, vigor, and tenacity to lead others to adapt to shifting customer preferences or change a business model that is no longer profitable.

Courage and Growth

The so-called Magical Square Mile defines the borders of the Massachusetts Institute of Technology (MIT). Each year, the magic inside this mile births 900 companies. In total, the MIT start-up engine has launched 25,000 companies, created 3.3 million jobs, and generated $2 trillion in annual revenue, which ranks it as the world's eleventh-largest economy. MIT's secret sauce includes 45 years of insight into entrepreneurship, outstanding science and engineering research guided by pioneering new fields, and a 150-year-old culture of *mens et manus*, Latin for "minds and hands."[8]

We want to return to the importance of vulnerability and courage since the pairing of these two words is the first concept taught in MIT's entrepreneurship program. It may be counterintuitive, but senior leaders who have impressive experience starting and growing new ventures are taught that vulnerability is the birthplace of innovation. New ventures require lots of detours, mistakes, and dead ends that force innovators to get comfortable with being vulnerable.[9]

Innovation is often linked with failure, and for this reason, vulnerability is, in fact, an early phase of courage. Success in innovation usually comes from making mistakes and learning from them, a process that can be costly, embarrassing, and/or painful. Even when we accept that mistakes are a necessary part of innovation, failure is still resisted, rejected, and avoided. We end up playing it safe when the fear to fail trumps our desire to innovate. While no one wants to fail, innovation happens only when people are willing to fail. This is why getting comfortable with vulnerability is just part of the innovation drill.

When we fear failure, we walk away from our boldest ideas. Instead of being original, we sell conventional products and familiar services. But great entrepreneurs and innovators have a different response to the fear of failure. Yes, they're afraid of failing, but they're even more afraid of failing to try.

After a mistake, even successful innovators can shut down and withdraw, rather than come together to resolve problems. Innovation becomes even less likely when the first reaction to failure is to ask: "Who is to blame?" If teammates are to offer support rather than blame, to reveal inadequacies rather than hide, and to learn from mistakes rather than repeat mistakes, they need to be vulnerable. This takes courage. If an organization wants to cultivate its people to be open to a world that comes with loads of uncertainty, then it will need to cultivate courage. This includes learning to question our conduct and the possibility of being mistaken. It takes a boatload of courage for one person to say to another with sincerity, "I'm sorry. I was wrong. Next time, I will try to see things from your perspective."[10]

Taking courage in a slightly different direction takes regret into account. Regret and courage have an interesting relationship. In work and in life, there are two kinds of failure: actions and inactions. You can fail by starting a venture that goes out of business or by not starting a venture at all. You can fail by getting left at the altar or by never discussing marriage with your significant other. Most people fear the actions they'll regret more, so they never start. We cringe at the anguish of declaring bankruptcy or getting rejected by the love of our life. But we are dead wrong. Teddy Roosevelt captured this brilliantly in his 1910 "man in the arena" speech ("Citizen in a Republic"):

> It is not the critic who counts; not the man who points out how the strong man stumbles, or where the doer of deeds could have done them better. The credit belongs to the man who is actually in the arena, whose face is marred by dust and sweat and blood; who strives valiantly; who errs, who comes short again and again, because there is no effort without error and shortcoming; but who does actually strive to do the deeds; who knows great enthusiasms, the great devotions; who spends himself in a worthy cause; who at the best knows in the end the triumph of high achievement, and who at the worst, if he fails, at least fails while daring greatly, so that his place shall never be with those cold and timid souls who neither know victory nor defeat.[11]

When people reflect on their biggest regrets, they wish they could redo their inactions more than their actions. "In the long run, people of every age and in every walk of life seem to regret not having done things much more than they regret things they did," observed psychologists Tom Gilovich and Vicky Medvec. They summarize this regret: "The most popular regrets include not going to college, not grasping profitable business opportunities, and not spending enough time with family and friends."[12] Ultimately, what we regret is not failing in things we did, but failing to act.

Courage and the Unknown

The unknown universe of launching a new venture is very different from taking responsibility for something that already exists. Managing operational risk is very different from managing innovation risk. One way to build the courage needed to launch a new venture is to start by answering three questions:

1. Do you want it? If you are not motivated, then give it up.
2. Do you have the means? If you do not have all you need, use what you have.
3. Is it within your affordable loss? If not, lower the risk.[13]

In part, the courage to act can be developed when you know what you are up against. Courage takes into account the assessment and management of risk, which is omnipresent. It can help to know what is at stake by completing a risk assessment of macro, industry, and financial trends and issues such as these:

- *Macro issues* include terrorism, cyber security, global warming, demographic changes, pandemic diseases, inflation, economic contractions, unemployment, interest rate changes, political instability, and general turmoil.
- *Industry issues* include the impacts of globalization and technology on products and services, shifts in consumer preferences and competitive responses, regulatory changes, and increases or decreases in the power of suppliers, retailers, or manufacturers.
- *Financial issues* include breaking a bank conveyance, high debt levels, and cash shortages.

Those issues and others present both threats and opportunities to organizations. Interestingly, rarely do these types of issues sneak up on an organization. In fact, one study found that in 199 out of 199 cases, the problem that brought an organization down had been discussed and dismissed.[14] Spotting disruptive forces is one thing. It is quite another to change because cultures are often committed to existing organizational structures and existing processes. In contrast, breakthrough innovations often cut across organizations horizontally. Silos are vertical. The R&D stovepipe is separated from the sales stovepipe. Each stove cooks independently from the other. A fragmented, internal focus is a recipe to calcify the culture. Creativity and innovation are fed best by functional experts who integrate, rather than separate, their efforts to respond to external change.

Let's continue with processes. As organizations mature, and often in response to risk, layers of processes are added. Each process on its own adds value—Lean standards, quality, strategic pricing, safety, talent management, pay for performance, and so on. The problem arises when metrics focus on whether people are using the tool, rather than on whether they actually need the tool. In other words, the tool becomes the end rather than the means. When this happens, the process tail starts to wag the innovation dog. You know that things are off the rails when people spend more time writing reports than interacting with customers.

Essentially, it's the rigid application of processes that dampens employee initiative and engagement. Whenever rigidity and rules replace virtue, thoughtful entrepreneurial spirit and intelligent risk taking get squashed. However, a note of caution is also in order here. If you are ready to create an innovative culture as part of an existing organization, prepare to be misunderstood. Hostile financial, operational, and human resources bows shoot arrows at innovative pioneers. Silos that war against each other unite to pound a new business model into the traditional model. We have seen the enemy and he is us![15] This is why it is vitally important to rely on antidotes to risk-averse cultures:

- Rather than rely on fragmented silos, we need interdisciplinary teams.
- Rather than being tough on people, we need to be tough on processes.
- Rather than accepting risk-averse cultures, we need to create intelligent risk-taking cultures that learn from mistakes.
- Rather than praising the past and being paranoid about the future, we need to empower innovators to launch and grow new ventures.
- Rather than protecting successes, we must put products out of business before competitors do.

THE COURAGE TO OPEN THE CIA

When the message is "do not stray from your silo," it takes courage to solve systematic problems that rest outside a person's duties. Carmen Medina, retired CIA deputy director for intelligence, created an informal Rebel Alliance at the CIA. The group questioned assumptions and the status quo in response to the

CIA's failure to share information it already possessed that could have prevented the terrorist attacks on September 11, 2001. Medina developed a novel approach to intelligence sharing that was awarded a Service to America Medal for activities that improve homeland security. That's right. The CIA, the preeminent spy organization for the United States, made us safer by improving how it shared information.[16]

The core idea was encouraging people to become "good" rebels in pursuit of a noble goal, recognizing that trouble awaits you (Table 3.1). This message is relevant for innovators: no matter how noble your goal, prepare to be challenged by those who are scared of change and/or those who treat the status quo as sacred. Even if you are a benevolent rebel, expect to be misunderstood at best and shunned at worst when you call out problems. With these cautions understood, the odds of a leading change increase when good rebel qualities are practiced instead of bad rebel qualities.

GOOD REBELS	BAD REBELS
Change rules	Break rules
Create	Complain
Ask questions	Make statements
Are mission focused	Are "me" focused
Are passionate	Are angry
Are optimistic	Are pessimistic
Generate energy	Sap energy
Attract possibilities	Alienate people
Socialize opportunities	Vocalize problems
Wonder if	Worry that
Pinpoint causes	Point fingers
Believe	Doubt
Are social	Are social loners

TABLE 3.1 Actions and Characteristics of Good Versus Bad Rebels

Source: Adapted from Carmen Medina, "The Heart of Innovation: Building Trust and Encouraging Risk," CIG Summit, Baldwin-Wallace College, Berea, OH, April 12, 2012.

In brief, good rebels strive to serve the organization. Bad rebels strive to serve themselves. Good rebels are not motivated by recognition or money. In fact, many avoid attention. The central motivation of the benevolent rebel is to make a difference. What the good rebel needs to learn is how to take intelligent risk without being reckless. Medina suggested there is a rebel inside us all. However, from the C suite to the lowest level of an organization, people are rewarded for conforming. Fear of failure leads to risk aversion, resistance to change, and complacency. In contrast, a clear purpose that creates a culture of collaboration is energizing. In Medina's view, "Optimism is the greatest act of rebellion."[17]

Courage and Risk

In 1979, Monty Python's comedy *Life of Brian* was released. Brian plays the part of the unenthusiastic prophet who doesn't want the job. He yells to a group of followers, "I have one or two things to say."

The crowd yells back, "Tell us. Tell us both of them."

Brian cries out, "Look, you have it all wrong. You don't need to follow me. You don't need to follow anyone. You must think for yourselves. You are all individuals."

The crowd responds compliantly, "Yes, we are all individuals."

Brian says, "You are all different."

The crowd parrots back, "Yes, we are all different."

A quiet voice says meekly, "I'm not!"[18]

Absurd as this scene may seem, it neatly matches what psychologists have discovered about our conduct in groups. Cultures affect conduct far more than people acknowledge or admit. People consider themselves to be individuals, but a surprising amount of what we do and think is really prompted by group-action and groupthink. Too often people act as passive bystanders rather than as active and courageous participants.

This is why "just do the right thing" statements do little to encourage people to speak up against unethical acts. That's because when people do speak up, they are not sure they will still have a paycheck. When it comes to courage, often the problem isn't being confused about what we should do. We want to do the right thing but not if the price is higher than we can bear or beyond what is even fair. We know what we should do, but we don't know how to do it. So we observe what's wrong, but we feel too weak to make a change. A useful antidote to passivity is bystander education. This involves practicing virtues in low-stress circumstances to prepare for high-stress, high-stakes situations.

The goal is to decrease the number of bystander witnesses who do nothing or, worse, contribute to harming others. Let's use fraud prevention to make clear the value of bystander education. When it comes to preventing fraud, the only chance an organization has is courageous bystanders. Auditors and regulators cannot catch fraud without the aid of courageous bystanders. This is why silent bystanders represent an enormous reputational risk to all organizations. Research reveals three factors that can give rise to fraud (Figure 3.2):

FIGURE 3.2   Three Factors That Give Rise to Fraud: Perceived Pressure, Opportunity, and Rationalization

Source: Adapted from Donald R. Cressey, *Other People's Money: Study in the Social Psychology of Embezzlement,* Patterson Smith, Montclair, NJ, 1973, p. 30.

- *Perceived pressure:* People sometimes feel pressure to cut corners to hit monthly targets. Pressure can lead people to overstate or understate billable hours, adjust economic forecasts, adjust earnings, inflate product capabilities, or understate the time to provide services.
- *Opportunity:* People sometimes think they can get away with stealing. An ethical organization puts controls in place to reduce opportunities for code of conduct violations. They also prosecute people who break the law. That said, any reasonable organization would much rather help than punish people. Besides, prevention usually costs less than punishment.
- *Rationalization:* Some people rationalize that an organization won't miss money or equipment. They can also convince themselves, since their actions have not been uncovered, that the organization deserves to take the loss. Rationalization can also include believing that the means justify the ends. The leader misrepresents earnings so that everyone on the team can earn a bonus for hard work.[19]

Organizations put controls in place to mitigate risk associated with opportunity. However, organizations lack the tools to mitigate risk associated with pressure to perform and rationalization. Given the huge reputational risk of fraud, it is vitally important and beneficial to add the tool of bystander education to the risk management kit.

Bystander education starts with a simple premise: knowing does not lead to doing. The list of ethical challenges might be long, though the list of reasons for ethical lapses remains pretty short. "I didn't know how to say no. Everyone was doing it. I didn't think I would get caught."

So why don't bystanders speak up when they observe fraud? Bystanders often believe they will not be able to influence the offending individuals, especially if the offenders have more power than they do. They may fear the price they would be forced to pay. They fear becoming outcasts. They might harm their careers and jeopardize their financial health. Any rationalization will do!

The people who successfully navigate the pressure to perform and the rationalization to not act when they observe fraud first get clear about virtue. They start with the premise that most of us would like to behave in accordance with virtue, though we need help living as our best selves. This is why the focus is more on practicing virtue than knowing virtue. This is why we practice what we want to do under pressure by pre-scripting our convictions out loud with respected listeners. We learn to be courageous by breaking courage down into manageable parts and by practicing in low-stress situations so that we are prepared for high pressure.[20]

Here is a critical benefit of integrating bystander education into an ethics program. The directors of character education at each service academy have reported that bystander education reduces ethical lapses.[21] *Bystander intervention* is an evidence-based method, the goal of which is to increase the percentage of people who step up or speak out when they witness behaviors that could harm others. Bystander intervention empowers individuals to go from inaction to action by practicing courage.

First, we need to understand what stops us from being courageous when we want to be. People overestimate that knowing will lead to doing. And they underestimate the difficulty of putting courage into action. We all have faced situations in which it was unclear how to raise concerns, even when we knew that what was going on was wrong. When this has happened, we have rarely acted for personal gain. Rather, we were uncertain as to whether we could make a difference or whether the price we would have to pay would be too high. That is why more rules do not help us challenge authority or challenge peers whose conduct is harming others.

Few of us are idealists who will act courageously under any circumstance. Most of us are pragmatists who balance self-interest with selflessness. Sometimes we get sucked in by cynicism.[22] In addition, under threat, we don't think clearly. Emotion takes over, and our brains start to work against us rather than for us. When we are scared, our brain shuts down the prefrontal cortex—that is, the thinking part of the brain—making us less flexible and creative in solving situations that involve conflict. The good news is that with practice, we can learn to control our emotions and competently protect ourselves and others. This is part of bystander education.

To learn courage, replace blame with humility. Practice courage by acknowledging weaknesses. Arrogance is a sign of weakness and fear. Humility is a sign of strength and courage. Arrogance aims blame and pain at others. Humility is open to our shortcomings, including the difficulty in "how" to practice courage.

When we are humble, we more readily accept how easy it is to misunderstand the motivations of others. I can observe your behavior and not have a clue why you did what you did. Heck, we are often unsure why we do something ourselves, never mind understanding why someone else does something. So we get into trouble when we assume that we know what someone else is thinking. Most people who do unethical things are basically good people. Who hasn't felt trapped or forced into doing something he or she didn't want to do? So a bit of grace goes a long way by giving us insights about human follies uncovered by behavioral economists. We suffer from a host of irrational conduct that includes but is not limited to the following:

- *Groupthink:* Like the people in *Life of Brian*, we fail to think for ourselves.
- *Confirmation bias:* We make sense of the world by choosing to process information that confirms our current beliefs, rather than discovering what is actually happening.
- *Fear of loss:* We fear loss about twice as much as we hope for gain. This is why fear too often drives our decisions.[23]

Once the barriers to courage are understood, the enablers of courage can be applied. A powerful start is to get very clear about the kind of person we aspire to become. What is the very best version of ourself? We are also more likely to strive to be courageous when the people around us are open about their imperfections and mistakes, especially our leaders. We don't trust people who claim only strengths and don't mention shortcomings. To err is human, and we don't trust people who won't admit to mistakes. When leaders can share their flaws and errors, we can more easily allow ourselves room for mistakes and opportunities to learn. People of character embrace vulnerability not out of comfort or discomfort but out of their understanding that character development depends on being open and vulnerable.

The strongest courage enabler is to acknowledge what is at stake. We have worked with hundreds of corporate controllers and find that an exclusive emphasis on rules in financial reporting has a major flaw: it misses the question of the purpose of financial leadership, which depends on understanding the powerful impact that financial decisions have on people's lives and organizational health. Controllers are the stewards of the organization's resources. In this sense, they are keepers of the culture. Financial leaders help the organization make decisions that strengthen the enterprise. To this end, financial leadership is founded on trusting and meaningful relationships. Trust is earned, based on who the financial leaders are (their character), as well as their competence (their ability to create and report financial information that is both accurate and transparent).

It is far more effective to tap into people's positive desire to excel. The same is true in healthcare. Physicians who want women to get a mammogram are more convincing when they describe the benefits of early detection than they are when they inform patients about the disease they may develop if they do not get a mammogram. Gain sharing is better than risk mongering.

We suggest better tools rather than more rules. For example, we can use tools from one sector (aviation) in another sector (healthcare). Interestingly, the way pilots practice aviation safety principles has been applied to surgery teams. Pilots don't want to crash a plane, and surgeons don't want medical errors. That's the easy part. The harder part in both cases is avoiding near misses and death.

What improved aviation safety were formal pre- and postflight briefings, safety checklists, and empowering any member of the flying team to speak up. What helps in surgery is preoperative "huddles" when the team comes together to outline the plan for the case. This includes the surgeon actively inviting teamwork and the team being reminded that if someone observes an error, to flag it so that it can be corrected and prevented from becoming worse. Checklists in flying and in surgery mitigate the risk associated with members of the team viewing their job too narrowly. For example, nurses can limit their jobs to preparing the patient only preoperatively. Or nurses can view themselves as being members of a team that is committed to the larger purpose of protecting the patients' health from the time they enter the hospital until the moment of discharge.

Let's return to fraud. It may be less than obvious how a positive, purpose-driven approach prevents deception. To see how this works, consider the boss who wants to adjust quarterly statements to improve a bonus for her hardworking team by counting revenue that has been billed but not booked. Over 100 controllers discussed this common problem in a series of virtue-based seminars that included a section on bystander education. Remember, the role of the controller is to ensure accurate financial reporting. So it would seem completely reasonable that the way for the controller to stop the boss from booking unrecognized revenue would be to start with accounting rules. Right? Wrong.

Rather than starting with rules, start with questions. Appeal to a shared purpose of virtuous conduct that de-escalates, rather than escalates, conflict. Once introduced to the virtues, a sample of nearly 200 leaders from 27 nations revealed that people wanted permission to be virtuous, independent of nationality. In fact, there was a statistically significant change in the statement "Do you want permission to be virtuous?" after the seminar compared to before.[24] Once leaders understood the personal and strategic benefit of virtue, they wanted permission to act this way. Ethical action is the same as strategic action. Sometimes we succeed, and sometimes we don't. But just because success isn't guaranteed, it doesn't mean we don't try. We need to move from "Can I can be virtuous?" to "How can I practice virtue?" The following section explains how.

Strengthening Through Scripting

Scripting involves practicing answers to questions out loud with a trusted colleague. We mitigate risk by practicing how to respond to a problem like fraud before it happens. Imagine a leader who wants to recognize revenue in this month's financial statements but that revenue hasn't yet been earned. Maybe he wants the bonus for his team. Maybe he is under incredible pressure to pay for a child's medical bills. Who knows?

Remember, we are often wrong when trying to guess a person's motives. Besides, challenging a person's motives or calling someone out for being unethical rarely goes well.[25] Rather than challenging someone's motives or her integrity, practice asking or making some variation of the following three questions and two statements in descending order. Here are the questions, followed by examples of potential answers to each:

1. "Is there any reason we are doing this?"
2. "Could we rethink our plans?"
3. Good, bad, good response.
4. "Is there anything I can say to change your mind?"
5. "If you are unwilling to change your mind, then this is what I'll need to do."[26]

The goal is to get to the right outcome without blowing up the relationship. The first question to leaders who want to recognize revenue that hasn't been earned is this: "Is there any reason we are doing this?" This question will lead most leaders to pause and rethink the request to perform a questionable activity. If they still insist, then we ask the second question: "Can we rethink our plans and double-check with the CFO to make sure our decision is acceptable?" If needed, statement 3 ups the ante: "To strengthen the company, we need accurate financial information [*good*]. If our financial information is inaccurate, we erode trust in our decisions [*bad*]. Since we always strive to earn people's trust, let's ensure that our decision reflects accurate financial information [*good*]." Questions 1 and 2, and statement 3 will resolve the vast majority of ethical lapses. Goal achieved: maintain the relationship while ensuring that integrity prevails.

However, let's say you have an ornery leader who won't give up. Remember that it's not clear whether she is under financial distress, wants to help others, or is just plain greedy. We don't know, and there isn't much upside to challenging motives. Question 4 asks, "Is there anything I can say to change your mind?" And if you have to take it to the wall, then our last resort is to move from a question to a statement: "If you insist that we count unrealized revenue, then I'll need to go to the audit committee of the board to ensure that our financial reports are accurate."

Rarely, if ever, do we need to resort to statement 5. Yet too often, people under pressure jump to question 4 and statement 5 far too soon. The result is that they might get to a good outcome, but they blow up the relationship in the process. The evidence is that questions 1 and 2 or statement 3 usually save the relationship and the company's integrity. Questions 1 and 2 and statement 3 also express true curiosity on your part to understand the reasons for the action since you cannot easily guess someone's motives.

In sum, those who are effective bystanders are more likely to be clear about wanting to strive to be virtuous, even under pressure. They anticipate situations in which virtue will be challenged, and they share out loud with a respected listener what they would do. When we approach dilemmas in a less confrontational and less self-righteous way, we calm down the amygdala and kick in the prefrontal cortex. To live a life committed to the virtues requires that we understand ourselves and others by reducing the impact of pressure to perform and self-justifying behavior.

Even though corporate ethics programs are designed to protect the most important corporate asset, reputation, bystander education is a missing piece. This process recognizes that you already want to be courageous but that you may not always know how.

The same is true in medicine. We want doctors with integrity and professionalism, and we want a safe environment in hospitals. To achieve these goals, doctors in training—from the earliest years of medical school—must learn to have voice in service of the well-being of their patients. When the "North Star" of "patients first" is clear, the required actions of the educated bystander are also clear. Even junior doctors in a very hierarchical system will speak out and be commended for doing so when bystander education is practiced.

Voluntarily, and for reasons of enlightened self-interest, organizations would be well served to add bystander education to their ethics tool kit. Of course, some form of compliance and risk management is essential in preserving an organization's reputation. However, what if organizations spent a fraction of the costs associated with compliance and risk management to create a culture of virtue and integrity? The value is to teach leaders how to rely on courage in the face of pressure to perform, rather than to recite codes of conduct.

Developing Courage and Grit

Gandhi, Nelson Mandela, and Martin Luther King, Jr., lived remarkable lives that bent the curve of history and continue to inspire many today. However, rather than limiting our notion of courage to extraordinary acts in the face of danger and injustice, it is better to expand our understanding of courage to something that fits all of us. Lead change.

Resolve a conflict effectively. Take an intelligent risk. The foe is not some unknown enemy but rather anything that prevents or corrodes the good.

Courage is not a gift of nature. We learn about courage from our life experiences. Aristotle said that virtue is in our power, assuring us, "Where it is in our power to act, it is also in our power not to act."[27] One act of courage is just that: one act. It is not yet a habit. Nor is it yet part of our character. To act with courage requires repetition that is habit-forming. Courage is something we might hope to have, but until we act, it is not real. Even if courage becomes habitual, we all still fail and sometimes fall short of our convictions.

It may seem as though risk takers have some inherent courage. They do not. Courage is learned, as is cowardice. There is no such thing as courageous DNA or, for that matter, cowardly DNA. Another word for learned courage is *grit*, which Angela Duckworth defines as passion and perseverance for long-term goals. Grit is about having stamina to create a future reality that takes months and years. Someone with grit lives life as a marathon rather than a sprint.[28] When passion and perseverance continue over a long time, demonstrating an unwillingness to give up—that's grit.

Grit is not the same thing as stubbornness. Stubborn people tend to hang on beyond reason or sometimes for the wrong reason. Stubborn folks cling to ends that serve their desires or lock onto means that lack merit. This isn't the case for gritty people, who are internally motivated to hang in there irrespective of circumstances. The gritty have a kind of "can-do" attitude that sees them through rough spots and sets them on course for a longer haul if necessary. They are not stupid. To be stupid is to do something that has no possibility of becoming reality. To be stubborn means "I won't learn." To be gritty means "I want to learn, grow, and get better."

Grit is not necessarily associated with intelligence. In fact, sometimes gritty people have an advantage over those who are intellectually brighter. One way to think about intelligent people is that they process information and come to conclusions faster than the rest of us. When success is slow in coming, and ideas for addressing problems are scarce, the intelligent people might too readily give up because they are used to achieving a good outcome quickly. People more used to working hard to succeed might be more willing to correct mistakes and be grittier, and they might have an advantage over people who are used to success coming easily.

Persistent folks tend to be open to being wrong. They'll keep trying. Gritty people consider admitting to their mistakes as progress rather than an indictment of their ability. They tend to understand failure in the same fashion. Failure becomes a problem they can work on, rather than a defeat that stops the game.

All this has to do with learning and growing from mistakes and adversity—the pursuit of personal growth by being challenged by our failures rather than being comfortable with our successes. John Hagel talks about the "comfort zone" and the "learning zone."[29] Our comfort zone is the place where we are living risk free, or so it seems. It is the place where it is easy to get by, where we play it safe, and where we back away from trying anything new. It may be comfortable, but in the business or healthcare worlds, it is a dangerous way to proceed. Imagine if neither doctors nor patients participated in clinical trials of new drugs or new procedures! If that happened, progress would stop in its tracks, and we would be using the same treatments we used in the 1930s. To succeed requires stretching out of our comfort zones.

The goal of creating a future adds purpose, which makes grit even more powerful. Purpose provides vision, direction, or reason for grit to happen. Purpose gives passion a focus, and perseverance adds duration to the equation. The goal is not persistence. The goal is a moral purpose that commits our life to something bigger than self, which requires grit to accomplish.

Persistence depends on *resilience*, which in Latin means "to jump again." When, not if, adversity comes our way, do we overcome, or do we get overwhelmed? Adversity includes trauma, which can be chronic, such as abuse, sickness, or divorce. Or trauma can be acute, such as experiencing an act of violence. Chronic stress is more cumulative, though less intense, than acute stress.

Research on our response to trauma reveals something quite interesting. After a significant trauma, most people recover and become resilient over time. Whether we manage to get to the other side of sadness depends on how we think about trauma overall, not the trauma itself. This is critically important because our response is in our control while the horrible event often is not in our control.[30]

It comes as no surprise that sadness is the core emotion we feel after a significant loss. What is less clear is the constructive role that sadness can play in helping us be courageous when we face loss. Bereaved people report that living with sadness is like living life in slow motion. As a result, they pay less attention to the world around them and their normal everyday concerns and more attention to turning inward. Sadness turns our attention inward, enabling us to take stock of our situation so that we might start to adjust.

Interestingly, with sadness comes an accuracy that promotes deeper and more effective reflections. Research has demonstrated that when people are made to feel sad, they are more accurate in how they view their abilities and performance. When people who are angry are compared to people who are sad, it's the sad people who demonstrate greater resistance to stereotyping. When people are sad, they are more likely to make accurate judgments about others.[31]

This isn't to diminish the deep pain and sense of loss that comes from trauma. It is difficult to make sense of a tough event when we are still emotionally charged, though given adequate time and coaching, we can learn to regulate our emotions and reframe a negative experience into more positive terms. Optimism is a strong predictor of how we get to the other side of sadness.[32]

We can learn to become more optimistic by developing an internal locus of control (*conviction*), rather than being defined by circumstance. This involves a shift from explaining bad events as our own fault (*global explanation*) to concluding that one event does not mean something is wrong with our life (*specific explanation*). When we shift from "I can't change the situation" (*permanent*) to "I can change myself or the situation" (*impermanent*), we become more resilient.[33]

Here is the important point: these are cognitive skills or how we think, which means that they can be learned. When we learn and practice framing adversity as a challenge, we become more flexible in the face of adversity in a way that promotes growth and resilience. In contrast, when we view adversity as permanent, then we become inflexible and less resilient. We lose hope.

Now this certainly is not a recommendation to go out and experience some trauma in your life. In fact, our advice is that when it comes to trauma, avoid it! While the pain isn't something any of us want to experience, what we do know about trauma is this: when courage is combined with other virtues, people can get to the other side of trauma. Perhaps this means they are both wounded and a bit more whole. Maybe they are not fully recovered, and it is no longer possible to go back to a situation no longer available. But getting to the other side of sadness does mean that we are healing.

What helps us recover and build resilience is to be surrounded by people who care about us when times are bleak. Relationships buttress resiliency. Beyond simple bumper sticker fixes, the good news is that sound research demonstrates that we can overcome, rather than be overwhelmed, when, not if, unwanted trauma pays us a visit.[34]

PROFILE: ARTASHES GAZARIAN

To act with courage means that we have chosen a greater benefit (purpose) than individual comfort and achievement. This obviously is a huge endeavor, literally a lifetime's work. Without courage, none of the other virtues is possible. Artashes Gazarian was involved in plucking Lithuania from the former Soviet Union orbit in the late 1980s.

Born in a Siberian labor camp, raised in Belorussia and Ukraine, Gazarian earned social science degrees in St. Petersburg, Russia. He was a plant manager in the former Soviet Union, despite not being a member of the Communist Party. In the mid-1980s, Gazarian moved to Klaipeda, Lithuania. This is when President Gorbachev of the Soviet Union was pursuing *glasnost* ("openness") and *perestroika* ("restructuring"), which Lithuanians and others decided to take advantage of, although in a way that Russia did not agree with. When Moscow learned of "disunity" efforts, Gorbachev quickly demanded a meeting with underground leaders, including Gazarian. Gorbachev told his Lithuanian comrades that *perestroika* did not mean independence. Tanks would make the benefit of unity clear, if this point was not understood by Gazarian and his fellow underground leaders.

To avoid war, Gazarian and other Lithuanian leaders formed a strange alliance with the KGB and Soviet commanders stationed in Klaipeda. Issuing orders in Moscow was easy. But local Soviets found that it was not easy to execute those orders to gain control of this Baltic nation. To avoid war, local Soviets warned Gazarian and his fellow Lithuanian leaders about their fellow citizens who were involved in incidents that could spark a war. Local Lithuanians warned the Soviets about troops who treated citizens cruelly that could spark street riots. Both sides policed their own and each other, hoping for a peaceful outcome.

In late 1989, the Berlin Wall fell. The Iron Curtain toppled not only in Germany but throughout Eastern Europe. Lithuania won independence. Gazarian became Klaipeda's deputy mayor, responsible for economic affairs. He sold state-owned enterprises and property to anyone who would invest in Klaipeda under one condition: if after two years, the owner had created wealth and jobs, they would receive the property for free. As a result, Lithuania grew its economy without state funds. His idea was soon adopted nationwide, and it was later applied throughout east and central Europe.

The story of Gazarian is a bold story of courage. The Lithuanians we interviewed who shared this experience talked about feeling alive, emboldened by shared sacrifice and commitment to freedom. Their relationships with each other "encouraged" each other.

One of the things people of courage learn is what risks are worth taking. Gazarian wonders about people who are scared to risk speaking up in a meeting. He chides: what idea would you give your life for? Gazarian's standard of courage is impressive, but it is probably too high a bar for most of us. We will see later in Chapter 7 on hope that hope and courage are intertwined. If hope is not possible, it's an illusion or wish-dream. The same can be said for courage. Using courage to take a risk that has no chance of succeeding is not really courage. The reason we act courageously is to make things better for ourselves and for others. We act courageously because doing so gives us reason to hope for a better future. In contrast, simply falling on our sword as a martyr leaves in place the very thing we wanted to change.

PROFILE IN COURAGE: JAKE

Acute lymphoblastic leukemia—a cancer of the bone marrow—was the diagnosis for Jake, a freshman collegiate lacrosse player. "It all started with yellow eyes," wrote Emma Harding, a fellow athlete and writer for the university sports news. Jake was sitting in the dorm room with some of his friends when one of them said to him that his eyes were yellow. During a visit to the health center, Jake was told to rest for a couple of days. That did nothing to help. Jake's commentary is more colorful. "I was just a vampire. I was completely white, and even the warm-up lap (for lacrosse), which is, what, a 50-yard jog, made me dead after."

Jake dropped out of school to begin a rigorous regimen of chemotherapy. He lost significant weight. He lost his hair. But he did not lose his heart! He became the lacrosse player who had cancer. He never played one minute, and yet he had tremendous impact not only on the lacrosse team but on the university's athletic program as a whole. He became a leader. He modeled courage.

His sophomore year found Jake back in school. Instead of returning to the lacrosse field, he returned for more chemotherapy. He had to begin facing the fact that he might never play lacrosse again. His bones were brittle. He had long-term goals of serving in the military. Those plans were threatened. What did not change was the courage that Jake brought to every experience.

Jake has been part of a student athlete leadership experience in which the athletes study the seven virtues and learn how these virtues play a key role in effective leadership. Typically, the goal of the class is to think about the virtues in relationship to their sports and their roles as leaders with their team. On one occasion, seven leaders from an engineering company were visiting the athlete class. Jake briefly shared part of his story. Stories have power, and his story had a powerful effect on those seven men and women.

Terry was one of the executives who heard Jake's story. He is a pretty traditional, old-school steelworker. He is not formally educated, but he is smart and thoughtful. He does not play lacrosse.

His field is the factory, where he supervises and leads a team to high performance so the company can win in a competitive marketplace. Like Jake, he is learning about the virtues in order to make himself a more effective leader. Like Jake, Terry has faced his own share of adversity. In a way, he is also a man of courage.

The next day Terry sent an e-mail to leaders. Terry wrote, "I very much enjoyed sitting in with the students. The lacrosse player is an exceptional young man. His words touched my soul. . . . There are very few people in this world who can open up that way and in a moment can bring tears to a 57-year-old steelworker's eyes . . . tremendous honesty and power." Jake's vulnerability was a sign of strength to Terry.

Terry's words were shared with Jake, who was touched: "I did not meet Terry. I really wish I did though. That is so nice that he sent that e-mail. I obviously do not play lacrosse because of my current health problems, but I love being part of the team. It is just kind of hard to relate all this stuff we have been talking about back to my current sport, so I figured the next best thing is cancer! I look at the battle of having cancer as just one big lacrosse game, and it helps me put things into perspective. I have always loved talking about it, and helping people is something I really love to do. I would much rather help someone than have someone help me."

The closing that Terry wrote in his note to Jake was powerful. He said, "Your brother in virtue, Terry." The two men are different in almost every way imaginable, except that they are brothers in virtue. And so it is for all of us who want to know and use these virtues, like courage. In courage, we become brothers and sisters in virtue. We become a team.

COURAGE TOOL KIT

Courage is doing the hard right without any assurance that the outcome will be favorable. This is why courage comes with risk. We don't always want to pay the price, but we might have to in order to be brave. Even though courage does not come with guarantees, that does not necessarily mean we should fall on our sword. In fact, the opposite is often true. It is not always clear whether we should blow a whistle or work for change from the inside. We need wisdom, not just courage. What follows are two reminders on how to increase courage to promote growth and to mitigate risk.

De-escalate Rather Than Escalate a Conflict

The purpose of bystander education is to get to a good outcome without blowing up a relationship. This is achieved by asking or making some variation of the following four questions and, if needed, one statement, in descending order:

1. "Is there any reason we are doing this?"
2. "Could we rethink our plans?"
3. "Since we want to have a good outcome and avoid a bad outcome, how can we respond in a way that is good? Good, bad, good response.
4. "Is there anything I can say to change your mind?"
5. "If you are unwilling to change your mind, then this is what I'll need to do."

Evaluate the Affordable Loss

The point of evaluating affordable loss is to define the level of risk that we are prepared to take in order to explore a growth opportunity. We often don't know whether a jump into the unknown will result in a favorable outcome. We can define and manage the level of loss we are prepared to accept by answering three questions:

1. Do you want it? If you are not motivated, then give it up.
2. Do you have the means? If you don't have all you need, use what you have.
3. Is your new initiative within your affordable loss of money, reputation, or opportunity costs? If not, lower the risk.[35]

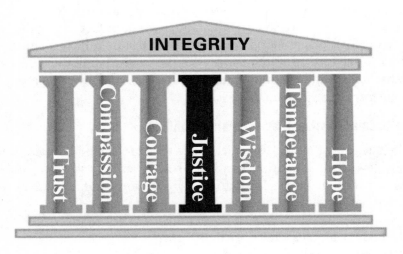

FIGURE 4.1 Pillars and Pediment: Justice

Source: Copyright © Parker Hannifin.

CHAPTER 4

Justice

Our ego is not our amigo.

*If you are neutral in situations of injustice, you have
chosen the side of the oppressor. If an elephant has its foot
on the tail of a mouse and you say that you are neutral,
the mouse will not appreciate your neutrality.*
—DESMOND TUTU[1]

So what is justice? Common meanings of *justice* are "law," "rule,"
"code," and "sanctioned by law." Justice is often defined as fairness or
equality. Equality is easier to determine because it involves less judgment. "Fair" is clearly not the same as "equal," though these words tend
to be used interchangeably. Fairness can be trickier because we have to
"justify" our decision.

Here is a story about the Ethical Protectors program to introduce
the virtue justice.

THE ETHICAL PROTECTORS

Artie, a former New York City police officer, is about to demonstrate what to do when attacked by a guy who is six inches taller
and 40 pounds heavier. In the same fashion that an announcer
at a boxing match introduces a fighter to an audience, he tells
his audience—a group of New York and New Jersey police

officers—"I'm 5 foot 7 inches, and I weigh 180 pounds. All right, I'm 190 pounds." He has an easy nature despite horrific flashbacks from his 20 years of service as a New York City cop. Artie yelled "Stop!" to a cyclist racing through a barricade toward the Twin Towers, during the terrorist attacks on September 11, 2001. Artie was too late. The cyclist was cut in half by a plate of glass blown from the Twin Towers just before they collapsed.

Tonight Artie looks pleasant, a bit plump, and badly over-matched. On the mat, the big guy attacks Artie, but in two quick moves, the larger man's body hits the ground with a resounding thud. An audience of police officers, who are not easily impressed, were very impressed. One says, "Hey, I don't think the guy's arm goes that way." Another says, "It does now!" The big guy doesn't dare move, hoping his arm will still work when Artie decides to give it back. Artie calmly and politely asks, "Now, sir, was that really necessary? I would like to treat you like a gentleman. Would you be willing to act like a gentleman?"

Artie releases his attacker's arm so he can remind cops that it takes about two hours to process an arrest. When you fingerprint a guy, his elbow is right next to your face. If you are elbowed to the head, you will get to learn about concussion protocols. If you retaliate, you will get to learn about police abuse. Rather than file for worker's compensation or fill out reports to defend yourself, Artie recommends using your power to make a friend.

Artie is part of a group of former police officers and Marines who teach current officers what it means to be an "ethical protector"—that is, a person who protects life, self, and others, *all* others. Remarkably, "all others" includes the enemy. In this program, Marines and police officers practice character as part of learning the martial arts. The hierarchy of conduct is very clear: lead with character, de-escalate conflicts without force, and if force is needed, use the martial arts in defense. When they have no choice but to use the martial arts, they are reminded to disarm. Don't dismember! Marines warn the officers that training someone in the martial arts without teaching character is like giving someone a loaded gun without teaching her how the gun should be used. The officers and Marines on Artie's team serve in the Ethical Protectors Program designed and led by Jack Hoban, a retired Marine captain. In 1996, the Marines started to rethink hand-to-hand combat, as wars with clear front lines were replaced with wars where there were no fronts. Robert Humphrey, who had survived the Battle of Iwo Jima, and Jack Hoban, who had taught other Marines the martial arts, led the initiative. Their goal was to integrate "winning the hearts and minds" of the locals into martial arts training. To do this, Marines needed to integrate ethical training as the foundation to teaching soldiers how to operate in a battle where the difference between insurgents and civilians was blurred. Marines also needed to be persuaded that ethics was best learned by teaching the martial arts, rather than being blitzed by PowerPoint slides.[2]

Hoban started with the Marine core values of honor, courage, and commitment. While these values are noble in purpose, without care, honor can become conceit, courage can become martyrdom, and commitment can become zealotry. Since the enemy holds the same values of honor, courage, and commitment, what is different about Marines? The answer: the universal commitment to protect life—self and others, including all others. Ethical protectors put others before themselves. This protection has extended to the enemy (all others) as long as they have stopped taking life. To be clear, self and others (all others) doesn't sweep away the harsh reality that Marines do kill people. Protecting life has not precluded taking life as long as the enemy was killing.

Hoban's first hurdle was to redefine a warrior as a person who kills only to protect others. The second hurdle was to recognize that protectors are far more ferocious than killers. A mother lion protecting a warthog dinner from a pack of hyenas will fight some. A mother lion protecting her cubs will fight to the death. The third hurdle was to stop the practice of dehumanizing the enemy to make it easier for cops to arrest people they looked down on as "trash" or Marines to kill Asian soldiers they referred to as "gooks." Hoban wanted it to be clear that killing people just because they disagree with our beliefs is indefensible. Everyone deserves to be treated with respect and dignity, even the enemy. This is justice embodied.

Steely-eyed Marines reminded Hoban that they were facing a ruthless enemy who terrorized civilians and beheaded soldiers. Being soft against a callous adversary will get innocent people killed. Hoban argued that treating people with respect and dignity is not going to make a Marine less capable of doing what needs to be done. Besides, in a world of 24/7 news cycles, a single Marine involved in an unethical act splashed on CNN will destroy a military strategy faster than anything that the enemy can do.[3]

Not everyone will agree with the practice of "ethical protection" as the best way to win a war against insurgents. Even if you agree with this high standard, it takes plenty of strength and practice to treat everyone with respect, regardless of how they treat you. Character can seem quaint and old-fashioned when someone is faced with life-and-death decisions. Heck, it can seem quaint when someone cuts us off on the highway. When we are threatened or disrespected, rage and indignation take over. We readily replace self and others (all others) with "If you mess with me, I'll mess with you."

This is why our ego is not our amigo. Bloated egos lead us to take things personally. And when things get personal, our thinking gets fuzzy. Slaying our ego is wickedly difficult to do, but it is essential if we hope to treat others (all others) with respect and dignity.[4] Doing so is just.

Justice: The Most Complicated Virtue

Langdon Gilkey bemoaned to a colleague, "My God, Bertram, the root of the demand for equal treatment . . . is not the outraged sense of justice for the other fellow. . . . It is the frustrated desire to get for yourself all that is coming to you. Self-interest, of course, is also the root of our desire to get more than our neighbor, and that is one reason, isn't it, that life is so damned complicated."[5]

We all are capable of putting personal concerns for our comfort in front of our concern for the needs and wants of others. We may not speak up when a hardworking, high-performing, but quiet staff person does not receive a well-deserved bonus, though we feel outraged when compensation, promotions, and professional recognition are offered to others when we think the rewards should have gone to us.

Law follows society's vision of justice, not the other way around. This means that we decide what is just and then pass a law. For example, throughout most of human history, it was legal to pollute the earth. Our views in this respect have changed. Consequently, we changed laws. So, today, we are fined if we pollute.

But what is legal and what is ethical can be quite different. The rule of law ensures that contracts are binding, which helps ensure "just" business practices. The rule of law also ensures that legally negotiated contracts permit executives to walk away with millions, even when customers were deceived, wealth was destroyed, and employees lost jobs. So the distinction between law as rule and ethics as exception to rules is important to understand. Law is what we have to do. Ethics is what we should do.

We might wonder in an unfair world whether we are at a disadvantage if we do more than the law requires. Perhaps that is true in some cases, though there is at least one reason to view virtue as a competitive advantage. Virtue increases engagement. Keep in mind that *moral* is the root word of *morale*. A moral or just work environment is not only fair and pleasant. It is key to engagement. If I do not think you are being fair with me and/or my team, for whatever reason, I am not likely to engage fully. I am not likely to reveal all that I know, nor will I share what I am imagining or even discovering. Instead of being eager, I will probably be tentative. Instead of being open, I am more likely to be guarded. Instead of being quick, I will be slower and more likely to hold back. Remember our discussion of discretionary effort in Chapter 1 on trust? Folks are unlikely to exert the discretionary effort that is key to achieving high performance unless there is trust and they perceive themselves as being treated justly by the organization.

A moral work environment depends on wisdom as well as justice. There is a reason that a law degree is titled jurisprudence. Justice (*juris*) is the desired end, and wisdom (*prudence*) is the essential means. Jurisprudence certainly involves rules. We recognize that creating and applying rules often fails to acknowledge that the purpose of rules is to unite people. An effective rule is moderate and flexible. Wisdom balances firmness and kindness, according to the virtues of practical wisdom and justice.

Let's apply the idea of moderate and flexible rules to nursing homes. Sadly, too many nursing homes warehouse the elderly more than help them to live well. This is not to suggest that nursing home caregivers are callous. In fact, the vast majority of nursing home caregivers take their duty to keep the elderly safe seriously. They also want to treat the elderly with "dignity," though it is far easier to put this word in a brochure than it is to really create a culture of dignity. It is easier for nursing homes to rely on numbers to precisely measure and enforce rules to monitor grandmother's physical health than it is to create a culture of dignity.

What number would we use to measure her dignity? An emphasis on rigid metrics and rules ensures that caregivers monitor whether grandmother skips her medication, loses weight, or hurts herself. What metrics and rules would relieve grandmother from the three great plagues of nursing homes: boredom, loneliness, and helplessness? To bring life to the elderly requires shifting from a culture governed by metrics to a culture governed by helping people to live life well. We can "check all the boxes" by complying with all the regulations and still miss the essential point.

An interesting study compared a nursing home united by the purpose to live well with another that was focused on metrics. The treatment nursing home created a policy that encouraged pets, plants, flowers, and an on-site childcare program. The control nursing home focused on the rules and routines. The difference between the treatment and control nursing homes was stunning. Required prescriptions per resident in the treatment nursing home were half that of the control nursing home. Use of psychotropic drugs like Haldol, prescribed for agitation, decreased significantly. Surprisingly, even deaths were less, by 15 percent. The study couldn't offer a numerical explanation for the differences in results. However, the researcher was clear that the treatment home replaced boredom, loneliness, and helplessness with spontaneity, companionship, and helping others. Rather than rely on metrics to achieve these goals, they relied on meaning.[6]

Admittedly, ideas about meaning are far more complex and abstract than metrics. This is one of the reasons why justice is arguably the most complicated virtue. Some cultures define justice by what's best for the community rather than the individual. Justice can be defined by what serves the greatest good. Justice can be defined by human rights—we don't kill the old and feeble because they pose an expense to the young and strong. Justice can be defined by an abstract principle: do the right thing, the right way, for the right reason. Injustice can be guided by Machiavellian standards. Fortune favors the bold, so the means justify the ends. Machiavellian standards in particular can lead to claims of hypocrisy.[7]

Hypocrisy: What Happens When Justice Is Missing

Here are six sentences from Enron's 65-page-long ethics code:

Respect: We treat others as we would like to be treated ourselves. Ruthlessness, callousness, and arrogance don't belong here.
Integrity: We work with customers and prospects openly, honestly, and sincerely. When we say we will do something, we will do it. We have all worked hard over the years to establish our reputation for integrity and ethical conduct. We cannot afford to have it damaged.[8]

Clearly, these ideas stayed in the ethics manual, while senior leaders committed fraud. The company defaulted on its obligations, costing shareholders billions, and thousands of employees were stripped of their retirement savings. During a speech to the Association of Certified Fraud Examiners, a business leader cautioned that ethics was more about culture than codes of conduct. "Culture starts at the top. But it doesn't start at the top with pretty statements. Employees will see through empty rhetoric and will emulate the nature of top-management decision making. A robust code of conduct can be emasculated by one action of the CEO or CFO." The speaker? Andrew Fastow, the former CFO of Enron, who spent more than five years in federal prison for committing fraud.[9]

While it easy to spot hypocrisy in others, with a bit of honest reflection, we can see our own hypocrisies. None of us is immune from saying one thing and doing another or from rationalizing our conduct as selfless when we are, in fact, acting selfishly. Human frailties such as denial, rationalization, and blind spots make it unrealistic to eliminate being a hypocrite. Striving to act on our better nature is especially tricky when we are given power. According to Abraham Lincoln, if you want to test someone's character, then give that person power.[10]

The University of California at Berkeley Psychology Department used cookies to test Lincoln's insight. Students were organized into teams of three. One team member was randomly selected to be the group leader. After the leader was selected, the team was asked to fix problems, such as cheating and binge drinking. After a half hour, researchers brought each team a plate of four cookies. If you expected that a pause or discussion about the fate of the extra cookie would follow after each person ate his or her cookie, you would be wrong. In each case, the randomly selected leader grabbed and gobbled the fourth cookie quickly and with gusto. The leader did not eat the extra cookie because he or she was more virtuous or added more value. The person simply believed that rank had its privileges.[11]

Author and former investment banker Michael Lewis thought that this simple experiment captured what he observed on Wall Street. Leaders who were lucky to receive extra cookies believed that they deserved them. Maybe they did. Or maybe "justice" is in trouble when morality meets power. Lewis's comments are backed up by research that demonstrated that power can increase selfishness and reduce consideration for others.[12]

Few people begrudge an extra cookie in the form of high compensation for leaders who use their power to benefit society with valuable products, jobs, and tax bases. Citizens start calling for "justice" when corporate cookie monsters grab excessive compensation and leave crumbs or empty plates for shareholders, employees, and taxpayers. So the takeaway from the extra cookie story is to understand that if we are not careful, power can replace compassion with inattention to the concerns of others. Power can undermine justice.

Profits Before Principles

The Great Recession evaporated $5 trillion from investments, such as pension and retirement funds, tossed 8 million people into unemployment, and ejected 5 million people from their homes. And this was only in the United States.[13] The great credit crunch, or what we would call the "great character crunch," nearly blew up the planet's financial systems.

In the short term, putting profits before principles might seem advantageous. But over the long term, the financial health of an enterprise is put at risk when principles are ignored, as these examples illustrate. Financial company stocks were hammered for generating profits when they placed consumers in loans they could not afford. Pharmaceutical companies' images and stock prices were bruised when nongovernmental organizations (NGOs) and the media aggressively challenged strategies that put profits before the lives of HIV/AIDS victims living in developing nations. Fast-food, alcohol, and tobacco companies' stock prices have all been pummeled when NGOs and regulators have attacked promotions of unhealthy eating, drinking, and smoking habits.[14] The way to create an especially nasty ethical stew is to pour a weak potion of financial performance into a boiling pot of a profits-before-principles culture and then add lots of pressure to perform.

The Return on Assets (ROA)

Despite the fact that organizations have focused intensely on creating a performance-driven culture—that is, the ability of firms to leverage their assets as measured by their return on assets (ROA)—results have been declining for decades. The ROA is an important number because it reveals the efficiency with which leaders leverage assets to generate earnings.

Here is a stunning fact: the ROA for U.S. public companies is only a quarter of 1965 levels.[15] In other words, a 50-year decline in ROA has meant that leaders have increasingly required more capital to make less money. That's just the kind of pressure that leads companies to become "serial restructurers." This means jobs are cut continually in hopes of future growth that never comes.

The ROA can be improved in the short term by reducing costs

through layoffs and outsourcing. But over the long term, the ROA decreases when cost reductions weaken the firm's core competencies. Acquisitions can buy revenue, which, when done well, improves the ROA through growth and scale. However, when done poorly, acquisitions bloat bureaucracies, which adds costs, calcifies decision making, and reduces ROA.[16]

The Dirty Dozen and the ROA

The layoff is, sadly, an all-too-common justice issue in the VUCA world in which we live. It is not without reason that layoffs make some people bitter and angry. Even when I keep my job, it is hard to watch valued colleagues lose their jobs because the firm lost money and not because the people who were laid off did something wrong. No one will be surprised that organizations lose the trust of their employees after a layoff. To be even more precise, organizations can expect that a dozen unattractive behaviors will grip their culture after a layoff.

We present to you the "dirty dozen":

1. Decreased trust
2. Less information sharing
3. Loss of accessible leadership
4. Centralized decision making
5. Escalating political infighting
6. Increased interpersonal conflict
7. Decreased morale, commitment, and loyalty
8. Loss of teamwork
9. Decreased innovation
10. Increased short-term crisis mentality
11. Increased resistance to change
12. Risk aversion[17]

When too many employees exhibit the "dirty dozen," the benefits of an improved ROA are short term. The cost savings made possible by the layoffs will give the ROA a bump in the short term. However, the cost savings aren't sustainable if disengagement settles in.[18] This presents leaders with a vexing VUCA conundrum: how to balance financial stability and employee stability?

To improve financial stability, sound VUCA strategy includes fewer fixed costs and more variable costs, especially when it comes to compensation, because employees typically represent 50 to 85 percent of an organization's total costs. Variable costs provide a buffer to revenue fluctuations, which is why companies increasingly hire part-time employees, outsource noncore functions, and, unfortunately, also lay people off. To avoid the attention of activist investors—wealthy individuals or groups who use their deep pockets and influence to obtain seats on a company board—publicly traded companies must pay attention to excessive costs or to poor ROA. If the leadership team won't effect changes to improve metrics like the ROA through restructuring and layoffs, then the activist investors who gain board seats will force these changes.

While leaders are paid to deliver financial results, here is what followers want in their leaders: trust, compassion, stability, and hope.[19] The virtues of trust, compassion, and hope can be offered by any organization to help navigate VUCA if an intentional virtue plan is well designed and practiced to strengthen the culture. It is employee stability that presents an especially tricky conundrum. Clearly, most people seek stable employment. However, a steady job depends on steady revenue funded by two key stakeholders: customers and investors. Both expect superior value propositions or they will take their business and money elsewhere. In other words, a steady job depends on delivering superior value to customers and investors. And superior value depends on an engaged workforce, which is a function of leaders exhibiting trust, compassion, stability, and hope.

So what happens when an organization faces market headwinds so severe that layoffs are necessary to survive? For organizations that "practice virtue," there is silver lining in the dark cloud of workers' losing their jobs. The virtues act as a buffer against the "dirty dozen." When leaders exhibit courage and compassion, they legitimize virtuous behaviors. When employees observe gratitude or witness forgiveness, it starts a mutually positive reinforcing cycle. When virtue is practiced well, it is contagious.[20]

Our research has revealed that virtues such as trust, courage, compassion, and hope improve morale, as well as prevent dysfunction in the face of adversity that can include layoffs. Employees who experience virtue are more helpful to customers, more empathetic, and more respectful toward colleagues. Virtue helps us absorb the blow of a layoff and bounce back with resilience and toughness.

Of course, there is a long list of workplace injustices besides layoffs. We might still be angry or disappointed for not receiving the raise or promotion we thought was our due. We may still be upset for being treated disrespectfully by a colleague or customer. We might be steamed by someone who is making a fat salary and not earning his or her keep.

From the individual's perspective, learning to handle injustice, especially when we can't effect change, is a practical life skill to develop. From an organizational perspective, the critical commitment that has to be made by boards and senior leaders is this: put principles before profits.

Principles Before Profits

People can limit their view of principles before profits by defining justice to mean following the law. No less, but no more. In other words, organizations earn a "license to operate," the right to profit, by adhering to rules and regulations. So organizational principles about justice are governed by what is legal, rather than what is virtuous. Here is where things get tricky. As financial performance declines and the pressure to perform match is lit, there are plenty of temptations to cut corners. Enter the compliance industry. It seems reasonable to increase the number of rules to reduce the likelihood of unjust business conduct. Yet, unless an organization is careful, a singular focus on ethics defined as compliance with a set of rules can stunt a company's efforts to innovate and take intelligent risks.[21]

Organizations earn a "license to operate," merely by adhering to rules. The exception to the rule is when organizations achieve excellence ethically, which goes beyond compliance with rules. Doing so leads to a personally fulfilling and socially rewarding life. In fact, the call for business to help solve the world's problems grows increasingly stronger. In 2016, Edelman completed its sixteenth annual trust barometer that surveyed 33,000 people from 28 countries. Edelman's trust barometer doesn't use the word *justice*. Yet the link between justice and trust becomes clear enough in Edelman's finding that 80 percent of respondents agree with this statement: "A business can take specific actions that both result in profits and improve economic and social conditions in the communities where it operates."[22] Edelman's research concludes that people want business to make life better for others, while they also profit.

Edelman reported that in 2016, trust in business was the highest it had been in 16 years, at least among 15 percent of respondents defined as the informed public or elites. The income of informed elites places them in the twenty-fifth percentile of all wage earners. In 75 percent of the 28 countries surveyed, trust in business was over 50 percent among elites, which again were 15 percent of the population. In contrast, trust levels in business were below 50 percent for 85 percent of society. The trust gap between the elite 15 percent and the mass 85 percent was 31 points in the United States, 29 points in France, 26 points in Brazil, and 22 points in India. Despite this trust gap, business was more trusted than government in Mexico by 44 points, in South Africa by 44 points, and in the United States by 12 points.[23] People viewed business as better equipped to lead change than government and nongovernment organizations.

According to Edelman, the role of CEOs and employees is critical in building trust. Trust is earned when leaders demonstrate three qualities prized throughout the world: honesty, ethical conduct, and competence. In fact, 80 percent of respondents believed the CEO's personal values mattered a great deal. However, CEOs were viewed as underperforming when it came to integrity and engagement. Engagement was especially important because society trusted what employees said about an organization more than they trusted what senior leaders said.[24]

Our research has demonstrated that senior leaders, former offenders, production line workers, students, and physicians, among others, believe that virtue preserves an organization's reputation and its financial assets. Importantly, people want permission to be virtuous. Our experience reveals that virtue is not something people need to be sold on. Virtue is how people, from a variety of countries and cultures, across many industries, want to live and work.

Let's take the business case of virtue first and value second a step further. If we are to improve the ROA, then we must prevent reckless-ness, but not risk taking. This means adhering to the law is the baseline expectation, although the aspirational goal is to practice virtue. Virtue first and economic value second. The order matters a great deal. To extract value, we first must create value. Before we get rich, we have to enrich others.

Michael Porter has proposed the idea of *corporate social value* (CSV). He argues that business has lost societal trust because it limits the purpose of business to creating economic value. He believes that businesses miss new customer opportunities by being blind to broader social issues.[25] If businesses address these issues, they will be rewarded with increased economic wealth. Politicians pile onto the problem by trying to solve social ills at the expense of business.

Porter argues that business and government are stuck in an out-dated false choice between economic efficiency and social progress. Rather than fall victim to the tyranny of either-or thinking, organiza-tions can create economic value by solving societal problems. While opportunities for traditional product development are limited, oppor-tunities for businesses to add social and economic value are vast. Citizens want the government to resolve challenges, such as global warming, but businesses could take these problems on themselves.[26] For example, Parker Hannifin, where one of the authors is a senior executive, designed consolidated natural gas (CNG) dispensers used to fuel truck and bus fleets worldwide to reduce emissions and lower energy costs. In 2015, the Greater Cleveland's regional transportation system purchased Parker Hannifin's CNG dispensers, which will save more than $200,000 over the life of each bus while reducing annual emissions of CO_2 by 100 tons. This means that the region's air quality will improve because the entire fleet will have decreased greenhouse gas emissions 30 percent by 2017.[27]

Solving the complexity of global warming is one thing, but let's consider another business. Chick-fil-A, the fast-food restaurant chain headquartered in Atlanta, Georgia, attracts customers more through community involvement and hospitality than through advertising, thus lowering its cost of sales dramatically. The company's incredible growth was kick-started when the founder's sister needed a place to eat lunch. She told her brother, Truett Cathy, Chick-fil-A's founder, to put a store in the mall where she worked. This advice turned chicken into a golden goose. Chick-fil-A's growth was fueled by America's mall building binge in the 1960s and 1970s. More malls, more Chick-fil-A stores, more sales. The good times hit a big snag in 1982 when a recession and 17 percent interest rates put the brakes on mall building. Unfortunately, when times were still good, Cathy issued a corporate bond to pay for a new corporate headquarters. He wasn't about to default on the bond, so he pulled his leadership team together to figure out how to grow the business. The team wondered if Cathy understood that there was a recession? He said that he did, in fact, know there was a recession, but he just did not plan to participate.[28]

At the time, the leadership team was composed of a group of 30-year-olds who were very capable and very frightened that they would lose their jobs. Putting a piece of chicken between two pieces of bread may not seem very complicated. Yet things can get pretty tense when you struggle to grow a business during a recession. The epiphany moment came when the team concluded that they didn't have a sales problem—they had a fear problem!

How do you cope with fear? They concluded they needed to be very clear on why Chick-fil-A existed. Interestingly, this is the same question that legendary leadership expert Peter Drucker argued that all organizations should first answer. The team certainly understood that profit was the lifeblood of the company, though profitability was not the reason the company existed. The "aha" moment was coming to the conclusion that they did not own the business; they were stewards of the business. So the team created a set of principles founded on stewardship, hospitality, and making an emotional connection with customers and colleagues. As the team aligned around this purpose, fear loosened its grip.[29]

Guided by stewardship, the hierarchy of purpose was now clear: customers would come first, employees second, and profits last. The business case for putting principles before profits was that a great brand could not be built on a weak culture. How has it worked out? In 2000, Chick-fil-A sales were $1 billion. In 2015, sales were $6.8 billion. That's a lot of chicken![30]

In 2014, Truett Cathy passed away. The group of 30-year-olds has mostly retired, and a new, highly qualified leadership team now runs the show. Can a new team, one that hasn't experienced the shared adversity of their predecessors, sustain ever-increasing sales? Time will tell. Can a set of principles that includes a commitment to a faith-based approach be exported to other companies? Probably not, because each organization must find its own set of principles to follow. But the fundamental question that can and should be asked of leaders of any organization is this: "How will we deal with fear?" And a healthy way to address fear is to answer the question: "Why do we exist?" Or, put differently, "What is our ultimate concern?"[31]

Our Ultimate Concern

Thinking about our ultimate concern is a way to get at the question "Why do we exist?" We don't need to look for an "ultimate concern" because we already have one, according to Paul Tillich, an influential twentieth-century theologian. Tillich's idea of ultimate concern is defined by whatever we take with total seriousness. The powerful can take power with ultimate seriousness. A cynic takes cynicism with ultimate seriousness. A leader can take profits before principles with total seriousness.[32]

It's worth getting a purpose, if for no other reason than it helps us live longer. Purposeful people have a 15 percent lower risk of death compared with those who said that their life was without purpose. Finding a life's direction and setting overarching goals contributes to longevity, regardless of when we discover it, though the earlier we find a purpose, the earlier its protective effects may be able to occur.[33]

Tillich suggested that we subject our ultimate concern to critical inspection and reevaluation. A worthy ultimate concern involves a purpose that is greater than ourselves. A clear purpose centers us in a world that can otherwise easily disorient and confuse us. The struggle of veterans is often not to forget the war but to re-create the intense purpose they had when they were in the service. This is true for mothers and fathers who step out of the workforce to raise children or reenter the workforce after raising children. It is true for people who retire after a meaningful career.[34]

The search for meaning represents one of the deepest truths of being human. Viktor Frankl, psychiatrist and Auschwitz survivor, put it this way: "The way in which a man accepts his fate and all the suffer-ing it entails, the way in which he takes up his cross, gives him ample opportunity—even under the most difficult circumstances—to add a deeper meaning to his life. He may remain brave, dignified, and unself-ish. Or in the bitter fight for self-preservation he may forget his human dignity and become no more than an animal. Here lies the chance for a man either to make use of or to forgo the opportunities of attaining the moral values that a difficult situation may afford him. And this decides whether he is worthy of his sufferings or not."[35] As Friedrich Nietzsche said, "He who has a why to live can bear with almost any how."[36]

While Frankl's story is about clarifying our ultimate concern through suffering, Jim Collins provides interesting insights about our ultimate concern when it comes to success. The success of Collins's book *Good to Great* created a challenging dilemma. Collins wasn't sure whether he should stay on the Stanford faculty or start a com-pany. Fortunately, he was in the position to ask Peter Drucker for advice. Drucker, 87 at the time, asked questions and listened to Col-lins for almost a whole day. And yet Drucker offered no advice. At the end of the day, Collins anxiously asked Drucker, what to do? Drucker responded to Collins's angst with three observations. First, he thought Collins worried a lot, and he didn't see that all of that concern was doing him much good. Second, he thought Collins was overly con-cerned with success, even though he had been exceptionally successful and had every reason to believe this would continue. Drucker's final observation was a question: Why don't you focus on being useful?[37] Now, that is a question that has value not just to Collins, but to all of us. A good question is the first step to discovering a compelling answer.

PRACTICING JUSTICE: THE ALLEGORY OF THE CHARIOT

Unlike compliance training that assumes we don't know what is right, Plato believed that our life's mission was to remember what we already know is right. He used the allegory of the chariot to teach his followers how to be useful, or how to "aim at the good," so we can redirect ourselves when we are up to no good. The chariot in his story is pulled by two winged horses, one mortal and the other immortal. The dark horse is mortal: prideful and unresponsive to whips and spurs (rules). The white horse is immortal: honorable and modest, guided by words rather than by a whip (exception to the rule). In the driver's seat is the charioteer, trying to get two strong-willed animals to "aim at the good."[38]

The horses pull in opposite directions, and the charioteer struggles to get them to work together. The best charioteers soar to catch a glimpse of the edge of heaven before they sink back down to earth. And all do sink back to earth. The best that the charioteer can do is "aim at the good," so the fall is shallower, and the ability to soar again gets a bit easier.[39]

The charioteer represents reason (lover of wisdom), the dark or mortal horse represents appetites (lover of gain), and the white or immortal horse represents spirit (lover of victory). If we aren't careful, the dark immortal horse runs our life, seeking nothing higher than eating, drinking, sex, and money. The consequence can be a tire around our middle, an addled brain, financial grief, and, if things really go into the dumper, time in the slammer. The other extreme is viewing all desires as wrong. Love even for a spouse is reduced to lust and food nothing more than fuel.[40]

Plato argued that a properly trained dark mortal horse generates as much energy to pull the chariot as the white immortal horse. The chariot soars highest when both horses are aligned. To become an ace charioteer means not to indulge the dark mortal horse or the white immortal horse too much or too little, but to harness passion in a positive way. Enjoy sex through love and commitment. Enjoy food and drink with family and friends and in moderation. Appreciate what wealth can buy, but avoid having money become paramount. Good charioteers train their white and dark horses to work together by being centered on virtue, a worthy ultimate concern.[41]

Plato's charioteer trusted rationality. Jonathan Haidt grants more power to emotion. Haidt explains that our emotions are like a bull elephant. As the rider of the bull elephant, we believe that our thoughts are in charge. Haidt points out that if the emotional equivalent of a six-ton pachyderm wants to go left and the rider wants to go right, then left it is. A "just" path is what we seek. However, the bull elephant's power is fueled by emotions of anger, grief, or anxiety, which makes the righteous path elusive. Guiding the charioteer or the pachyderm depends on the little rider (our rationality) and the big beast (our emotions) moving together.[42]

As Benjamin Franklin said, "If passion drives, let reason hold the reins."[43]

Better or Bitter?

Among the most critical skills that the charioteer and elephant rider have is to become better rather than bitter when injustice smacks us upside the noggin. The best among us earn our admiration by responding to injustice with grace and with grit. Nelson Mandela was released after 27 years of being imprisoned unjustly. His first act of freedom was to forgive his jailer. When asked why he would forgive someone who took 27 years of his life, he said he did not do it for the jailer; he did it for himself. Unless he forgave his jailer, he would be imprisoned forever by anger. If he was full of hate, he couldn't lead South Africa to reconcile its unjust apartheid history.[44]

Part of being human is to carry around resentments—about past perceived or real injustices. Spending energy on these resentments can prevent us from enjoying our relationships and responsibilities. Think of a time when you were treated unfairly, and chances are a wave of emotions washes back over you, making you mad or sad all over again. In reliving our injustice, we might ask if it is doing us any good. Positive change surely doesn't start with a negative mindset. As Frankl suggested, we need to move beyond being a victim and make meaning out of our suffering.[45] It certainly isn't easy to watch someone treat us unjustly without consequence. And it is important to underscore that forgiveness is not necessarily the same as reconciliation.

Sometimes there is little to be gained by continuing a relationship with someone who is intentionally deceptive, indifferent to our concerns, or worse. However, if we can forgive, we will be able to free ourselves. Perhaps we can learn to forgive someone not because he or she deserves it but because we don't want to carry around the resentment. One way to begin to get past these resentments is to identify the hidden benefits of those negative experiences. By focusing on benefits, the costs can be made to seem smaller and, therefore, less controlling of our lives. Of course, it is exceedingly difficult to forgive others who have harmed us.

When we learn to forgive, we let go of resentful feelings toward someone who has harmed or insulted us or one of our friends or loved ones. When people forgive, they slowly transform their negative feelings and attitudes toward that person into positive ones. There certainly is no easy way to overcome anger or sadness caused by injustice. Yet it is worth considering that forgiveness and compassion are more powerful than hate, if we can do it. With practice and the benefit of time, we have a chance to get better rather than bitter after an unjust experience.

Here is a really important point. Like Mandela, we don't just forgive to improve relations with others. We forgive to prevent being consumed by hate. People who are good at forgiving have less stress, less depression, and better health. People who are good at forgiving also have better relationships with others. This is because forgiving helps them to repair their relationships—especially if the offender has also apologized and tried to make amends. Forgiveness helps coworkers rebuild positive relationships after a conflict. Forgiveness reduces the desire for revenge, which is a major cause of negative behaviors in the workplace. Also, when companies ask customers for forgiveness when they make mistakes, it helps to rebuild customers' trust. In a word, forgiveness produces great personal and organizational benefit.

Reflect on a time when you were harmed by someone. It could be something minor or something serious. Take a few moments to identify some positive consequences of the event that you were not expecting. Perhaps you became aware of personal strengths you did not realize you had. Perhaps a relationship became better or stronger, or you became a stronger or wiser person.

Here is a benefits-finding exercise and examples that might include the following:

1. What happened when you learned the importance of forgiving?
   Other relationships in my life grew stronger.
   I learned about qualities to look for in friends.
   I learned to stand up for myself.
2. In what ways has your life improved?
   I became wiser (that is, slower to trust in relationships, less naïve).
   I became more aware of other people's feelings.
   I became less worried about pleasing others.
   I learned how to deal constructively with my anger, and learned how to keep a cool head.
3. How have you become a better person?
   I discovered strength I didn't know I had.
   I became kinder, less selfish.
   I learned more about how to be a good teammate.
   I learned how to be grateful for what I have.[46]

"We had the experience but missed the meaning," cautioned T. S. Eliot in "The Dry Salvages" (1941).[47] Two people can both experience injustice. One gets better, and one gets bitter. Through wisdom, one converts an unjust act or even a traumatic event into strength and insight, though not without pain and loss. She manages to work through the loss to come through it on the other side as a more resilient person. It is unwise to be full of hate such that wrath or depression dominate our feelings.

Our Ego Is Not Our Amigo

Even if we want to forgive, our ego gets in the way sometimes. This is a growing problem because our egos are getting fatter just like our waistlines. Since the 1980s, narcissism has increased at the same rate as obesity. The downside of growing egos for us and society is that there is clear evidence that narcissism decreases honesty and increases aggression. The moral of the story about Narcissus is that he didn't fall in love with who he really was. He fell in love with his reflection.

Today, we don't have to limit admiring our appearance to a single reflection pool. Thanks to social media, we can feed our ego instantly by blasting our achievements and accomplishments around the world.

Rather than putting our ego on a much-needed diet, we can waste our life trying to look good to others.[48] Clearly, treating others with respect and dignity is superior to worrying about our appearance. However, the rub is this: slaying our ego is wickedly hard.

So if we believe our ego is not our amigo, then what? We first need to be clear about who we want to be. Second, we are well served to understand that under pressure, our brain forces us to focus on self-preservation over concern for others. Third, through practice, we can combat our ego and neurology to create more meaningful relationships—not perfectly, but better than we used to be. Otherwise, if our ultimate concern is to protect our ego, then we will take things very personally and struggle to take into account the concerns of others.

The essence of ethics concerns our relationships with others. We are not surprised when a two-year-old or a teenager puts self before others. Even as adults, we are all capable of putting self before others. Narcissism isn't an either-or proposition—even an otherwise humble person can get a fat head, and even a fat head can be humbled. As we become more responsible, we often improve putting others before self. So a simple test of character is whether we put others before self, at least most of the time (Figure 4.2). We certainly should consider our interests too. Yet, often our interests are best served when we serve others. When we are completely selfish, most of the time, things don't turn out very well for us.

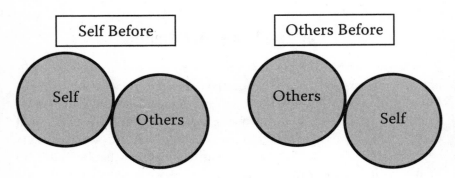

FIGURE 4.2   Self Before Others Versus Others Before Self

Source: Adapted from Robert Humphrey, *Values for a New Millennium*, Life Values Press, Maynardville, 1992.

Now here is the really hard Marine justice standard: put others before self—all others. Not just family and friends but strangers too. Not just people from our country but people from other countries too. Not just people who treat us well but even those who disrespect us. So we treat others—all others—with respect. This does not mean that we don't stand up for ourselves or others. It does mean we do so respectfully.

Compliance training presents ethics as "what" and "why." What should we do? Why should we do it? The harder question is this: "What does it take to make us virtuous, given all the distractions, temptations, and complexities that lie in our wake?" If ethics were as simple as compliance training suggests, then acting with justice and compassion would be easy. If this is easy, why then are justice and compassion often absent? Our knowledge will not save us from ourselves. Like eating right, exercising regularly, and getting adequate sleep, virtue is less about what we know and more about how we live. We need to become better charioteers by practicing to do what we already know is right.

Compliance often underestimates that when rules collide with habits, it is not going to be a fair fight. Aristotle taught that we learn to become better at things through practice. Bridge builders get better as they build more bridges. Higher surgical volume is a major driver of higher surgical quality and better outcomes.[49] We become more just by doing just acts.

Jack Hoban's Ethical Protectors program that we discussed in the beginning of this chapter teaches police officers how our brain works. The reward centers of our brain activate when we observe fairness toward others or toward us. In contrast, the amygdala lights up when we experience fear and anger, meaning we go into fight-or-flight mode. Under pressure and stress, our brain's response is designed to be intentionally limited. The amygdala governs our feelings. A threat both perceived and real triggers the amygdala to shut down the prefrontal cortex—that is, the thinking part of our brain. The amygdala protects us by focusing us on a small amount of information and reminds us about similar dangerous experiences.

The evolutionary nature of our brain is that we kept the parts that helped our prehistoric ancestors when a dinosaur was hunting them for dinner. The amygdala helps us survive by delivering a quick response within our whole body so we can avoid becoming the dinosaur's dinner. We haven't jettisoned this part of our brain, even though millions of years have passed since dinosaurs roamed the earth. As we put down our spears and picked up more schooling, our brains evolved to develop a prefrontal cortex.

JUSTICE TOOL KIT

How does justice interact with the other six virtues? It does not live in a vacuum as a virtue. We earn trust by developing healthy habits that slay our ego. When we practice justice and compassion, we increase trust. Trust makes it easier to lead change and innovate. Trusting cultures make us fast, agile, and creative. Also, we will need to practice courage to put principles before profits. It takes courage to live by a conviction to serve others—all others. Courage lays the foundation for persistence and resilience.

We will need to practice temperance to create habits of caring, fairness, trust, courage, and hope. Our habits define who we become.

We will need to practice wisdom, which starts by recognizing that we are all capable of hypocrisy. Even when we try to be virtuous, we will fall short of being perfect. But the good news is this: wisdom also reveals that we get better through reflection, support, and practice. We improve continually by practicing the humility, gratitude, and optimism of hope.

When we "aim at the good" to serve others—all others—with respect, our strategies and our tactics will be smarter. It also happens to be a better way to live.

What does it mean to practice justice? Try to put the concern of others, all others, before our concerns. Simple and very hard (Figure 4.3).[50]

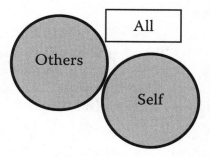

FIGURE 4.3   Putting Others (All Others) Before Self

Source: Adapted from Robert Humphrey, *Values for a New Millennium*, Life Values Press, Maynardville, 1992.

Justice is by far the most complicated virtue because there is no objective standard for what is fair. While we can't wring the complexity out of justice, we can simplify how we might practice justice. Here are some suggestions for how justice can be practiced.

Self and Others (All Others)

Our standard is to be just, and that is a very hard standard to achieve. It means to strive to treat people with respect and dignity independently of how others treat us. Admittedly, this standard is aspirational, which becomes clear when someone does something as simple as cutting in front of us in line.

The goal isn't to accept negative behavior. The goal is to understand the other person's negative behavior. The purpose isn't to become a doormat. The purpose is to de-escalate rather than escalate a conflict. When we manage to live up to the standard of self and others (all others), we lower our blood pressure, remain saner, and stay out of trouble rather making things worse for ourselves and others.

Pausing and Planning

When you are about to have a tough discussion or you are being attacked in a meeting, practice the pause-and-plan strategy. Deactivate your amygdala, and activate your prefrontal cortex by breathing. Take 60 seconds to breathe deeply four to six times. You will feel better, and you will think more clearly.

Better, Not Bitter

Depression and denial are not good places to be. Yet it is incredibly hard to grow from loss. The point is not to deny the pain of a significant loss. The point is to grow and gain perspective. Complete the benefits-finding exercise presented earlier in the chapter to sort out how you can gain strength from adversity rather than falling victim to loss.

Stakeholder Perspective

We tend to view injustice narrowly from our own perspective or from the perspective of just one stakeholder, such as employees. When a significant shift in strategy or policy happens where you work, take into account the big three: (1) the people you serve (customers or patients), (2) your teammates, and (3) who owns or funds your enterprise (shareholders and donors). Ask how an organizational decision affects not just you but each of the big three.

When we consider the impact of a decision beyond only ourselves or only the people we know, we gain some appreciation for how hard it is to be just to everyone who has a stake in a decision.

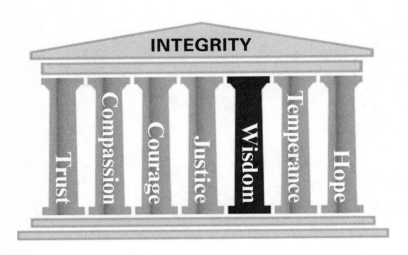

Wise-to-Unwise Spectrum

Disciplined reflection	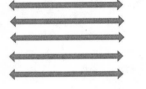	Busyness
Common sense		Poor judgment
Foresight		Short-sighted
Reasonable		Unreasonable
Proper means achieve proper ends		Means justify ends

FIGURE 5.1 Pillars and Pediment: Wisdom

CHAPTER 5

Wisdom

Leverage strengths and manage weaknesses.

To different minds, the same world is a hell and a heaven.
—RALPH WALDO EMERSON

Acting with wisdom is doing the right thing, in the right way, for the right reasons. Being wise allows us to navigate complicated workplaces and complicated situations. Being wise allows us to analyze the current state and embrace multiple and complex realities, weigh future possibilities, and make plans.

Consider the example of &Beyond in South Africa, which wisely both manages Phinda, a wildlife preserve, and serves the local community.[1]

STEWARDS OF A COMMUNITY AND A WILDLIFE PRESERVE

In Portuguese, *cobra de capelo* means "snake with hood." Spitting cobras bite to eat and spit to defend. While deadly, this serpent spends most of its time evading people and animals. When it is in danger or cornered, the snake fires venom through its fangs at the eyes of whatever blocks its escape. And it excels at spitting, hitting the eyeballs that it targets 8 out of 10 times, from up to 10 feet.[2]

Tyler, a 25-year-old naturalist who is part of a team that manages Phinda, a private nature reserve in South Africa near the coast of the Indian Ocean, is cavalier about spitting cobras. Tyler talks about the "snake with hood" as if he is letting you know where the bottled water is stored: "By the way, we share the grounds with a spitting cobra. Good to see you wear glasses. That will help protect your eyes. Should you see the cobra in the house, not to worry. Just give us a holler. I'll get the tongs and put it back underneath the house where it lives." The good news: the spitting cobra evades well and goes undetected during our stay. The bad news: each night, we fear the nightmare of accidentally stepping on the "snake with a hood" while going to the loo in the dark.

Tyler works for &Beyond, a for-profit venture that manages Phinda, which is owned by the local community. *Phinda* is a Zulu word meaning "the return." In 1991, Phinda was the site of one of Africa's most ambitious reintroductions of the Big Five—the leopard, lion, rhinoceros, buffalo, and elephant. &Beyond makes money housing, feeding, and guiding the tours of Americans, Europeans, and Asians who have the means to pay for a safari. The company shares a percentage of its profits with the local community that lacks the means to pay for schools, healthcare, and roads.

Each day, Tyler and other &Beyond naturalists monitor animal life in the morning and afternoon to ensure that foreigners have animals to see. Phinda is a 170-square-kilometer, fenced-in reserve that, while large, is not so large that nature would take care of itself once the Big Five and other animal species were reintroduced. Intense management is required to ensure that, for example, the lions do not multiply too rapidly at the expense of the cheetahs. Researchers conduct prey/predator experiments to understand if the zebra population could survive the reintroduction of wild dogs. Periodically, the land must be burned so that the chestnut-colored nyala can hide in the underbrush. The naturalists do not bother monitoring the giraffe herds because they leave the other animals alone and eat what others cannot reach.

&Beyond shifted the burden to pay for reserve management to its naturalists, making it clear that they had to learn to "wash their own hands." This phrase means become self-sufficient by earning enough money to pay salaries and operating costs. The naturalists learned to become entrepreneurs by charging volunteers to learn about conservation. The conservation experience attracts mostly students studying biology and ecology at English or U.S. universities with an occasional middle-aged adventurer supplementing this free labor pool. The volunteers pay to keep records of animals that the naturalists spot and, in exchange, they get an up-close look at the Big Five.[3]

Is the story of &Beyond an example of wisdom in how a private nature reserve can balance the ecology and the economy? Not to the satisfaction of some environmentalists who want nature, not humans, to manage nature. However, Phinda's relatively small size requires intensive management to prevent animals and people from bumping into each other, thus endangering both. It is also a challenge to ensure biodiversity and avoid inbreeding in a relatively small land mass occupied by very large animals.

Some critics claim that South Africa needs to worry more about jobs for their people than land for their animals. Jobs are a critical antidote to heartbreaking poverty. Yet, when economic growth comes at the expense of animal life, both jobs and animals are extinguished.

Ecotourism protects animals, while employing about 10 percent of South Africa's workforce.[4]

Wisdom rejects the jobs-or-animals argument as a false choice. In contrast, innovation and, in this instance, wisdom involves making unobvious connections between two seemingly contradictory goals. Jim Collins argues that the "tyranny of the *or*" should be replaced by the "genius of the *and*."[5] Straddling two seemingly contradictory goals (environmental preservation or economic growth) demands a healthy dose of wisdom. As F. Scott Fitzgerald said, "The test of a first-rate intelligence is the ability to hold two opposed ideas in the mind at the same time, and still retain the ability to function."[6] In this regard, &Beyond and its leaders show wisdom.

Wisdom and Experience

"When I told my wife that I needed to write a paper about wisdom and I didn't know what to say, she laughed," said Stanley, an MBA student. Stanley's Romanian wife told him the only wise thing he ever did was marry her. He continued, "She said the only reason I make fewer mistakes now is because she's my wife!"

Stanley's wife understood wisdom as a "true and reasoned state or capacity to act with regard to the things that are good or bad for man."[7] *Prudence* is another word for wisdom. In Latin, *prudentia* also means "foresight, practical judgment, and discretion." Thomas Aquinas concluded that "prudence seeks action that is reasonable—that makes sense."[8] However, common sense is not so common! Wisdom is not a matter of a high IQ or formal education. In fact, sometimes the reverse seems true. People with common sense often lack a formal education, while well-educated people might have little or no common sense. There is no shortage of human tragedies caused by unwise book-smart people who got themselves and others into trouble. This is why we need leaders who have both people and street smarts, not just book smarts. Look out when leaders are missing all three!

All cultures lift up the virtue of wisdom that is hard won through experience in which adversity is overcome. Since wisdom capitalizes on experience, age is associated with being wise. As people age, they start to count time until their death, while young people count time from when they were born. When people realize that they are vulnerable and that life can be swept away in a heartbeat, paradoxically, they are better able to see what is important and what is not. Aging is about loss, which can teach us how to come to grips with health, talent, and time limitations. As people start counting years to live, they feel the pressure to set priorities and clarify purpose. When time is understood as limited, the wise spend less time on what bothers them and more time making a difference.

The young can also acquire a carpe diem perspective, especially when it appears that their horizon has been shortened. Young people exposed to life-altering events, such as the September 11, 2001, terrorist attacks in the United States or the outbreak of SARS in Asia, have demonstrated a similar reordering of priorities as older folks.[9] When the young or relatively young live through a serious illness or crisis, their view of life is suddenly stark and clear, revealing new insights and the potential birth of wisdom. People might come back from adversity wounded, but they also come back more whole.

Wisdom and the next virtue, temperance, are the means to an end. Thus, wisdom is always a part of the process for reaching some goal, but it is never the goal itself. Recall that *jurisprudence* links "prudence" or "wisdom" with "justice," which means "wise justice." Justice is the proper end, and wisdom is the proper means.

Wisdom certainly includes knowledge, but it is more than knowledge. Wisdom adds understanding to knowledge. Often, wisdom adds the dimension of practical skill to knowledge and information. Wise people learn to become more pragmatic than idealistic or self-righteous. Plato softened his notion of educating "philosopher kings" to a more modest standard. He came to realize that the real challenge of leadership is finding common ground among people who do not always like each other, who do not always like the leader, and who do not always want to live together.

Vice competes openly with virtue in every organization, every day. For that matter, vice competes with virtue inside each of us every day. People gossip, are jealous, and yell at their children. We let our worst side surface. When people bring out the worst in themselves, they bring out the worst in others. At times, hardworking people are not rewarded with prosperity and unvirtuous deeds go unpunished. When employees are part of an unethical culture, even the most virtuous people will struggle to do what they know is right.

Thankfully, the opposite is also true. When people are part of a culture that lifts up virtue, it is far easier to bring out their better nature. In our experience with over a thousand leader and team evaluations, follow-on coaching, and continuous assessments, the virtues work in Asia, Europe, North and South America, and Africa. Here is one example. In 2015 and 2016, we conducted seminars that were attended and evaluated by approximately 300 leaders representing 28 nations in locations such as London, Frankfurt, Johannesburg, Shanghai, and Seoul. The most striking attribute of the evaluations was their similarities rather than the differences. When we compared pre- and post-seminar survey results for the 300 leaders who attended, nationality was statistically unrelated to ratings. Our research revealed that once people were introduced to the virtues, they wanted to be encouraged to be virtuous. Our conclusion was that regardless of their country of origin, people want the opportunity to develop wisdom rather than to have it suppressed.

This is certainly not a novel finding. The universality of the virtues can be traced to a period known as the Axial Age, which occurred between 22 and 26 centuries ago. An explosion of philosophical and religious ideas was birthed in Greece and China during this period. There is no evidence that people like Aristotle and Confucius knew each other, although they lived at about the same time. Yet, independently, Western and Eastern philosophers identified and practiced virtues in ways that are more similar than dissimilar. In this sense, the virtues are neither Eastern nor Western. The Chinese leader Lao Tzu, who lived in the sixth century BCE, stated: "Watch your thoughts; they become words. Watch your words; they become actions. Watch your actions; they become habits. Watch your habits; they become character. Watch your character; it becomes your destiny."[10] Heraclitus, the Greek philosopher known for his views on change being central to the universe, observed, "Character is destiny."

The good news is that wisdom is learned, like all the virtues. Wise people are bred; they are not born. We can shake the traits that are used to label us. Here is a fun study to make this point. Shy males entered a waiting room, not knowing that they were in an experiment. A total of six females sat next to the shy males and talked to them for 12 minutes each. The experiment was repeated the next day so the males received 144 minutes of female attention. Shortly after the experiment, these formerly shy males gained a confidence boost and started to date, when many had not done so before.

Six months after the experiment, the psychologists conducting the study told the shy males what had really happened. Knowing that they had participated in an experiment didn't matter because a change in attitude had already changed their shy habits. A total of 144 minutes that involved six females doing nothing more than being interested in a shy male changed their self-perception. Before the experiment, these shy males had developed a habit to shy away from approaching females. After the experiment, the males in the study had replaced their shy habit with a newly learned habit to interact with females. The males were pleased with the outcome and called the experimenter asking if he was doing other experiments![11] Like the young males in this experiment, we can learn to be wiser with the right boost.

First we make our habits, and then our habits make us. In the short term, we get a booster shot to change from a book, a seminar, or a coach. Over the long term, we return to old habits. Traditional training is about information. Once informed, we are trained. Intelligence is about a fixed body of knowledge, often impersonal and clinical and, oddly, not social. In contrast, wisdom is deeply personal and adaptive. Lasting change takes into account how we perceive the world. Lasting change also focuses on behavior and habits. Wisdom involves clarifying who we want to be, training our emotions, and engaging in a journey of self-cultivation that is, at moments, both crucial and mundane. We practice every day how we interact with others and the activities we pursue. We aren't just who we are. We can make ourselves into better people all the time.

Barriers to Wisdom

The seven deadly sins—pride, greed, lust, envy, gluttony, wrath, and sloth—are the strongest competitors of the seven classical virtues. Most of us have given all seven sins a very thorough test drive at some point in our lives. We learn they are called "deadly" for a reason: they offer one certainty, and that is misery. Charlie Munger, a business partner of Warren Buffett for 50 years, offered four surefire ways to be miserable:

1. Be unreliable. You can counter all the other virtues by not doing what you say you are going to do.
2. Do not learn from the experience of others. Do not learn from failure. Self-destruct due to drugs, resentment, and envy of success.

3. When you face adversity, quit. Even the most fortunate and advantaged can ensure misery if they collapse in the face of trouble.

4. Avoid Einstein's belief that success is driven by "curiosity, concentration, perseverance, and self-criticism." So be sure to reframe any new insight that challenges your current worldview into what you already believe.[12]

Munger's misery list helps us wrap our heads around wisdom by showing us its antithesis and what happens in the absence of wisdom. This isn't to suggest that developing wisdom is easy. Each day, organizations full of messy, complicated people bump up against messy, complicated problems. Office politics distract teams from serving customers and patients better than the competitors do, although that doesn't stop virtue competing openly with destructive office cultures, envy, and complaints about workloads.

A former CEO was asked how he would describe his job. He said he was running an adult daycare center: "Sally, you can't have Phillip's office. Harry, if you don't come in on time, you are going to have trouble keeping up with the other kids. Pierre, please learn how to play and work better with the other children." In other words, when the office is focused on politics, it is not focused on innovative ways to better serve customers and patients.

Wisdom is about choices. In this sense, when we are wise, we control our own fate. People can choose envy and excuses, or they can choose wise conduct. Each day, our choices determine how our character will shape our destiny. Wisdom is also an advantage, especially when wise and engaged teams compete against unwise and disengaged teams.

Soft Is Hard

Wise leaders understand the relationship between intangibles, such as leadership, culture, and teamwork, and the tangibles, such as revenue, margins, and market share. In the twentieth century, leaders focused more on tangible assets than on people. It's not that people didn't matter, but wealth was created by leveraging "hard assets," such as land, equipment, and cash. Hard assets still matter in the twenty-first century but the business model has switched to emphasizing soft assets. Increasingly, hard results, such as revenue and profitable growth, are made possible by soft methods, such as engaged talent.

Organizations that own fewer hard assets lower their fixed costs, resulting in more financial flexibility. Since on the other side of VUCA is more VUCA, organizations must carefully consider their staffing levels. A VUCA world rewards flexibility, so that not if, but when, revenue declines, the core of the organization is protected. A financial buffer is created by spending less on fixed assets, like land and offices, and relying more on variable costs, such as interns, part-time workers, and contractors. As organizations strive to contain fixed costs, some part-time workers and recent graduates struggle to secure full-time jobs.

The reason that organizations must be especially careful about staffing levels is that 70 percent or more of an organization's operating costs are associated with total compensation (wages and benefits). In other words, people are the most expensive line item on virtually any organization's income statement. So the financial challenge is converting an enormous investment in human capital into cash as quickly as possible. To achieve this goal requires an engaged workforce. In a typical organization, approximately 30 percent of the workforce is fully engaged, 50 percent is modestly engaged, and 20 percent is disengaged. If human capital were viewed similarly to any other investment, with only 30 percent of assets generating a solid return, it would be logical to conclude that this was a lousy investment.[13]

Arguably, this shift from hard to soft assets makes the capacity to cultivate employee engagement among the most vital leadership tasks of our age. Since engaged people increase the chances of future growth, wise leaders want to maintain or strengthen the 30 percent who are already fully engaged and move some of the 50 percent of employees who are modestly engaged toward more engagement. At the very least, wise leaders try to minimize the problems that come with the 20 percent of employees who are actively disengaged. Sound engagement strategy can be summarized like this: start by making the strong stronger. Start with the fully engaged to understand what is going well and then do more of it. Start with what is right rather than with what is wrong.

Here is a key insight about engagement from Gallup. The direct supervisor accounts for 70 percent of the variance in engagement scores. Amazingly, Gallup polls has also reported that most people would rather clean their homes than spend time with their boss![14] This is not a knock on bosses. It raises the issue of whether bosses understand what motivates people.

Researchers who reviewed 120 years of research from 92 quantitative studies that included 15,000 individuals and 115 coefficients discovered that the relationship between salary and satisfaction was weak. These findings are consistent with Gallup's research, which is based on 1.4 million employees from 192 organizations in nearly 50 industries from 32 countries. So the answer to the question "Can money buy engagement?" is "No."[15]

We don't want to be misunderstood on this point. Money matters. If people don't receive competitive wages, even the mission and the culture may not keep them. Think of money as a threshold ticket: people need to make enough money so they think less about money and think more about their work.

Money is necessary for us to live, but money is not sufficient to cultivate a passionate staff. If employers are not careful with incentives, they start treating people like Pavlovian dogs doing tricks for treats. Offering incentives to professionals like teachers assumes that they can be conditioned to do what is needed because they are motivated to gain rewards and avoid punishment. Employers are just as likely to select the wrong incentives that stop people from doing what is right. For example, healthcare reimbursements have been based on how many patients doctors see and how many procedures they do. With volume-based incentives like these, the perverse and unintended consequence can be doctors' doing unnecessary procedures. This is not how physicians and nurses want to do their work. They want to do the right thing for the right reasons in the right way. It's just that volume incentives could possibly nudge doctors toward prioritizing volume over patient care. It is this realization that has given rise to fully integrated, salaried physician systems. Perhaps it is not coincidental that healthcare organizations that are structured this way—like the Mayo Clinic and the Cleveland Clinic—are rated the numbers 1 and 2 hospitals in the United States today.

What about rules? We need rules for sure, though when we rely exclusively on rules, there are inevitable unintended consequences. Too many rules erodes the skill to practice wisdom.

What about metrics? We certainly pay attention to the activities and the results that are measured. Numbers help leaders compare, and numbers also make hiding difficult. While numbers can help drive accountability, it is wise to acknowledge that numbers are subject to sampling error—data collected from a sample that is too small can misrepresent the larger population. Numbers are subject to measurement error—we are not measuring what we think we are measuring or the results over time differ. Correlational data are too often used to make definitive casual conclusions. Corporate metrics, such as revenue by employee, indicate high or low productivity, but they don't tell an employer why. Perhaps high productivity numbers are associated with improved technology, wise staffing, or thoughtful processes.

An incorrect use of a metric can look like this. Since the direct supervisor accounts for about 70 percent of the variance in engagement scores, let's hold the supervisor accountable for her team's engagement score. Let's set a goal that at least 40 percent of all employees must be highly engaged and tie this result to the supervisor's merit pay. This perverse use of extrinsic motivators to encourage engagement driven by intrinsic motivation causes the engagement tail to wag the relationship dog. The goal is not a high engagement score. The goal is creating trusting and caring relationships. Engagement is a by-product of how people are treated. The order matters. Trust and caring relationships must come first; engagement then follows.

When work involves people, it involves virtue. Yet, in a world of incentives, punishments, and metrics, the link between soft methods like virtue and hard results like profit can be missed. Leaders who are brilliant readers of financial statements too often fail to read how morale problems stirred up by disengaged employees cost money. Low morale means that there is an absence of trusting and caring relationships. When this happens, low morale will generate only 30 cents of value for every 1 dollar spent. In contrast, Gallup claims that engaged workforces have generated up to 147 percent higher earnings per share (EPS) for companies compared to competitors who lack engaged workforces.[16]

APPLIED WISDOM: LEVERAGE STRENGTHS

An effective way to increase engagement is to focus on strengths. Why strengths rather than weaknesses? Disengagement goes up when leaders ignore their colleagues or focus on their weaknesses. Approximately 40 percent of a workforce is disengaged when the boss ignores them. Similar to a marriage about to go bad, when apathy hits, the relationship is in trouble. The level of disengagement decreases to 20 percent when the boss focuses on their weaknesses. If the focus is on weaknesses, the thinking goes, at least those involved still care. Here is the remarkable number: when the boss focuses on strengths, only 1 percent are disengaged.[17] Playing to people's strengths is good math.

To be clear, leveraging strengths does not translate to ignoring weaknesses. It does mean that lifting the level of performance from pitiful to mediocre is not exactly a winning formula. The smarter and quicker path to high performance is to offset the weakness of one person with the strength of another.

A strength-based approach has a simple premise. People are more productive and more satisfied when they use their strengths more often. Of course, individual strengths need to align with an organization's strategic priorities. Depending on the person, teams might have many or few opportunities to align individual strengths with organizational priorities. Either way, even a modest opportunity to increase the time that people rely on their strengths improves individual satisfaction and organizational productivity.

If teams decide to do so, exploring ways to leverage individual strengths and manage weaknesses could start tomorrow. Over the long term, a culture can be strengthened further through hiring and promotion decisions. Who is hired and promoted is among the clearest statements of virtues that an organization can make.

In making hiring and promotion decisions, we can consider talent based on competence and character. While there is a risk in trying to simplify the world into a grid like the one in Figure 5.2, taking into account both character and competence offers a powerful way to think about hiring, firing, and promotion decisions:

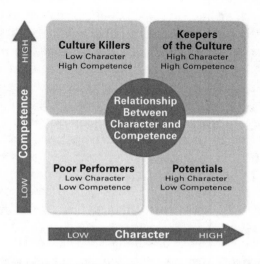

Keepers of the culture possess high competence and character. These are the people whom leaders should drive to work each day. These are the people to build a team around.

The *culture killers* on the team are those with high competence and low character. A con artist can score a 10 on emotional intelligence competence, but a 1 on character. High competence and low character is an Enron waiting to happen. If someone scores low on character, the employers hope that person is dumb and lazy. It is easier to foil the unethical, dumb, and lazy than the unethical, ambitious, and smart. This is why smart rainmakers who destroy morale are an organization's worst nightmare. It is extremely hard to jettison cancers when they pay the bills. However, what leaders tolerate defines them. Our ethical boundaries are clear when leaders let culture killers walk all over people, as long as they make it rain. Typically, when leaders do cut the cancer out, people who have been held back by the culture killers are then freed to step up. Perhaps not immediately, but eventually, performance increases rather than decreases because one superstar performer can't outperform a good team.

Potentials are those who are high in character but low in competence. Clearly, some threshold level of competence is needed to do the job. With that qualifier in mind, since *virtue* means excellence, an investment in high-character people is a good bet.

Poor performers possess neither competence nor character. They are especially unpleasant by offering neither value nor virtue. Unless they pick up their game and demonstrate an openness to change, it is time to go. What should be done with poor performers is not complicated, although how a relationship ends often is.

The message here is to be careful when character and competence are decoupled because high competence and low character are a dangerous combination. Organizations get into trouble when they trust in competence and forget about character. Think of the difference between a doctor who is brilliant and principled and one who is brilliant but unethical. The impact of these two individuals is totally different, even though both are highly competent. Whom would you like to be treated by?

Hiring for Character and Training for Competence

There is a strong business case to hire for character and train for competence, though this is not so easy to do. What gets in the way is invisible bias. People are just not that good at making hiring decisions, although they too often think otherwise. Here is the evidence behind this statement. Most organizations proclaim the benefits of attracting a diverse applicant pool. Despite good intentions, researchers from MIT and the University of Chicago have revealed that employers come up short. Researchers sent identical résumés to employers with one exception: their names. Some résumés used African-American stereo-typically black-sounding names, like Lakisha Washington, and others used white-sounding names, like Emily Baker. The result? White names received 50 percent more callbacks for interviews than black names.[18]

Similar studies found similar results when the application suggested the person was Muslim, an ex-offender, a mother, gay, or disabled even though the qualifications were held constant. We are children of the Enlightenment who have been taught that the conscious mind knows all. Yet what leads to poor hiring decisions is unconscious bias.

Making accurate assessments of a person's ability is more the exception than the rule. There are two human shortcomings that are especially difficult to overcome during interviews: *confirmation bias* and *similar-to-me syndrome*. Confirmation bias means that people look to confirm what they already know, rather than recognizing new facts. When it comes to interviewing, having confirmation bias means that employers are at risk for judging a person in the first five minutes of a conversation based on what they already think about their competence and character, rather than what might be the candidate's true characteristics and potential.[19]

Similar-to-me syndrome means that employers look to hire someone like themselves, rather than hiring someone who offsets their weaknesses. Studies have demonstrated that the best predictor of who gets hired has more to do with the characteristics of the interviewer than those of the interviewee. If the hiring manager has been an athlete, she values hiring athletes. If he worked his way through school, he wants to hire people who did the same. People look to hire someone more like themselves, rather than looking for what will truly drive performance.[20]

The limitation of confirmation bias and similar-to-me syndrome is that employers miss the mark in serving customers and patients. Consider these two scenarios: (1) You are an engineer building a product for a user. (2) You are a physician treating a patient. Who do you think the user or the patient is? Write down everything you think you know about the person you are trying to help. Chances are, your list is incomplete in a way that prohibits your understanding of your user and the help she really needs.[21]

To mitigate the risk associated with our bias requires that we start by understanding why this happens. Biases are mental short-cuts. They exist partly because the human brain cannot process all the information that bombards us, so we fill in the blanks. Combating unconscious biases is challenging because the biases don't feel wrong. They actually feel right. However, in order to create a work environment that supports and encourages diverse perspectives and people, it is necessary to recognize and challenge bias. Not only is it the right thing to do but it is also in the organization's best interests. Diverse talent is likely to produce services and products that work for diverse customers.

If you want to address your biases, you need motivation and wisdom to make the unconscious conscious. The person's name on the top of a résumé and his or her address do not correlate with potential performance. The year a person graduated from college does not tell you how well that person will perform in a particular job.[22]

While the school that an applicant attended does not correlate with performance, the applicant's character does. Sounds good, but not so fast. Our hiring dilemma is that we can objectively evaluate what matters least (for example, demographic features, where the applicant went to school) but not what matters most (character) because assessing someone's character is subject to bias. It is easier to observe character over time than during an interview. We can evaluate character after we have seen how well someone works with others and how they respond to adversity and pressure.

The risk of bias can be mitigated when everyone on the interview team looks for the same behaviors of giving, grit, growth mindset, and gratitude (4Gs). Here is evidence that the performance virtues matter:

- *Givers* who learn not to be doormats consistently outperform takers, although the negative impact that takers have on a culture is double or triple the positive impact of a giver.[23]
- *Growth-mindset people* can outperform people with a fixed mindset by two times when confronted with a challenge even though both groups have the skills to succeed.[24]
- *Gritty leaders* outperform quitters. Grit is a by-product of passion. Passionate people report innovating twice as frequently as dispassionate colleagues.[25]

- *Gratitude* builds fortitude to recover from setbacks and to stay resilient in the face of adversity. Grateful people are 25 percent more alert, alive, and awake than ingrates.[26]

These data make clear that the "performance virtues" defined by these 4Gs are critical performance differentiators, yet they are difficult to measure and evaluate during the limited time of an interview. Let's break down the 4Gs—giving, grit, growth mindset, and gratitude—so that employers are at least clear what they should look for.

The first G is *giving*. Givers often seek opportunities to serve others. Givers are adept at building genuine trust. They have the ability to develop a strong network of relationships that increases engagement and sparks innovation. When employees act like givers, they facilitate efficient problem solving and coordination and build a cohesive, supportive culture that appeals to customers, suppliers, and team members alike. A willingness to help others to achieve their goals lies at the heart of effective teamwork, collaboration, innovation, and service excellence. During the hiring process, look for individuals who share knowledge, offer assistance, and contribute to others without seeking anything in return. A valuable way to protect a culture is to screen for and exclude takers—those who try to get other people to serve their ends while carefully guarding their own expertise and time. Eventually, takers negatively affect team cohesiveness and erode the culture. Adam Grant reports that a taker's negative impact on culture is double or triple that of a giver's positive impact.[27]

The second G is *grit*. Gritty people generally demonstrate a strong passion that drives them to take on challenges or achieve excellence in whatever they do. Their resilience and persistence enable them to maintain effort and interest over time despite facing setbacks and obstacles. Angela Duckworth defines grit as "perseverance and passion for long-term goals" or "the tendency to sustain interest in and effort toward very long-term goals."[28] In other words, it means sticking with your goals and plans for the future—day in, day out, not just for the week, not just for the month, but for years—and working really hard to make that future a reality. Gritty people tend to have developed a strong sense of hope and plenty of courage to keep them going during the tough times. Key indicators of gritty individuals described by Duckworth are these:

145

- *Goal directedness:* Knowing where to go and how to get there
- *Motivation:* Having a strong will to achieve identified goals
- *Self-control:* Avoiding distractions and focusing on the task at hand
- *Positive mindset:* Embracing challenge and viewing failure as a learning opportunity[29]

The third G is a *growth mindset*, a term coined by Carol Dweck.[30] Her research demonstrated that growth-mindset individuals believe you can get better, smarter, and more collaborative. People with a growth mindset are always trying to figure out how to learn, grow, and develop themselves further. They know that success is about hard work, trying, effort, and being open to advice. In contrast, fixed-mindset individuals believe you either have ability or you don't. They tend to avoid experimenting and learning. People with a fixed mindset tend to avoid challenges because they believe that if they fail, it is because they lacked ability.[31]

The final G is *gratitude*, which is a by-product of humility, self-awareness, grace, and wisdom. Quick to acknowledge and reward the contribution of others, a grateful person demonstrates a profound understanding that success is seldom achieved only by one's own efforts but most often through the support and backing of others. A lack of gratitude is related to taking, and the presence of gratitude is related to giving. Takers are most likely to use "I," "me," and "my" pronouns and take personal credit. Givers are more likely to use "we," "our," and "us" pronouns and to share achievement. Grateful people have a tendency to live a reflective, intentional, and self-disciplined life. They look for and find the positive in situations, and because of this, it may be easier for them to develop compassion and empathy for others. While ingrates are quick to blame others, grateful people are likely to own mistakes and share what they learned from their mistakes.[32]

Looking for the 4Gs in potential employees is a sound strategy. Giving and gratitude are pro-social behaviors that build trust. Grit and growth mindset drive high performance. The order matters. A secure base of trust and care helps people strike out to be boldly innovative. However, accurate assessments of the 4Gs are hard to come by if we are not prepared to see ourselves as flawed judges of character. We agree with Pogo: "We have met the enemy, and he is us!" If we are prepared to acknowledge our shortcomings in evaluating others, then here are four ways to mitigate bias:

1. Ask people to lead the hiring process who have a track record of hiring high performers. Based on the facts, choose the person who is good at selection versus the person who wants to select.
2. Grant the hiring manager veto power in the hiring decision without granting unilateral authority. Hiring managers start out with high standards, but their standards drop when jobs go unfilled and pressure to fill them goes up.
3. Put together a diverse hiring team, and make sure to compare evaluations. This simple step helps overcome bias.
4. Compared to unstructured interviews, structured interviews help mitigate the risk of bias and increase the chances of a good hiring decision.[33] Structured interviews that elicit insights about the 4Gs help everyone on the team look for the same high-performance behaviors.

Performance Evaluations

Like hiring, evaluating people is fraught with bias. Rats offer insights to why people view performance evaluation as unappealing as dental work. Do you think your private thoughts affect a rat's behavior? If you said no, surprisingly, you are wrong.

A research study brought people into a lab to run performance tests on rats. Signs that said "dumb" were placed next to the stupid rats, and signs that said "smart" were placed next to the brilliant rats. Even though these signs were completely bogus, the "smart" rats performed twice as well as the "dumb" rats. The interesting part of the study is that all of the rats in the experiment were average. No rat was dumber or smarter than another. Yet, the use of "smart" and "dumb" signs to label the rats' intelligence changed how the researcher touched the rats. Smart rats were handled more gently, and dumb rats were handled more callously. How rats were handled affected performance, not just by a little but twice as much! In other words, private thoughts did affect the performance of a rat.[34]

So what does this mean to people? We stand closer or farther away from people we like or do not like. We make more or less eye contact. The differences in our interactions are so subtle that we are largely unaware of how we relate to others. Even though we are unaware of the differences, the impact on performance is profound. Students perform differently based on what teachers expect of them and how teachers treat them. Military trainers can make soldiers run faster, and mothers can influence the drinking habits of their teenagers based on expectations and level of care.[35]

What happens to rats labeled as smart or dumb also happens to people who are stacked and racked during performance evaluations. If managers are not careful, performance evaluations are a version of the rat experiment. Are you smart or dumb? Clearly, managers need to evaluate performance, but the current approach isn't driving high performance. In fact, only 8 percent of companies report that their performance management system is valuable, and 58 percent report that it is a waste of time.[36]

The idea that performance evaluation improves motivation was birthed by Frederick Taylor's time and motion studies. A century ago, employees like assembly-line workers or coal miners could easily be measured on parts produced by hours worked. The goal was to increase pay for people who exceeded performance outcomes and to cut the pay of or fire people who failed to perform. This made sense then.[37]

So what's changed in the past 100 years? First, performance evaluations have evolved to become legal tools to protect organizations from lawsuits. When the goal is to mitigate legal risk, evaluations emphasize following rules more than encouraging high performance. The theme of trusting and caring relationships that runs through this book often is not considered during performance evaluations. Think of a performance evaluation like a three-legged relationship stool. One leg is mutual trust, the second is shared goals, and the third leg is mutual respect. Remove any one of the three legs, and the stool can't stand. And when working relationships are strained, one or more of these three legs is lacking. Formal performance evaluations are needed least when the three legs of the stool are sturdy. Sadly, performance evaluations are needed most when they are least effective—to resolve problems of distrust, lack of shared goals, or mutual disrespect. Let's look at one more shortcoming of traditional performance evaluations. In a VUCA world, goals shift, strategies evolve, and priorities change. People work on projects with different teams and bosses throughout the year. Often, people have responsibility without authority, meaning that they often cannot control results. Yet, annual performance evaluations assume a stable world and clear responsibility. Goals are set, and then results are measured 12 months later.

Given challenges in managing effective relationships and rapidly shifting priorities, it should come as no surprise that traditional performance evaluations contribute more to disengagement than engagement. This is why companies like Microsoft have abandoned forced rankings that increased power struggles and decreased collaboration.

So what do we put in place of traditional annual performance evaluations? Google argues that compensation decisions should be separated from development decisions. Extrinsic compensation conversations simply don't mix with intrinsic coaching conversations.[38]

Again, this is not to suggest that compensation doesn't matter. Everyone needs to make a living. The critical insight to understand is that motivation isn't bought. Motivation is cultivated by a compelling purpose, an opportunity for mastery, and empowerment to be self-directed.[39]

Clearly, results matter, which is why it is important to understand that high performance is driven far more by intrinsic than extrinsic motivations and far more by coaching than controls. Perhaps more organizations will replace annual performance evaluations with ongoing feedback about how employees add value and ongoing coaching to contribute to their growth. This means that managers will need to learn how to coach well.[40]

Coaching

Imagine if performance evaluations started with two questions: (1) "What do you do well?" and (2) "How could you do more of it?" Consider how infrequently, if ever, you have been asked these two questions. For that matter, how often have you asked these two questions of others? Just as we do not always know our weaknesses, we also do not know our strengths. Performance evaluations are more often deficit-based with a focus couched nicely as "areas for improvement." While deficit-based thinking is about understanding and preventing problems, a strength-based approach is about excellence.

So who can help us learn about our strengths? Mentors and coaches can be incredibly valuable in helping to develop character and competence, though their approaches differ. Mentors give advice based on their own success and expertise. Mentoring can be a great thing, but mentoring isn't coaching. Coaches help people clarify their own goals. While mentors place themselves at the center, coaches place the learner at the center. Good coaching helps people uncover and develop their goals through self-discovery. Put simply, coaches ask nonjudgmental questions, and mentors more often offer advice based on what contributed to their success. Both mentoring and coaching have value, though coaching is an especially powerful way to help people grow. The Massachusetts Institute of Technology reported that well-coached entrepreneurs were seven times more likely to secure funding and grow their business at three and a half times the growth rate of entrepreneurs who were not coached.[41]

Since the best athletes in the world need a coach, why wouldn't the rest of us benefit from great coaching too? A few lucky leaders are able to hire an executive coach. For most of us, we need an option that costs less or, better yet, is free. How about a trusted friend? Reach out to someone you know, like, and trust. Of course, there is more to coaching than liking and trusting someone, but without this, coaching isn't likely to work.

Clearly, your known or liked or trusted friend isn't trained as a certified coach, but that doesn't mean she can't be helpful and at least apply some basic coaching methods. The mission of good coaching is to establish a safe environment, diffuse emotion, and meet someone where he is. The best coaches promote self-discovery by revealing blind spots, rationalization, and denial. Good coaching involves relationship building, achieved through empathy, and active listening. Empathy means that it's all about the learner, and it's not about the coach. Good coaching relies on empathy to look for strengths and possibilities while avoiding judgment. There is a stronger payback to leveraging a strength, rather than focusing on deficits, weaknesses, challenges, barriers, and adversaries. When you focus on problems, you have more problems. When you focus on possibilities, you have more opportunities.

Effective coaching is founded on listening and questions. Active listening is easier to understand than to do. Good coaching relies on levels 2 and 3 and avoids level 1:

- Level 1: *Internal*—listen, though we focus on ourselves.
- Level 2: *Focused*—listen to the words and emotions of the speaker.
- Level 3: *Global*—listen for tone, energy, and what isn't said.

Effective coaches ask *"what"* and *"how"* questions, not *"why"* questions. A *"why"* question is a judgment question that certainly makes sense in many circumstances, but not when it comes to coaching. Strength-based coaching explores possibilities while avoiding judgment.

This concept of the value of strength-based thinking has important lessons for doctors when they take on leadership roles. An internal conflict arises between the need for physician-leaders to embrace a strength-based leadership approach and an opposite "deficit-based" approach that doctors use in diagnosing patients' symptoms. This tension between doctor as healer and doctor as leader requires role mindfulness and nimbleness in transitioning between healing mode and leadership mode. Let's take a slightly deeper look at this tension that comes from doctors' training as healers.

Doctors are trained to think about problems because patients come with symptoms, which are clues to hidden issues. In thinking about a patient's symptoms, doctors are trained to generate a *differential diagnosis*—basically a list of all the potential causes of a specific symptom. The more seasoned the doctor, the broader the list of differential diagnoses and the more elegantly the list can be narrowed to identify the specific cause of the patient's problems.

This way of thinking is time-honored and works very well for making diagnoses. The problem is that it trains doctors to see the world through a "problem-focused" lens—or what is sometimes called "deficit-based thinking." The unintended effect of being a deficit-based thinker is that, although the approach works beautifully for being a healer, deficit-based thinking handicaps doctors when it comes to solving organizational challenges and leading. The antidote to deficit-based thinking is *appreciative inquiry*, which is a strength-based approach. Instead of asking, "What is the problem with this situation?" which is a deficit-based approach, consider the power of asking, "What opportunities do we have with the talent in the room?" This is an appreciative question and invites different solutions. The lesson for doctors who are leaders is that they must take a "time out" when they go from a clinical setting to an administrative function so that they can switch from deficit-based to appreciative thinking.

Back to coaching and strength-based thinking. As an aspect of strength-based thinking, good coaching is built on the growth mindset. Carol Dweck was retained to help a professional sports team develop interview screening questions for prospective players. Her suggestion was simple: "Ask the recruits what they expect at the next level of play (competition) and what they would have to do to prepare or change."[42]

Dweck cautioned that people are not good at predicting future success based on current assessments. We don't know how people might perform with the right commitment, effort, support, and training. What research continues to reveal is that commitment, effort, support, and training separate equally talented people. People with a growth mindset understand the power of "not yet,"[43] acknowledging that they have not yet achieved the results they want. However, they believe that with practice they have the capability to become better. There are three simple steps to the not-yet strategy:

1. Recognize that your brain is like a muscle. When you take on challenges, you get smarter. Your brain is, in fact, malleable. Neurons are connected when challenges are confronted, thus enhancing brain development. When challenges are avoided, the opportunity for brain development is lost.
2. Understand the difference between a growth mindset and a fixed mindset. Table 5.1 contains a summary of a growth versus a fixed mindset.

GROWTH MINDSET	FIXED MINDSET
"I can learn anything."	"I am either good at something or not."
"When frustrated, I still persevere."	"When frustrated, I give up."
"I want to challenge myself and those around me."	"I don't like to be challenged."
"When I experience failure, I learn from it."	"When I fail, it is because I lack ability."
"If you succeed, then I am inspired."	"If others succeed, then I feel threatened."
	"My abilities determine everything."

TABLE 5.1   A Growth Versus a Fixed Mindset

Source: Adapted from Carol Dweck, "The Power of Believing That You Can Improve," video file, TED Talks, November 2014, https://www.ted.com/talks/carol_dweck_the_power_of_believing_that_you_can_improve.

3. Rely on a not-yet strategy when desired results haven't been met. This means that through reflection, effort, deliberate practice, learning from mistakes, and seeking advice, you can get better and achieve the desired results. You just haven't done so yet.[44]

As the practice of a growth mindset has spread, Dweck has grown concerned about the practice of a false growth mindset. A *false growth mindset* strives to make someone feel good independent of the actual outcome. A well-intentioned teacher and manager who learn about the growth mindset can incorrectly praise for effort regardless of results. Dweck makes clear that praise without result is a consolation prize that suggests that outcomes do not matter as long as we tried. But results matter a great deal, and that is why the phrase "not yet" is so important. We have "not yet" achieved the outcome we want. However, goals can be reached through loads of effort, smart strategies, and coaching from others.[45]

WISDOM IS BRED NOT BORN

We are not the same person we were when we were teenagers, before we were married, before we had children, or after we mourned the loss of a family member. So the issue isn't whether we can change. The challenge is, how will we change? If we blame others or ourselves, it will be much harder to change. If we look for benefits that include ways to change our habits, change will be easier.

This view is not held by fixed-mindset leaders and teams who believe that people either have character or they do not. These people believe that character is a function of chemistry, the parents who raised you, or the neighborhood where you were raised. But they are very wrong. The most exciting, optimistic, and powerful idea of *Exception to the Rule* is this: character is learned, practiced, and cultivated. We can learn to give, to develop grit, to develop a growth mindset, and to be grateful, just as we can learn to take, to quit, to have a fixed mindset, and to be ungrateful.

Virtue is developed best when we feel responsible for our own growth. We are more motivated and perform best when we leverage our strengths and manage our weaknesses. And we develop faster still when we are part of a caring and cooperative culture.

There are no surefire ways to develop wisdom, though it certainly involves some sort of disciplined reflection and self-understanding. Otherwise, as T. S. Eliot cautioned, "We had the experience but missed the meaning."[46]

WISDOM TOOL KIT

Wisdom involves more than knowledge. Wisdom is about learning from experience, which requires disciplined reflection. The problem is that we are busy, and we do not take the time needed to reflect. We may be lost, but we are making great time!

Without disciplined reflection, we are less clear about where we are going, fuzzy about how to live by our convictions, and less able to learn from our experiences. Our default then becomes being busy, which is a very weak alternative to having a purpose.

Everyone reflects, so there is nothing novel about that. What is novel is having disciplined reflection on virtues. Consider the impact on developing our character if we asked and answered these four questions once a week:

1. "Did I reflect on the virtues?"
2. "In what acts of compassion was I involved (a private act to relieve the suffering of another)?"
3. "In what acts of social justice was I involved (righting a public wrong)?"
4. "Did I learn from my mistakes?" The question isn't "Did I make a mistake?" Rather, the question is "Did I learn from my mistakes?"

If you are looking for an even simpler way to practice disciplined reflection, Benjamin Franklin reduced four questions to two questions. Each morning, Franklin asked himself: "What good can I do?" Each night, he asked: "What good did I do?"

Here are three questions that parents can ask kids to help them practice virtue in school:

1. "Were you courageous today?"
2. "Were you kind today?"
3. "Did you learn from your mistakes today?"

Reflection helps us to pay attention to our life. Most of us don't lie, cheat, and steal. Most people are good people interested in being better people. This is why, for most people, practicing virtue is less about what harm we have caused and more about what good we failed to do.

Not-Yet Growth-Mindset Strategy

Apply three strategies to further develop a growth mindset:

1. Understand that your brain is like a muscle. When we do things that are hard and important, we get smarter. When we ignore challenges, we stagnate.
2. Understand the difference between a growth mindset and a fixed mindset.
3. Put into practice "not-yet" strategies.

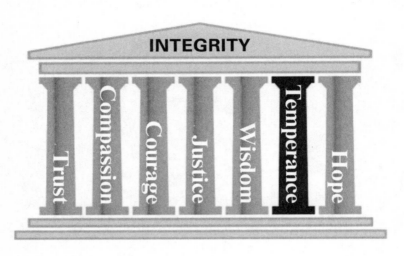

Temperance-to-Intemperance Spectrum

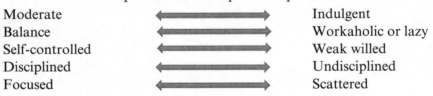

Moderate		Indulgent
Balance		Workaholic or lazy
Self-controlled		Weak willed
Disciplined		Undisciplined
Focused		Scattered

FIGURE 6.1 Pillars and Pediment: Temperance

Source: Copyright © Parker Hannifin.

CHAPTER 6

Temperance

To be virtuous is to be temperate—the
Greek middle way.

Calm is contagious.
—RORKE DENVER, FORMER NAVY SEAL AND TRAINER[1]

Temperance is about our habits. If we want to convert a tag line of
"calm is contagious" into a habit, then we need to practice temperance. Temperance comes from the Latin *tempus*, which means "time,
season, or right time." Temperance also implies patience, or waiting for
the proper time to do something. To be virtuous is to be temperate—to
do things in a timely fashion and in due season. This virtue deals with
how we spend our time and how we train ourselves to be better.

According to Thomas Aquinas, temperance governs the passions.[2]
This understanding of temperance comes from the Greek word *sophrosyne* or *enkrateia*, which simply means "moderation": the state of being
wise, or the idea of having self-control. Temperance is the master of
our urges and desires, so that we resist extreme behavior through
self-governance, self-control, and discipline.

As we mature, most of us learn how to "temper," or control, our
actions and ourselves. Temperance also seeks to balance our lives.
When life is balanced, there is less likelihood that self-indulgence
will become a problem. Through discipline and habit, we avoid two
extremes—indulgence and abstinence, workaholism, or laziness.

The virtue of temperance also addresses balance, which means that we have found the middle. The goal is not to take on more tasks but to create balance in our life—what the Greeks called the "middle way." As an example of the dire consequences of intemperance, classical mythology tells of Icarus, whose intemperance led him to fly so high the sun melted the wax off his wings, causing him to crash into the sea. His father, Daedalus, flew the middle way and stayed out of trouble. The point of the middle way is that no matter the situation, we can identify the extremes and locate the mean between them. How do we remain calm so we can fly the middle way?

Consider a story about flying the middle way—that is, responding to pressure to perform with learning to control what we can.

AMERICA'S CUP

The America's Cup is the oldest international sporting trophy and predates the modern Olympics by 45 years. It is yacht racing's greatest prize. In 1851, Queen Victoria watched the first America's Cup from the finish line. After seeing the United States win, the queen is said to have asked who came in second. The reply was "Ah, your majesty, there is no second."[3] This story may have been fabricated by an American reporter itching to take a shot at British imperialists. True or not, the story captures the way the America's Cup competition works. The winner is the defender, and everyone else is a challenger. In 2013, the United States defended the cup against the New Zealand challengers. Down 8 to 1 to New Zealand, the United States rallied to win 9 to 8 in one of the greatest comebacks in sports history. Ask the Kiwis. There is no second.[4]

Oracle Team USA is owned by Larry Ellison, the founder of Oracle and one of the world's wealthiest people. This gives Team USA a huge competitive advantage—access to the Oracle bank account to buy the best technology and the best sailors. The boats that compete in the America's Cup fly as much as they sail. They are built with a massive 13-story sail designed as an airplane wing combine with foils dropped below the surface to lift the boat literally out of the water. Sailors grind upside-down bicycle pedals that convert human power with sufficient energy to shoot a cata-maran through the water at very impressive speeds—up to 55 miles per hour.

In this winner-take-all culture, the team's top sailing coach doesn't talk about winning. That's right, the focus is not on winning but on doubling down on activities that sailors can control. The coach teaches sailors that winning is a by-product of self-control—temperance—and successful habits. The coach and sailors gather around a cockpit of three large flat-screen TVs. At the precise moment when the boat's speed was the fastest, or at any speed, for that matter, the team members can watch what they did and listen to what they said. The picture, sound, and data act like a mirror, revealing tactics and teamwork for all to see. The coach needs to say little because the video, audio, and numeric mirror tell all.[5]

This evidence-based approach to sailing is also used by physical trainers to ensure maximum fitness. Baseline data are collected on each sailor's strength, flexibility, and diet. These data are used to design a customized exercise and diet plan for each athlete. Actual performance on the boat is constantly linked back to fitness and diet habits. Older athletes are often more resilient than younger athletes, but they are not as fit. They need more time to recover from intense physical exertion, and some of their exercises focus on injury prevention. Younger sailors recover from physical exhaustion faster and are less likely to be injured. However, they may not have the resilience earned from grit under fire. Everyone is cross-trained in activities like boxing to ensure a particular muscle group isn't overused.

Now, we acknowledge that starting a chapter about temperance with a story about rich people racing yachts could be a head scratcher. Clearly, there are other ways to apply all this sailing and engineering talent, treasure, and time to more pressing societal needs. Ideally, the world would cheer at least as much for inner-city teachers and physicians who cure cancer as they do for fast sailors, fleet-footed soccer players, and basketball players who can slam dunk. But the point of this story isn't about societal priorities, as vital as that is. This is a story about doubling down on what we can control—our habits.

The 3As

The really important point of a chapter on temperance is this: character is learned both at the leadership level and at the cultural level. Of course, we are shaped by our DNA, by how we are raised, and by the culture in which we live. However, there also is far more room to transform leaders and culture than we might realize. In fact, we are wise not to underestimate the powerful imprint that culture makes on us above and beyond how we were raised.

The primary focus of a chapter on temperance is to put virtue into action. With this goal in mind, this chapter on temperance is organized around the 3As that guide us from gaining insight to doing: *awareness*, *attention*, and *action*. The 3As used here are different from the 3As of apologize, acknowledge, and atone for the purpose of restoring trust described in Chapter 1. The 3As of a commitment cycle go like this:

- *Awareness:* Gain Insight
  Gain insight into our strengths and shortcomings associated with each virtue.
- *Attention:* Focus
  After we are more aware of each virtue, it is easier to commit to an area of growth when we focus on one virtue and leverage our strengths.
- *Action:* Do
  It is not a virtue until we act, and to act we need tools. This chapter includes a robust individual and team tool kit, which is why it is the longest.

Now let's consider each A.

Awareness: Being Calm

Rorke Denver has provided leadership for all aspects of U.S. Navy SEALs training. As a Navy SEAL, he led special-forces missions in the Middle East, Africa, and Latin America. These experiences gave Denver unique insight into extraordinary leadership under intense pressure. Among his most valuable insights was that troops mimic a leader's behavior at a minimum, and, more likely, troops amplify a leader's behavior. This is why "calm is contagious" is such a critical habit for leaders to exhibit under duress. In contrast, when a leader lacks composure under fire, chaos or stupidity can become contagious.[6]

At its best, West Point offers an example of what "calm is contagious" looks like. One of the authors discussed with three West Point alumni how training has evolved from 30 years ago. Two of the three graduates were Army Rangers, and the third was a tank commander stationed in East Germany during the Cold War. When the three alumni reflected on how cadets are educated today compared to their era, they liked what they saw. All three remembered being screamed at while they applied a field bandage on a soldier in a gymnasium. Their military trainers screamed insults at them to induce artificial stress in the belief that if soldiers could not handle insults, then what would happen when bullets were flying?

Fast-forward 30 years: cadets now learn to apply a field bandage out in the field where the bullets really are flying. The training process simulates stress soldiers face on the battlefield. In a chaotic environment, the role of the leader is to lower anxiety, rather than to increase it, and to help cadets remember their training. "Calm is contagious" is not just a tag line. You have to train for it. This is the important takeaway for all of us. Under pressure, people default to their training.

NASA understands how to apply "default to training" concepts when teaching astronauts to walk in space. Space walking at 17,000 miles per hour tethered to a space station sounds pretty awesome. But even if you are the adventuresome type, here is something that can dampen your enthusiasm. Even the toughest and most resilient astronauts report being terrorized by a feeling of falling toward earth while walking in space. The space station is still under the influence of earth's gravitational pull, so astronauts out for a space stroll feel like they are being sucked into the abyss. Training will not eliminate this fear, but training can teach astronauts to cope with the fear.

The Neutral Buoyancy Lab is where astronauts practice space walking under water, which comes as close to simulating weightlessness on earth as possible. Astronauts practice for hours in a massive swimming pool 40 feet deep that includes a mock replica of the space station. Three safeguards protect astronauts from literally being lost in space: (1) handles to grab onto the space station; (2) tethering to stay connected to the space station should they slip; and (3) a propulsion system on their suit to reconnect to the space station if the handles and tethering fail. Astronauts train intensively and frequently so that when they experience the fear of falling, they know exactly where to reach for the handle, which helps them calm down so they can complete their mission.

NASA's thorough training deepens or changes people's habits so that people learn how to rise to the challenge they are being prepared to confront. The way habitual change is achieved is practice, practice, practice until people no longer need to think about the new habit. Contrast this kind of training with traditional education, which devotes limited if any attention to creating new habits. While training includes knowledge, good training goes a step further. The goal is to create a habit of being calm under pressure so that after the training, people will default to this standard.[7]

NASA's mission is "to reach for new heights and reveal the unknown so that what we do and learn will benefit all humankind." The military's mission is to "defend the Constitution against all enemies foreign and domestic." For physicians or business leaders, the best organizations have their own version of a "reveal the unknown" and "defend the Constitution" purpose statement, like "better care of the sick, investigation of their problems, and more teaching of those who serve," which is the Cleveland Clinic's mission. The best organizations make no apologies for high-performance expectations. Now imagine that the organization also says that because we expect so much, we owe you training to cope with the pressure to perform in a VUCA world.

Calming Our Brain

We can learn to be better teammates by gaining insights into how our brain works under pressure, when our interpersonal skills and teamwork are tested. The architecture of our brain is built on emotions. We feel first and think second, making it unrealistic to control our emotions under all circumstances. Executive functions, which include working memory, self-regulation, and flexibility, are the neurological building blocks that underpin resilience and perseverance. It is very difficult to achieve resilience, curiosity, and tenacity without first developing a neurological foundation of executive functions and the capacity for self-awareness forged by practicing virtue.

We do not need a deep dive into neurology to learn how to get our brain to work with us rather than against us. Simply understanding that we feel first and think second can be remarkably useful to helping us remain calm under fire. Recall that perceived or real threat triggers the amygdala to shut down the thinking part of our brain known as the *prefrontal cortex*. The amygdala helped us avoid becoming dinner for a prehistoric beast. Several thousand years later, we have put down our spears and picked up books. As we have evolved from a hunting society to a knowledge economy, we have developed a prefrontal cortex without jettisoning the amygdala. This is why we still feel before we think despite our neurological evolution.

It is easy to recognize when the amygdala is running the show. A colleague with an activated amygdala avoids eye contact, paces or moves away, and appears not to be listening. Stressed out people shut down new information to focus on the perceived or real threat at hand. When the person rejects any option you suggest, yelling or even getting physical will not work because the person's overstimulated brain is not accepting new insights.

When we are stressed out, we need the equivalent of a "time out" for two-year-olds. A rule of thumb is that it takes about 20 minutes to shut down the amygdala and reopen the thinking part of the brain. If we try to have the last word, we will retrigger the brain to shut down, which can take several hours rather than 20 minutes to reset. We help ourselves and our colleague with an overactivated amygdala by learning to open the brain's gate by paying attention to how someone responds to threats. Rather than giving more unwanted advice, we can shift to something enjoyable or give the person space without additional input. Once a person is no longer showing signs of amygdala activation, then it is time to reengage.[8]

In the end, we can only control one brain—our own. A very simple technique to reset the brain is to pause and plan. This means that when the feeling of flight, freeze, or fight kicks in, simply take deep breaths for 60 seconds. Try it. Take four to six breaths over a 60-second period by thinking only about inhaling and exhaling. To benefit from this simple exercise, sit up straight in a chair, close your eyes, and rest your hands in your lap. The favorable impact on self-control is impressive. Breathing is the means of stepping into our fear without becoming undone.[9]

Using Self-Control

Plato and Aristotle considered the goal of our existence to be the pursuit of excellence or virtue. Aristotle argued further that goodness can be developed by practicing virtue. We become just by practicing just actions; we become trustworthy by practicing trustworthy actions; we become courageous by performing courageous acts. Virtue is what we aspire to be when we are at our best. Rather than asking the rule-based question "What should I do?" virtue-based reasoning asks, "Who do I want to be?"

This isn't even to hint that it is possible to practice virtue flawlessly. A truly virtuous person is always an unrealizable ideal. Let's repeat the word *always*! We practice virtue for a lifetime, striving to improve habits like self-control.

Anyone who wants to improve needs to take this into account—that self-control is the capacity to change ourselves. The ability to control our emotions, thoughts, and behaviors enables us to stay focused, especially when things get difficult, unpleasant, or tedious. We rely on self-control to power through tough times and to push even when we are tired and even when we are jaded. Self-control separates the determined and successful from the easily distractible and discouraged.

Attention: Life-Work Balance

Here's the second A of the commitment cycle: attention.

The Sikh tradition pays close attention to temperance. This becomes clear once we understand that *Sikh* means "discipline" or "learner." Sikhs rely on meditation and yoga as the means of self-control over the "five thieves" (lust, rage, greed, attachment, and conceit).

While few Westerners travel to Yamuna Nagar Canal, it is an ideal place to gain insights into the Sikh tradition. This area is where the founding plant of Jamna Auto, a world leader in the production of commercial vehicle springs, is located. CEO Randeep Jauhar leads the family-owned business. Randeep Jauhar's father, Sadar Bhupindar Singh Jauhar, started the business and also founded Guru Nanak Khalsa College. In 1968, the college was opened on the five-hundredth birthday of Guru Nanak, the founder of Sikhism. This revered Sikh leader devoted his life to serving society's impoverished.[10] This is why the mission of Guru Nanak Khalsa College is contributing to India's economic growth by teaching bright, disadvantaged students technical and business skills founded on the Sikh tradition of social justice and self-control.[11]

Jauhar's father hosted a dinner that you could never prepare for nor ever forget. When we pulled up to his home, the car door was opened by a Sikh guard in military garb. A welcoming delegation of local business leaders and the Guru Nanak Khalsa faculty lined each side of a red carpet. Flower petals were spread at our feet, and we soon ran out of neck as each person placed a rose garland over our heads. Everyone we met bowed and said, "Namaste." *Nama* means "bow," and *te* means "you." So *namaste* literally means, "I bow to you." The gesture helps us replace the five thieves by focusing on the divine spark within each of us.

As we left Yamuna Nagar Canal to visit other parts of India, the struggle to reduce poverty and limit environmental degradation was visceral. Now all nations struggle to create jobs and protect trees, which implicates temperance. The extremes of rich and poor, cleanliness and degradation are in plain view throughout the country. For example, on a busy street in Chennai, it becomes clear India is a nation living in several centuries at once. Land Rovers and Mercedes-Benzes are surrounded by motorcycles, bicycles, and tok-toks. On one side of the road, beautiful corporate campuses house India's ignition to its economic growth, the information technology sector. On the other side, we see barefoot pedestrians, too poor for any other means of transportation.

Truck exhaust and dust make your eyes burn. Your nose takes in some nasty odors bubbling up from toxin-laced puddles next to the road. You watch a monkey jump impressively from one palm tree to another, reminding you that the road cuts through a subtropical ecosystem. In a single generation, India's vibrant economy lifted 150 million people out of abject poverty, almost half the population of the United States. Sadly, poverty is still the plight of millions more, and the cost of prosperity has been pollution.

Western nations increasingly have to learn to compete with hungry emerging markets like India populated by millions willing to do whatever it takes to release poverty's grip on their lives. Maybe it's just a hard, cold fact of our times that competing on a global stage means learning to accept a life of 24/7 connectivity. The benefits of globalization come with the price of business never turning off. Pervasive technology means that we never disconnect. Here are some facts to shed light on why we feel so distracted by technology:

- 204 million: Number of e-mails sent per minute
- 30: Average number of times an office worker checks his or her e-mail daily
- 8: Average number of windows open on a worker's computer at the same time
- 23 minutes: The length of time it takes to return to a task after being interrupted
- 221: Average number of times U.K. citizens check their phones daily[12]

It did not matter whether we worked with senior leaders or students in St. Petersburg, Russia, New Delhi, India, São Paulo, Brazil, or Pittsburgh, Pennsylvania—balance is always an issue. In fact, if we were to identify a single virtue that came up most often in over 10 years of working in emerging and developed countries alike, it was temperance. We met thousands of students and leaders who had thought deeply about how to make money, but far less deeply about how to make meaning. We have met a world full of high-performance leaders who are yearning for more balanced lives with the possibility of satisfying careers that provide time for family, friends, and community. Globalization, technology, and increased compliance demands rob us of discretionary decision making and time. While business often must operate 24/7, this does not mean that people have to do the same.

The number of hours in a week is 168. That's it. No more, no less—whether rich or poor, Indian or American, educated, or not. *Time* is the root word of *temperance*. Our use of time raises the question: "What are we living for?" It is interesting that society uses the phrase "work-life balance." We start by flipping the phrase to "life-work balance." Mahatma Gandhi was reputed to have stated, "Work is a means of living, not life itself." First, we need a life; then we work. Even if we get a life, it is not possible for us to always live a perfectly balanced life.

Temperance is the struggle to make the right decisions and to do the best we can at any given point in time.

Knowledge alone will not help us lead a balanced life because insight does not always lead to action. Even when I know I should move more and eat less, I don't. Like eating right and regular exercise, the solution to a balanced life is often in plain sight.

It is curious that we do not always do what is clearly in our interest. However, our irrational behavior makes more sense once we remember that our brain is wired to feel first and think second. In other words, we are not as rational as we might think. Part of being human is that we also have the infinite capacity to delude ourselves. Here are three common causes of delusion: denial, pride, and blind spots:

- *Denial:* A little boy cries, "My pants are wet, and I didn't do it!"
- *Pride before the fall:* The Romans welcomed a conquering general home with a spectacular parade, while placing a slave next to his ear whispering, "Remember, glory is fleeting."
- *Blind spots:* We lack a full appreciation of the negative impact that electronic screens (TVs, computers, smartphones) have on our relationships.

We want to pick up on the last point—being blind to our cultural obsession with electronics. An addiction to "screen time" over face-to-face time has consequences for our performance and relationships that largely go unnoticed. Here's why.

Screen Time Versus Face-to-Face Time

Technology has made physical presence far less important. Some people have traded their desks and offices for Internet access and smartphones. In an agrarian economy, home and work were intertwined. Technology has enabled us to go back to a form of that way of life because the percentage of work being conducted at home continues to increase. Punching a clock has its roots in manufacturing, when time on task required physical presence. Until recently, we might have said that doctors needed to see patients in an office, but today telemedicine is expanding treatment to include remote care.

Physical presence does not ensure optimal production. The fact that only 30 percent of a typical workforce is fully engaged makes it clear that my body may be in the building, but that does not necessarily mean that my brain is. If the job is completed, the number of hours worked and whether those are daytime or nighttime hours may be immaterial. Often, however, while employees appreciate flextime, managers are wary. For flextime to work, managers must be clear about their intentions.

If people understand the managers' intention, and they have control over what and how they complete their tasks, then their work becomes less stressful and more enjoyable. Of course, technology offers more than flextime. An American surgeon can conduct an operation in India remotely or vice versa. Cars and trucks can travel coast to coast without a driver. Consumers can shop for the cheapest airline ticket, hotel room, and rental car without leaving their home or talking to a person.

There are more technology blessings to be sure, though there are also technology curses. At a family dinner, everyone is connected outside the house, rather than talking to the person across the table. At meetings, colleagues take care of e-mails sent from people outside the meeting, while ignoring teammates at the meeting. E-mail creates a "respond immediately" mindset, so people juggle multiple tasks breathlessly to get more and more done in less and less time.

Clifford Nass, a psychology professor at Stanford University, has reported that nonstop multitasking actually wastes more time than it saves—and he says there's evidence that it may be killing our concentration and creativity too. One of the most interesting insights from Nass's research is that most people report they are very good at multitasking, but the reality is that they are miserable at it. Multitaskers experience a 40 percent drop in productivity, take 50 percent longer to complete a single task, and have a 50 percent higher error rate. Nass warned that excessive multitasking is diminishing our mental acuity in that we are changing our brain to be impatient and limiting our ability to concentrate. Those who multitask all the time cannot filter out irrelevancy. They cannot manage a working memory so they are chronically distracted. They are initiating much larger parts of their brain irrelevant to the task at hand.[13]

Multitasking is actually multiswitching. We are simply chopping up our attention into smaller chunks. We are switching back and forth between tasks rather than applying focused concentration. In other words, we are training our brain to spread our attention like peanut butter over a large span of activities. In this sense, the impact of multitasking is similar to attention deficit disorder.[14]

You could reasonably conclude it is our responsibility to control our use of technology and reduce multitasking by working on one application at a time. Tristan Harris, a former product philosopher at Google, asserts software engineers do everything they can to break down our self-control. Harris claims Silicon Valley intentionally teaches us bad habits so we get addicted to their devices. He explains software is designed to hijack your time by relying on variable rewards such as messages, photos, and likes that appear randomly. Variable rewards are a proven way to coerce users to check their phones compulsively. After all, Internet companies get paid based on how much time you spend on their site.

In response to the way our devices are designed for technology to control our time, he created an organization, appropriately named for a temperance chapter, Time Well Spent. Its mission is to encourage "do no harm" software engineering that promotes healthy rather than unhealthy habits.[15]

So our challenge is to replace attachment to our screens with attachment to people. In response to these negative technology habits, here is a pro-people hierarchy that any team could follow to create a "balanced," or temperate, way to benefit from technology's blessings and reduce its curses:

1. Talk face-to-face.
2. If face-to-face isn't possible, then Skype. If Skype isn't possible, then talk by phone.
3. If phone isn't possible, then text. A limited number of characters forces us to get to the point.
4. If text isn't possible, then e-mail. Some organizations go so far as to ban e-mails on the weekends.

Trust and care go up when we develop a habit to talk or phone first, and text and e-mail last. Technology can contribute to stress or reduce stress. It depends on how we use it. The best use of technology requires temperance.

Stress

Stress was invented in 1936. We didn't know what to call stress until it was studied in the twentieth century. Hans Selye borrowed the term *stress* from physics to describe the forces that produce strain on the body, similar to the way force is used to forge steel. Selye studied stress on rats. Lo and behold, things didn't turn out well for rats when they were tortured and abused. Cortisol levels soared, fighting went up, and life spans took a nose dive. All the surviving rats wanted to do was crawl into a corner and disengage from the world.[16]

Chronic stress isn't great for rats or people, though it is not a universal villain. The likelihood that a rat will bounce back from trouble depends on whether the rat is neglected or cared for. When mother rats lick and groom a stressed-out baby rat, the little rodent recovers and continues to explore its maze. When the mother rat ignores a stressed-out baby rat, the little rodent stops exploring the maze and cowers in the corner. When the brains of loved and lonely rats are compared, the hippocampus, the part of the brain that processes stress, is more developed in the loved than in the unloved rats.[17]

We are like rats. Among the most serious threats to a child's development is neglect—the absence of responsive and responsible caregivers. Neglected infants learn that their environment is unstable, unpredictable, and chaotic. And this isn't just true for children. It is the same for adults in work settings. When people feel a sense of belonging, like rats they are more likely to be resilient. So there is a critical insight here that is counterintuitive. Caring about people is not mushy sentimentalism. Caring about people makes them mentally tougher.

Upside of Stress

Do you try to avoid stress, or do you think stress is not so bad? For many, stress has come to mean feeling overwhelmed, experiencing daily hassles, or maybe far worse things, such as long-term trauma. Who the heck wouldn't want to avoid any of these? Yet viewing stress as a prompt to flee or fight is far too limiting. The evidence is that stress can make us smarter, stronger, and more successful. Rather than view stress always as a negative, we can learn to understand that stress tells us to pay attention to something we care about deeply. Stress gives us a heads-up to bring our A game because something important is at stake. We certainly don't stress out over things we are apathetic about.

In 1998, 30,000 adults were asked how much stress they had experienced in the past year, as well as whether they believed stress was harmful to their health. In 2006, researchers pored over public records to learn who had died among the 30,000. The study revealed high levels of stress increased the risk of dying by 43 percent. Makes sense, right? Well, here's the kicker. Those who believed stress was not harmful had lower death rates than those who reported high stress. Here is another interesting fact. Those who believed that people can be trusted tended to live longer than cynics.

Those findings are consistent with studies that reveal a strong relationship between stress and social interactions. People literally make us sick or well. Exposure to chronic social stress for an extended period of time increases susceptibility to catching colds. When we participate in supportive social networks, we enhance our immune systems and resist disease, even cancer.[18]

Even our most valued and trusting relationships are occasionally stressful. The passion and joy of raising a child comes with loads of stress, but also laughter. Entrepreneurs report that the pressure to make payroll weighs heavily on them, while they also find purpose and deep fulfillment operating their own enterprises. When it comes to career advice, the primary tip is "follow your passion." Sounds great, though the advice rarely comes with an important disclaimer. The word *passion* means "suffer." The reward of doing something meaningful requires sacrifice. This point is brushed over by commencement speakers telling graduates to follow their passions. It would be more useful to think of suffering the way Koreans do. In Korean, the phrase *good job* translates to mean "You have suffered!"

We can easily miss the point that passion for meaningful relationships and work comes with a stress invoice and suffering. We cannot create a meaningful life without stress, and we do not get stronger without suffering. This is not just philosophy and psychology. It is biology. For example, when levels of oxytocin are high, we are more likely to trust and help others. Oxytocin helps to suppress fear and reduce our flight-or-fight response. Our view of stress changes once we learn that there is an upside to stress. Once we learn about the benefits of stress, it doesn't just change our perceptions. It changes our biology.

When we view stress as harmful, these are our conclusions:

- It depletes my health and vitality.
- It debilitates my performance and productivity.
- It inhibits my learning and growth.
- Stress should be avoided.

When we view stress as making us stronger, these are our conclusions:

- It enhances my performance and productivity.
- It improves my health and vitality.
- It facilitates learning and growth.
- Stress can be positive and should be used.[19]

One of the many practical benefits of viewing stress as strengthening is that we are better able to thrive in a VUCA world. We learn to accept stressful events as simply part of living in a turbulent world. Sometimes we can remove the source of stress, and sometimes we change how we cope with what we cannot control.

People who strive to see the good in stress don't ditch the reality that stress has both downsides as well as upsides. This takes us back to temperance. The goal is to learn to fear stress less and to learn to respond to stress better. People who grow from stress learn to stand up for themselves as needed and to seek support rather than withdraw to cope with stress. People who double down on what they can control and let go of what they can't control can reduce their stress and increase their performance.

Learning to do all this by practicing temperance does not come to us in a prescribed how-to manual. Practicing virtue is much more artful than that. The virtues are interconnected, not linear. Compassion and justice are trust drivers. Courage and hope are character enablers. Wisdom and temperance are the means to support trust, compassion, courage, justice, and hope. Temperance is about balance, habits, and self-control. Temperance doubles down on free will rather than resigning to a life governed by fate and fear.

Fear and Free Will

Fear clouds how we see the future. Behavioral economics reveals that we have a negative bias, since we fear loss more than we hope for gain.

The irrational nature of a fearful future was captured by Michel de Montaigne 500 years ago: "My life has been filled with terrible misfortune, most of which never happened." A study tested Montaigne's fear by asking people to write down their worries. Then over time, they identified which worries actually happened. Surprisingly, about 85 percent of people's fears never happened. When misfortune did strike, 80 percent of the time people reported they handled adversity better than they expected. Even when things turned out badly, people reported that they learned valuable life lessons. This means that over 95 percent of our fears are exaggerations.[20] That which we fear the most only rarely befalls us!

So, given the powerful impact that fear has on our destiny, where does free will fit in? When we fear that our fate is more in the hands of our genes and neighborhoods, we wonder whether we are responsible for our actions. There is sound psychological research that we become helpless when we remove the belief that we can affect our fate. This is known as *learned helplessness*, a mindset that turns our decisions over to fate, rather than free will. Without free will, we are prisoners of fate.

Once we see how virtue alters ourselves and our small part of the world to be a bit better, then we accept the responsibility of free will. Clearly, we don't deny that some people get to play a better life hand than others. We can acknowledge our flaws, our fragmented lives, and, yes, sometimes a rotten fate and still see why the virtues are onto something important. We cannot always control our circumstances, but we can always control our response. Wise and temperate people learn to put down what cannot be controlled (fate), so that they can pick up what can be controlled (free will).

In her bestselling book *Eat, Pray, Love,* Elizabeth Gilbert wrote: "We gallop through our lives like circus performers balancing on two speeding side-by-side horses—one foot is on the horse called 'fate,' the other on the horse called 'free will.' And the question you have to ask every day is—which horse is which? Which horse do I need to stop worrying about because it's not under my control, and which do I need to steer with concentrated effort?"[21]

Action: Making New Habits

Temperance is about "concentrated effort" to make new habits by putting our foot on the 'free will' horse. So this is the chapter with the biggest tool kit to strengthen our habits organized first for individuals and then for teams. Let's start with individuals interested in creating "happy" habits.

Being happy seems like a great individual goal, although Aristotle reminds us that happiness is a by-product of doing what is worthy. Simply put, relying on our strengths to serve other people is key to enduring happiness and to creating an enduring habit. When we do, research reveals that happiness boosts a person's energy and creativity, fosters better relationships, fuels higher productivity at work, strengthens immune systems, and even helps people live longer.

What are the habits of happy people? They devote significant time to nurturing caring and trusting relationships with family and friends. They are first in line to help a co-worker or a stranger. They practice optimism and gratitude. They exercise weekly or even daily. They are committed to goals that are bigger than themselves.

Happy people also handle tough times well. Inside, they are the same as people who feel angst. And even the most self-controlled person can crack at times. What separates those who are calm from those who are full of angst is their strength in coping with challenges and adversity. They practice grace and grit under fire. Rather than share their own stress or crisis, they help others cope with their stresses and crises. Since they are charitable and cooperative, they are well liked and have a deep network of friends. They are more likely to get married and more likely to stay married.[22]

The aim here is to examine habits that help us live more significant and successful lives in good times and in rough times. Learning to change our habits is very different from learning to read financial statements. Habitual change cannot be learned in a seminar. We do not learn to be calm under duress by taking a test about self-control. We practice self-control by doing something that puts us under pressure.

We know that it is wise to spend more time caring about people and less time caring about stuff. We understand the benefits of eating less while moving more and sleeping more. We know this, but we do not always do it. The challenge is to create healthy habits around what we already know is good for us.

A word of caution. Before we jump into the temperance pool, consider common pitfalls in practicing virtue:

1. *Arrogance:* None of us has earned the right to be self-righteous when it comes to virtue.
2. *Sappy:* Platitudes that do not come off the wall are not likely to make much of a difference.
3. *Complexity:* Simple and frequent practices beat complex and infrequent practices.
4. *Fixed mindset:* An experimental mindset is key to practicing virtue, rather than a fixed mindset that concludes that you either have character or you do not.
5. *Willpower:* Sheer effort alone rarely does the job to change a habit. Making habitual change easier rather than harder is more likely to work.

So if we want to change or strengthen our habits, what do we do? Start with a compelling purpose governed by intrinsic motivation (become a more compassionate friend, parent, spouse, or teammate) rather than an extrinsic motivation (pay raise, bigger office, or new golf clubs). The idea that we are going to develop virtue through rewards and punishment runs counter to the essence of character. The motivation to develop virtue is intrinsic, not extrinsic. The logic of carrots and sticks does not explain why we choose to be virtuous. No carrot or stick will lead someone to internalize virtue. With these thoughts in mind, here are a variety of temperance tools that can help us create "happy" habits.

INDIVIDUAL TEMPERANCE TOOL KIT

Look Backward: When Did We Get Things Right?

We are more likely to change future habits by building on past strengths. In other words, before we go forward, look backward for when we got things right. We can reflect on the times when we managed to be virtuous by using a timeline. Historians use timelines to understand the past by exploring key people and experiences that shaped our past. Applied to our personal history, a timeline is a simple and insightful way to identify when we managed to be the best version of ourselves.

Here is how a timeline works. Whatever your age, divide that number by three. So if you are 33, you would divide your life into three parts: birth to 10, 11 to 22, and 23 to 33. Now, identify the key people and the key experiences that shaped you during these three phases of your life. Pay attention to when you overcame adversity. When were you most virtuous? When were your relationships caring, and when were you part of a purpose greater than yourself? While we can find plenty of examples of when we failed to act virtuously, we also were not totally absent in acting virtuously either. The purpose of the timeline is to look backward to when we have been at our best so as to live life well in the future.

Look Forward: What Would Be the Best Version of Ourselves?

The historian Doris Kearns Goodwin, in her TED Talk "Lessons from Past Presidents," quoted Harvard professor Erik Erikson: "The richest and fullest lives attempt to achieve an inner balance between three great spheres of life: work, love, and play." People who were dedicated to one of the spheres at the expense of the others are likely to be sad when they are old. In contrast, people who managed to pursue all three spheres with concentrated effort are likely to live a life filled with both achievement and serenity.[23] What might life look like if we managed to pursue all three spheres with concentrated effort?

LOVE

Theologian Martin Buber suggested that we view our relations with others along an It-Thou continuum.[24] At one extreme, if we view people merely as "its," we consider others to be objects to be manipulated for our personal gain. An "it" orientation reduces people to the means to make my life more comfortable and to serve my desires. Tyrants, such as Saddam Hussein, treated people as "its."

At the other extreme, we view others as "thous." We consider their welfare as central to our reason for being. This is the perspective of the servant leader. A "thou" orientation treats others with dignity and respect. A "thou" orientation recognizes empathy as the root of ethical conduct. In this instance, think of someone like Mother Teresa. Most of us operate somewhere between the extreme of Hussein's "it" and Mother Teresa's "thou." When we are at our best, we treat others as "thous." When we are at our worst, we treat others as "its."

We are back to free will. Good relationships do not happen by accident. They take time (tempus) and discipline (temperance). Most of us claim that our family and friends are critical to our happiness. If you asked family and friends to answer the question "How good am I at creating, caring, and trusting relationships?," what would they say?

Love isn't limited to family and friends; it also takes into account our communities. The word *philanthropy* means "love of humankind." Involvement in small groups, such as book clubs, athletic teams, and community theater, increases our social capital and well-being. Serving others is not just a nice thing to do. Unless people invest in their neighborhoods and professions, they simply do not work well.

WORK

We have more confidence to journey into the future (or to the unknown) when we are invited to start with existing strengths. Consistent with the literature on appreciative inquiry, our research demonstrates that an emphasis on what's right increases engagement, as shown in Table 6.1.[25] Frequently, leaders and programs focus primarily on gaps and deficits that are listed in the right column. We recommend starting with the strengths listed in the left column.

STRENGTH-BASED CULTURES	DEFICIT-BASED CULTURES
Focus on strengths—what's right	Focus on weaknesses—what's wrong
Create committed teams	Create compliant teams
Are customer- and patient-centered	Are mandate-centered
Highlight the positive	Highlight the negative
Seek to empower	Seek to control
Are flexible	Are fixed
Focus on potential	Focus on problems
Take intelligent, not reckless, risks	Avoid risks
Promote cooperation	Promote competition
Aim at the good	Aim at what's wrong

TABLE 6.1   Characteristics of Strength-Based Versus Deficit-Based Cultures

Source: Adapted from David Cooperrider, "The Concentration Effect of Strengths," *David Cooperrider and Associates blog,* April 22, 2012.

While leveraging strengths drives high performance, we want to emphasize again what a strength-based approach is not. A focus on strength is not the latest narcissism fad. A fat ego is a giant disconnect with the humble practice of virtue because people with an inflated sense of self-worth are unlikely to want to change. They are quite pleased with themselves, thank you very much, and, if anyone is going to change, it is you, and not them.

PLAY

Recreation actually means to "re-create." When we constantly put our nose down, working away without looking up, we lose perspective. Play helps us gain insights and perspective that otherwise would not occur to us.

Recreation isn't just about what we do but importantly with whom we do it. Whether our hobbies include bowling, bridge, or taking bows as an actress, doing it with people who bring out the best in us strengthens our ability to take on important and hard challenges in the other spheres of life—love and work.

THE 5CS

Now it is time to put meat on the bones of life-work balance. We would like to introduce you to a method that helps affirm or create a "best self" in love, work, and play life. You can remember the process by 5Cs: *company, challenge, competence, character,* and *conditioning.*

Here's how it works. The goal is to define what it means for you to live life well by applying the 5Cs to the three spheres of your life: love, work, and play. So in the case of company, identify people who bring out your best self in love, work, and play. Identify challenges you want to take on that are important and hard—growing a business, taking care of an aging parent, coaching disadvantaged youth. Identify your greatest competencies and strongest virtues to name and amplify what you do well at work or at home. Identify ways to build on your strengths of conditioning to contribute to better life-work balance.

Use five sticky notes to answer each of the following questions organized by the 5Cs. In answering each question, take into account the three spheres of your life—love, work, and play:

- *Company:* People Who Bring Out Your Best
  Who are the people who bring out your best self in love, work, and play?
  How could you spend more time with these people?
- *Challenges:* Purpose and Passion
  What important and difficult challenges are you passionate about in love, work, and play?
  What challenges would give you a clear sense of purpose?
- *Competencies:* What You Do Well
  What knowledge and skills represent your greatest strengths?
- *Character:* Who You Are at Your Best
  Which virtues are your greatest strengths?
- *Conditioning:* Physical Fitness
  How do you stay physically fit through exercise, diet, sleep, and disciplined reflection? Disciplined reflection is described in Chapter 5 on wisdom. Disciplined reflection is about paying attention to our life.
  What habits are your greatest strengths?

Now, it isn't possible to have perfect balance in all three spheres of life all the time. What is possible is to create a reasonable balance over time. This all starts by creating a vision of your best self by applying the 5Cs. Converting your vision into a reality is the second part of the exercise. We are on the prowl to identify discretionary time that you can repurpose toward the most meaningful parts of your love, work, and play life. Use three sticky notes to list your activities that take the most, modest, and the least amounts of your time. This should capture your life as it is today. When you review where your time goes versus where you want your time to go, now you have insight about how you want to repurpose where you put your energy. For example, if you want to spend more time with the people who bring out your best, then put them in your calendar. Put aside a Sunday evening to have family and friends over. Once a month, invite good friends out to dinner.

If you want to leverage your strengths more at work, then look to spend more time relying on your greatest competencies and greatest virtues. At play, look as much at whom you share recreation with, not just what you do. A book club, golf league, or community service with family and friends who bring out the best in us makes what we do more meaningful because of whom we do it with.

We can choose who we want to be going forward. Professionally and personally, the really good news is that small changes done with great conviction make a huge difference. Once we are clear about where we want to reallocate our time, our aspiration will not be our challenge. Our challenge will be making focused efforts and creating new habits. Now that we know where we want to spend our time, how do we create new habits to do this? Let's turn to the third A in the commitment cycle: action.

Action
START A STOP LIST

Since all of us are limited to 168 hours a week, rather than starting a to-do list, consider starting a *stop list*. What will you stop doing so that you can build capacity to grow personally and professionally? Here are some examples of what starting a stop list might consider:

- *Do fewer things well.*
  What can you stop doing?

- *Leverage your strengths as much as possible. Rely on teammates' strengths to offset your weaknesses.*
  The goal is to focus on what you do well and how you can do more of it.
- *Substitute screen time with face time.*
  Can you substitute spending time on screens (TVs, tablets, phones, and computers) with spending more time with people you care about? Respond to e-mails and phone calls once a day, rather than throughout the day. If this isn't possible, respond to e-mails in 20-minute chunks so you can devote more time to taking care of customers, patients, and colleagues and less time taking care of e-mail.
- *Focus efforts on one activity at a time.*
  The goal is to substitute multitasking with focused effort.

The point of these examples is to increase a precious commodity: discretionary time.

START DELIBERATE PRACTICE

Developing virtue is not just a matter of practice. It is *how* we practice. Deliberate practice doesn't mean practice more. It means practice better. Vince Lombardi, a hall of fame football coach in the National Football League, said, "Practice doesn't make perfect. Perfect practice makes perfect." When we are highly motivated, applying the following four elements of deliberate practice drives higher performance. You can apply these four steps of deliberate practice to develop a virtue or a competency:

1. Have a clearly defined stretch goal.
   A well-defined goal very easily finds its solution. Select a goal from the 5Cs that motivates you and that is both hard and realistic to achieve.
2. Devote your full concentration and effort.
   What gets scheduled gets done. Build specific times during the week to practice reaching your goal. There is no one-size-fits-all best practice to create healthy habits, but this is one approach. Make a list of a half dozen habits you want to practice. Focus on one habit at a time that you are intrinsically motivated to change such as those shown in Table 6.2.[26]

HABIT	WHEN	STARTING
Keep a gratitude journal.	Each night before bed	Starting on [*date*]
Have a date with spouse or partner.	Saturday evenings	Starting this Saturday
Exercise for 45 minutes.	Monday 7 a.m., Wednesday 8 p.m., and Saturday 10 a.m.	Starting Monday
Take a walk.	Each day just after lunch	Starting next month

TABLE 6.2 Habits to Be Practiced

Source: Adapted from Seph Fontane Pennock, "Positive Psychology 1504: Harvard's Groundbreaking Course," *Positive Psychology*, June 16, 2015.

Start with just one thing to change. Put it on screen saver, bathroom mirror, refrigerator, or, better yet, put it on your calendar. It becomes a habit when you no longer have to think about doing it. Update your list about every three weeks once you have strengthened your habit. Then try something new. The good news is this: a slight habitual improvement can make a dramatic difference.

3. Seek immediate feedback from someone you know, like, and trust. The most powerful tools in the high-performance toolbox are about relationships. Share your goal with a buddy and then seek voluntary accountability to stay committed to a goal you want to pursue.

4. Repeat, reflect, and refine.
   An important milestone is to practice virtue enough that it is no longer forced. This is best achieved by relying on virtue to enhance existing initiatives. Virtue is more likely to become a habit when practiced as part of meeting existing goals and operating normally. Substitute one habit (watching TV) with another (taking a walk with your spouse). What did you do right? How could you do more of it?[27]

There is nothing hard when it comes to understanding deliberate practice. That part is easy. To really excel, we can't kid ourselves. Select a goal you want to pursue for *intrinsic reasons* (you want to) versus *extrinsic reasons* (you should or have to). Then put deliberate practice into action.

Here is why deliberate practice is worth your consideration. We are all shaped by things we didn't choose—our family, the neighborhoods where we were raised, and our culture. We can be strengthened by our best experiences, best people, and our most trying times. We reduce being gripped by fear and troubled by our fate by paying attention to our life in ways that make a difference that we control.

TEAM TEMPERANCE TOOL KIT

Before we get started on ways that teams practice virtue, we will start with how teams should not practice virtue. Two cautionary notes concern what to do when, not if, the hypocrisy card is played and the importance of relying on a pull rather than a push strategy.

Hypocrite Card

Hypocrites appear to be virtuous, but their actions prove otherwise. Because we know that a leader will at some point say one thing about virtue and then do another, we can count on what we call the "hypocrite card" being played early and often. The mumbling about leaders "not walking the talk" could start this way. "All this virtue stuff is from la la land." Virtue has nothing to do with the way people treat each other where we work. Even worse, mumbling about hypocrisy happens out in the hallway and never makes its way into an open conversation.

A healthy dose of skepticism about the practice of virtue keeps a team grounded in reality. Skepticism is a good thing and should be encouraged. Since we are all flawed, that people fall short of our ideals should not come as a shock. This is why the practice of virtue needs to come with flashing yellow caution lights. The sign should read "Humans at Work." Despite their best efforts, expect them to mess up.

Here is what is easy to see—hypocrisy in others. Nothing hard about that. Here is what is not so easy to see—hypocrisy in ourselves. It is hard to see our own shortcomings because we all have a highly developed capacity to deceive ourselves.

Socrates said that the principal goal of life is self-knowledge, though he went on to warn that the principal barrier to self-knowledge is self-deception. We often justify our decisions after the fact. We struggle with "self-serving bias" when we think well of ourselves, our strengths, and accomplishments, and we skim over our weaknesses and failures. We are all capable of cutting ourselves a break while remaining tough on others. Robert Wright wrote, "Human beings are a species splendid in their array of moral equipment, tragic in their propensity to misuse it, and pathetic in their constitutional ignorance of misuse."[28]

Given human folly, it's best to deal with hypocrisy up front. Let's acknowledge that it should come as no surprise that every day, we will observe unvirtuous ways. Perhaps even in ourselves! Let's also acknowledge that we observe virtuous behavior daily, including in our own conduct.

We worked with a controller who had integrated a strength-based approach into financial reporting. On a conference call, he named and amplified the people whose virtues had contributed to favorable financial metrics. Before he could introduce how virtue strengths could be leveraged to take on performance weaknesses, a senior leader publicly took him to task. He was told in no uncertain terms that this was not the time to review what went well. What the boss wanted was accountability and ownership to fix the problems of the business.

After the meeting, a colleague pulled the senior leader aside. He pointed out to his friend that the controller was only trying to put into practice what he had learned at a virtue seminar. To the credit of the senior leader, he called the controller to apologize. He thanked the controller for helping the team adopt a more positive and constructive problem-solving approach. And he asked to be reminded when he strayed from the virtues. This story is a very realistic approach to the practice of virtue that makes clear that we fall short of our ideals. Rather than zeroing in on hypocrisy, it is more realistic and pragmatic to acknowledge that we are all capable of being both blindly shortsighted as well as spectacularly caring in how we treat others.

When we replace a focus on hypocrisy with a focus on compassion, second chances, and learning, we lift up the strengths of the human spirit. And this leads to the virtue, hope, coming soon. It is far better to practice virtue imperfectly than not to try at all. Besides, we all flunk the perfection test anyway.

One last cautionary note about what happens to us when we play the hypocrisy card. Calling out others for hypocrisy is not great for us. If in fact, we want to live by conviction rather than circumstance, then we can't let others lower our character standard. Remember the self-others (all others) standard in Chapter 4 on justice. The goal is to treat everyone with respect and dignity, independently of how they treat us. Why? Ultimately, we can only control our own conduct. Besides, who wants to put our character in the hands of others?

Push Versus Pull

They might seem like the same thing—"not to harm others" (typically the emphasis of compliance) and "to help others" (typically the emphasis of character)—since both involve treating people well. Yet, not harming a person is not the same as helping a person. On the *push* side, we are all capable of being "compliant" with rules not to harm others, while at the same time not giving a flip about helping others. Compliance demands that nondiscretionary expectations are met armed with sticks as needed. In contrast, the *pull* strategy of developing great character can take root only when relying on a strategy that is invitational.

Again, this isn't to suggest that compliance with rules is unnecessary. Dan Ariely's research reveals that cheating is contagious. Just as culture has a powerful impact on individual conduct to be virtuous, culture also can have a powerful impact on unvirtuous behavior. Ariely has run experiments on 50,000 people. The results? A handful of big cheaters and 30,000 little cheaters. People do not want to feel bad about themselves, so they cheat only a little. When people cheat a little, they can still feel good about themselves.

While big cheaters are small in number, Ariely reports they all started out as little cheaters. Big cheaters don't suddenly jump to the dark side. People do not start out to commit crime. Over time, they just wake up discovering that they have become criminals. Ariely's findings suggest that honor codes and brief reminders of doing the right thing can reduce cheating.[29]

Consider who teaches ethics at your organization now. Usually it's a computer. A computer can be used to inform regulators whether everyone completed the "ethics training." What does the computer teach you? Probably it teaches you to comply with rules, which, as Ariely's research reveals, can help reduce unethical conduct. However, after you take a course about rules taught by a computer, are you more ethical and empathic afterward?

Organizations have lots of experience teaching ethics as compliance but limited, if any, experience teaching ethics as character. Pushing character the way organizations push compliance will, at best, be harmless nonsense and, at worst, will lead people to wonder whether they just joined a cult. Since character is learned fundamentally differently from compliance, it is vitally important to consider what we teach and how we teach it.

Let's start with content by making a point that we want to emphasize. Just because a culture is unaware of and doesn't pay attention to character doesn't mean that virtue isn't affecting organizational performance.

The presence or absence of the virtues affects every culture, every day. So the open question is whether leaders are aware of the impact that virtues have on performance and whether they are paying attention.

Now, let's switch to the process of teaching virtue. For good reason, people run for cover when virtue is taught in a way that is sappy or self-righteous. By "sappy," we mean using a naïvely simplistic approach, long on platitudes and short on healthy skepticism. By "self-righteous," we mean an approach that is heavy-handed on indoctrination and short on self-discovery. We can't be so sappy that we are out of touch with the reality of human shortcomings or so arrogant that we fail to practice virtue with humility. A more helpful tone is to simply want to be a bit better than we used to be.

Getting Started: When Has the Team Been at Its Best?

By reflecting on when a culture has been at its best in the past, teams can leverage strengths to take on current and future challenges. One way to reflect on cultural strengths is to create a timeline similar to the personal timeline we discussed in the Individual Temperance Tool Kit. The purpose of a cultural timeline is to lift up a time when leaders and people were at their best. First, divide the history of the enterprise into three time periods. Second, look for key people and critical experiences that shaped the culture at its best during the three different parts of its history. Third, use the language of virtue to capture when people were courageous in times of adversity. Ideally, a historical timeline also reveals a sense of purpose that clarifies the reason that the enterprise exists based on how it has taken care of customers, patients, and staff.

Best Team Temperance Practices

Here are a couple of reminders in starting to practice virtue as a team. Few people would argue that strategy is more powerful than culture. This doesn't diminish the importance of strategy. In fact, the opposite is true. Strategy is so important that we must take culture into account to successfully execute a strategy. The key question is this: is your culture a tailwind or a headwind to your strategy? You can create more of a cultural tailwind by taking into account the following guidelines:

- *Are your decisions guided by principles first and profits second?* The order matters.

- *Do you rely at least as much on intrinsic motivation as extrinsic motivation?*
  This doesn't mean that money doesn't matter, because it does. It does mean that people on a mission are harder to beat than well-paid mercenaries.
- *Do you rely on soft methods to drive hard results?*
  This means that you work on engagement guided by virtue as the foundation for superior financial performance.

We don't reflect on virtues on Tuesday and then go back to sticking it to people on Wednesday. You want virtue embedded daily into operations. Consider routines such as these:

- *Staff meetings:* How can we integrate virtues into our regular meetings to enhance decisions?
- *Virtue moments:* Take five minutes to identify colleagues who made the team better and/or improved results by practicing virtue. After all, can you imagine that extraordinary performance will be achieved through cowardice over courage? Despair over hope? Distrust over trust?
- *Budgets:* Do we spend our money in a way that is consistent with the virtues?

Here is an example of how virtues guide budgets. The University of Louisville Medical School conducted a best-practice study in medical education that reinforced the value of coaching medical students. However, they lacked the critical mass of faculty to coach effectively. So they reduced the number of students enrolled from 100 to 80 to align with the number of faculty coaches available. They then increased the number of patients that medical faculty would see to make up for the revenue decline from enrolling 20 fewer students. The faculty concluded that more revenue wasn't a realistic option given the economic climate of healthcare. So the only way to live by their convictions was to repurpose existing revenue and costs to align the budget with their priorities.[30]

Strength-Based Meetings

Often organizations use numbers or metrics and colors to be precise about progress toward their strategies and to hold leaders accountable for results. Green numbers typically mean that a goal has been reached or exceeded. Yellow numbers mean caution in that results are mixed. Red numbers mean a significant gap exists between proposed and actual performance. Most meetings focus on red numbers and offer limited if any commentary on green results.

Starting meetings with green numbers has the practical benefit of getting our brain working with us (prefrontal cortex) rather than against us (amygdala). In most cases, people who have red results already feel bad enough, so there is no need to kick them when they are down. Trust certainly isn't part of cultures that are full of drama, where people put their energy into protecting themselves rather than taking care of customers and patients. When virtue is largely absent in a culture, it is like a smoke alarm going off in your kitchen. It is a blaring reminder that you are not safe and that you do not belong here.

Now imagine a culture where team members care about each other and have each other's back. These are teams where people feel valued, feel like they belong, and know they make a difference. This does not mean just be nice. These are teams that are very tough to beat. It's about building sufficient trust such that people help others who are struggling, rather than smirk when someone other than them is being slammed. This can be achieved by starting with green numbers and asking, How did virtue help us achieve these results? How can we apply what we learn from our green numbers to our red numbers? When we share stories about people at their best, we create bonds and connections greater than any forged by data. This does not mean that we ignore or throw out red numbers. It does mean that stories about when the team was at its best can be applied to areas where the team is struggling.

We will give the last words about temperance to Confucius and Benjamin Franklin. Confucius encourages us to be humble. In the *Analects*, Confucius argued that true humanity was impossible for most mortals, including himself. He recognized the difficulty of living simply, modestly, and in self-control.

Franklin's insights are a good transition to the next chapter, on hope. He offers a realistic and hopeful way to measure our ability to live modestly and in self-control over the course of our life. Franklin defined net worth by what remains when we subtract our bad habits from our good habits.

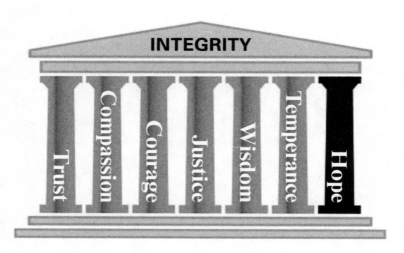

Hope-to-Despair Spectrum

Optimistic		Pessimistic
Grateful		Ungrateful
Future oriented		Stuck in the past
Humble		Arrogant
Reality based		Fantasy based

FIGURE 7.1   Pillars and Pediment: Hope

CHAPTER 7

Hope

Be better, not bitter.

We must accept finite disappointment, but never lose infinite hope.
—MARTIN LUTHER KING, JR.[1]

The virtue of having hope goes beyond the conventional dictionary definition of *hope*: "a feeling of expectation and desire."[2] Like temperance, hope is a matter of controlling our response to circumstances beyond our control, like adversity. Having the virtue of hope is about framing an adverse experience into one that offers growth, becoming "better not bitter." The stories that follow will exemplify this strength. By way of quick overview, we can become better rather than bitter by moving from a victim status to a strong survivor status.

Here's how in five steps, which are—like all the virtues—somewhat easier to describe than to actually adopt:

First, we become better not bitter by experiencing increased empathy. When we suffer, we are better able to understand the suffering of another.
Second, our relationships strengthen. Not surprisingly, as we become more empathic, the quality of our relationships improves.
Third, in the face of adversity, we acquire a deeper sense of

purpose. We learn to commit our life to something bigger than ourselves, which might include deeper religious and/or spiritual insights.

Fourth, we more easily recognize what it means to be vulnerable. Once we lose someone or a life we loved, we come to realize that what we care about deeply is ultimately temporary. Strangely, as we become more vulnerable, we also become stronger.

Fifth, we acquire a sense of urgency. We understand that life is fragile, and we don't want to waste the time we have left.

These adaptations to adversity, later discussed as *post-traumatic growth* (PTG), embody hope, the seventh of the virtues.

Consider some examples of the strength and liberating aspects of hope.

FORGIVING APARTHEID

Apartheid means separateness. Prior to World War II, a Cape Town, South Africa, neighborhood called District 6 was a multiracial and multireligious community. In 1966, the neighborhood was declared white by the apartheid government, which then proceeded to bulldoze residents' homes. By 1982, more than 60,000 residents had lost their homes and had been forcibly moved to same-race neighborhoods. Even though apartheid ended in 1994, District 6 still is a brown field absent any evidence that this was once a neighborhood for tens of thousands of people.

In 1945, Rita was born to a black father and a white mother in District 6. Her father taught her that dignity cannot be stripped away by another person. Sadly, this was a conviction she was forced to practice her entire life. Her father died in the early 1960s. In the cruel world of apartheid, his death was a blessing to her family. A mixed-race marriage violated apartheid immorality laws. If Rita's father had lived, the family would have been separated from each other.

Her mother's iron will rejected police demands to move, even as bulldozers knocked down her neighbors' homes all around her. But in 1981, the government was determined to flatten every house in District 6. Police made clear to Rita's mother that her home would be bulldozed, whether she was inside or outside. Her choice. Her mother moved and, then, died the day after her home was plowed under—a brutal casualty of apartheid.

In 2016, Rita worked as a tour guide at the District 6 museum. She retold her family's story to one of the authors during a visit to the museum. She had to remove her glasses to wipe away tears as she relived the pain of what happened with decades of anger boiling back up. She described being so consumed by hate that she wanted to strangle her oppressors. Slowly, very slowly, over a couple of decades, she learned to loosen the grip of hatred. As she learned to forgive, she released a dark emotional burden that had owned her for years. She was on the path of better not bitter.[3]

Here is a second, related apartheid story to illustrate the virtue hope, which is about being better not bitter.

OVERCOMING BITTERNESS

During apartheid, Sam was imprisoned at Robben Island off the coast of Cape Town not far from District 6. The prison didn't need a physical wall. The cold Atlantic Ocean reliably froze any prisoner who tried to swim for freedom. Sam was a soldier for the African National Congress (ANC) captured fighting against the apartheid government. Imprisoned, Sam "enrolled at Robben University" for 10 years. To the prisoners, the island prison acted as a university staffed by a faculty of fellow prisoners that included Nelson Mandela.[4]

Mandela, who spent 18½ of his 27-year prison sentence on the island, taught Sam to avoid being consumed by hate. Sam credits Mandela with teaching him to lead through consensus by listening carefully, especially when he had to work with people who had imprisoned him. This included his "warders," or prison guards, who were far too cruel too often.

One such guard was Christo Brand, who was Mandela's prison guard for 12 years. He was only 18 when he became a warder on Robben Island. He was told that the island's prisoners were South Africa's most dangerous, ruthless, and violent terrorists. Brand had buried a friend killed by people like Sam, so he came to his job programmed to hate. Then Brand discovered something strange. People like Mandela were not the "dangerous" criminals as described.

In a book he wrote entitled *My Prisoner, My Friend*, Brand depicted Mandela and prisoners like Sam as respectful and intelligent. In a remarkable turn of events, Brand worked in Mandela's administration when Mandela became South Africa's president. He also now calls Sam his friend. Today, they work together and watch rugby together on Robben Island, where they live with their families. Robben Island employs former inmates like Sam and former warders like Brand to share their stories with busloads of tourists who visit the island prison. Sam and Brand are part of Mandela's legacy to overcome hatred with forgiveness. As Sam transcended his hatred of Brand for being unfairly imprisoned, Brand transcended being part of an unjust apartheid system. [5] Both learned from Mandela to become better not bitter, which he expressed in a quote displayed in the lobby of the Iziko South African Museum:

> I knew as well as I knew anything that the oppressor must be liberated just as surely as the oppressed. A man who takes away another man's freedom is a prisoner of hatred; he is locked behind the bars of prejudice and narrow-mindedness. I am not truly free if I am taking away someone else's freedom, just as surely as I am not free when my freedom is taken from me. The oppressed and the oppressor alike are robbed of their humanity.[6]

Post-Traumatic Growth

The word *trauma* means "wound" in Greek, and the Persian poet Jalaluddin Rumi accurately asserted that "the wound is where the Light enters you."[7] We had a touching conversation with Rita about trauma after she shared her personal story. She had never heard the term "post-traumatic growth (PTG)" before. However, once the elements of PTG were explained to Rita, she repeated the word "yes" several times. At that moment, she recognized that PTG defined what she had experienced. She was able to imagine "where the light entered" based on how she had come to make sense of her experiences.

Post-traumatic stress disorder (PTSD) became familiar through the stories of soldiers returning from combat. Other traumatic events, such as the death of a loved one, a life-threatening illness, or being a victim of abuse are also sources of PTSD. Replace the word *trauma* with the word *adversity*, and we come to understand that suffering is universal. If we live long enough, we are all assured that unwanted trouble will find us.

When we find ourselves in an adverse situation, all we can control is our response—this is temperance. We can only hope to transform the cauldron of trauma into something good—this is where hope shows up. Rita converted a horrible life experience into a meaningful outcome by leading tours at the District 6 Museum. She reported that giving tours helped her make sense of her life by helping others focus on character, not skin color.

When it comes to trauma, the body keeps score. Our mind and our body are connected. Traumatic experiences can affect our bodily functions, such as going to the bathroom, eating, and sleeping. Trauma is not remembered clearly, but it is relived. We often distort our memories so we create our own reality. The story we use to describe the trauma can get stuck beyond the words we use. People who do not develop PTSD tell different stories than they told when they first experienced trauma. They focus on their growth and resilience.

We get to the other side of sadness by connecting with others. In contrast, disconnection from others weakens our resolve. The most resilient are surrounded by people who care about them. Having experienced trauma, people might seek therapy. More likely, people will seek the help of close family members and friends rather than a professional counselor.[8] Replace the word *therapy* with *supportive social network* and we learn how most people develop PTG.

Put negatively, the lack of social support is twice as reliable in predicting PTSD as the severity of the trauma itself.[9] Put positively, strong social support is an even better predictor of recovering from trauma than the level of resilience of the individual.[10] All this means that we are more likely to grow from adversity by telling our story to compassionate family members and friends who listen well and resist rushing in with solutions. We aren't cured, but we do heal. When it comes to apartheid, it makes sense that there would be no shortages of stories about bitterness rather than extraordinary stories of how ordinary people like Sam, Brand, and Rita became better. This is the broader lesson to all of us. Adversity offers us the potential, but certainly not the guarantee, to become better. Misfortune is not inherently beneficial, though it might be possible to take away something positive. Adversity offers a strong possibility to reveal our greatest insights and provide a new perspective on life.

The optimistic findings from PTG research are that most people are relatively resilient and recover from adversity. We experience distress and despair to be sure, but we also experience growth that can transform the devastation we feel into the advantage of resiliency and growth. While growth from adversity is common, how we experience adversity is not. Some people never ask "why-me" questions. Some people come to be defined by the adversity they experienced. Some people view their adversity as an event.

It was not until 1995 that we knew PTG was even an option! This is when Richard Tedeschi and Lawrence Calhoun's research revealed that we can grow from unwanted trouble. Adversity forces us to reorder our perspective in ways that we would not do under more stable conditions. The presence of growth does not mean the absence of pain. However, when growth takes root, some of adversity's negative impacts consume us less. We learn to acknowledge the pain of what happened without letting the pain own us. While we cannot change the past, we can shape a hopeful future.[11]

Humans are better equipped to thrive in hardship when they feel useful.[12] Self-determination theory holds that people need three basic things to be content: competency in what they do, authenticity in the way they live, and connection to others. These are all intrinsic to human happiness, and they far outweigh extrinsic values such as beauty, money, and status.[13]

Realism and Courage

Hope was the only thing left in Pandora's box once all the evils of humanity were released. The point of this myth was to explain that being human comes with plenty of evil, but it also comes, as Dietrich Bonhoeffer claims, with loads of hope. But we need to distinguish between realistic hope and delusional fantasy, as Bonhoeffer notes.[14]

Wish-dreams may be fun and fantastic, but fantasy has nothing to do with PTG nor hope. True hope is realistic and courageous because courage supplies the energy to hope. When hope links with courage, there is acknowledgment that possible solutions exist. According to William Lynch, the link between hope and courage is "the fundamental knowledge and feeling that there is a way out of difficulty, that things can work out, that we as humans can somehow handle and manage internal and external reality, that there are 'solutions'"[15] If we can harness realistic hope in the face of overwhelming adversity, we fare better than those who cannot.

Few people have lived by this statement more than Viktor Frankl. He survived a real-life Dante's inferno—three years in a Nazi death camp. The gate to Dante's inferno read, "Abandon all hope, ye who enter here,"[16] but by holding on to hope, Frankl survived hell on earth and lived to tell his story in his book *Man's Search for Meaning*. He described how people were treated as animals but responded with kindness.[17] Under these conditions, it would be logical to assume that self-survival would kick in. What didn't make sense was that some people gave up food when they were hungry and a blanket to a fellow sufferer when they themselves were cold. Even in the midst of humiliation, torture, and death, a small number of prisoners rejected self-preservation and chose character.

Frankl wondered what was different among those who gave from those who took, despite the extreme suffering that all experienced in the Nazi camps. He concluded that the difference was neither wealth nor poverty, the presence or lack of education, culture or lack of sophistication, or a particular religious tradition or a secular view. The commonality among those who managed not to give up their humanity in this horrific circumstance was they had a deep purpose in life. They all believed that even though they could not control the trouble that found them, they could always control their response.

Frankl left no room to excuse a lack of character due to victim status. He believed that we have complete control in our choice to be responsible, even in the hopeless Dante inferno of a Nazi death camp. Interestingly, he also found that those who responded to their situation well were realistic about hope. Realizing that their fate might be sealed and there was no room for wishful thinking, they accepted their reality with integrity. Yet, as Frankl points out, these were the individuals who were more likely to survive the ordeal.[18]

Here is the important insight that Frankl offers us. Hope is a decision—response to a choice. For that matter, so is despair. Frankl coined the term "tragic optimism," which described his horrific experience this way:

> The way in which a man accepts his fate and all the suffering it entails, the way in which he takes up his cross, gives him ample opportunity even under the most difficult circumstances, to add a deeper meaning to his life. He may remain brave, dignified, and unselfish. Or, in the bitter fight for self-preservation, he may forget his human dignity and become no more than an animal. Here lies the chance for a man either to make use of or to forgo the opportunities of attaining the moral values that a difficult situation may afford him.[19]

It is not necessary to undergo an experience as traumatic as surviving a death camp to understand the broader implication of this transcendent view of organizational life and of leadership. Leaders have control over their culture. When we create cultures where people choose to look out for each other, we feel safe with each other, which helps us do battle with the external forces that cannot be controlled. Otherwise, we spend our time and energy protecting ourselves from our teammates, which weakens our chances to succeed and contributes to despair rather than hope.

Here is the really important takeaway: when something goes wrong, and it always does, virtue-based teams quickly reassess, change, and grow. When teams combine courage with hope and when leaders create cultures in which hope prevails—including modeling hope and courage in their own actions—favorable outcomes are far more likely.

Modeling courage and hope is especially important when it comes to integrating an acquisition successfully. Whether integration teams are aware or not, the presence of virtue creates a solid foundation for a new organization. The absence of virtue will crumble the cultural platform on which the financial synergies depend.

Brave cultures glued together by hope are the only truly sustainable competitive advantage and the root cause of any merger's success or failure. Competitors can match price and even can match products over time. Competitors cannot replicate a brave culture. Virtues act as a vital buffer to fear and uncertainty during the integration process. Cultural integrations go far better when courageous leaders make clear the new entity's commitment to practice virtue, and that embracing virtue is a condition for staying on board.

The alternative to practicing virtue during the integration process is not a pretty picture. When fear replaces hope, self-preservation kicks in, breeding toxic doses of ego-based behavior. A fat ego prefers a healthy dose of denial, a sense of entitlement, and a commitment to the status quo. A fat ego can breed contempt, which is especially toxic to cultural integration during a merger or acquisition. The warning signs of ego and contempt include an aggressive sense of control, significant emphasis on personal achievement, self-righteous resentment about failures, defensiveness, overconfidence, and denial. Things turn especially ugly when contempt is directed at people who have been excluded from a group or declared unworthy. Rather than the creation of one team, the acquirer is anointed the winner and the acquired the loser. Life does not turn out well when we are united by contempt, fear, and hate. When people serve themselves first, they find that few others want to work with them, buy from them, supply them, or invest in them.

Self-serving conduct does not go well in medicine either. In 1978, Marvin Weisbord recognized that traditional medical training can breed tendencies to self-advancement that conspire against the very outcomes that doctors want for their patients. He said, "Science-based professional work differs markedly from product-based work. Health professionals learn rigorous scientific discipline as the 'content' of their training. The 'process' inculcates a value for autonomous decision making, personal achievement, and the importance of improving their *own* performance, rather than that of any institution."[20]

Weisbord was pointing out that this focus on individual self-development can conspire against recognizing the value of working together. Other medical leaders like Dr. Tom Lee describe traditionally trained doctors as "heroic lone healers."[21] Yet, being a heroic lone healer, a gladiator armed with facts and self-interest, can create behaviors that pervert the very goals that doctors have to heal their patients. Much evidence shows that patients do better when all their healthcare providers, including doctors, work together as a team in service of their patients' recovery or healing.[22]

The result of these important observations about teamwork in healthcare is that leading medical institutions are now teaching teamwork to their caregivers. For example, at the Cleveland Clinic, team building is taught at all stages of medical training—as part of the first week of medical school, as part of the curriculum for chief residents, and as part of leadership training to doctors, nurses, and administrators who are identified as emerging leaders within the organization. Indeed, leadership training is becoming widespread in medicine as medical institutions, medical societies, and educational institutions appreciate its importance to the mission of providing superb care and promoting health.[23]

The favorable impact that teams who trust and care for each other has on patient outcomes makes clear that this virtue stuff isn't just the hope we will be "nice." It is far tougher than that. It is learning from the struggles and stories of others and finding ourselves "aiming at the good" during the process. Life is both more pleasant and more productive when we are united by hope, affection, and purpose. Hope does not involve being sappy, which is a form of submission that ignores the hard tasks we confront. Hope does not involve cynicism, which resigns us to avoid doing what we know is right. We can learn to replace cynicism with reality-based optimism.

Optimism Versus Pessimism

As Gimli in *Lord of the Rings* said as he and his friends were taking on the enemy, "Certainty of death, small chance of success—what are we waiting for?"[24] That's the kind of optimism that leads a team to take on any foe—real or imagined. In contrast, grumpy and bitter isn't exactly a launching pad for greatness.

In the 1960s and 1970s, Martin Seligman set out to answer the question of whether people are born with a DNA-endowed sunny disposition or the DNA of a perennial sourpuss. He tested how animals responded to electric shocks that they could neither prevent nor avoid. These now shell-shocked animals were then given opportunities to prevent or avoid pain. Despite the chance to avoid trouble, they didn't. Seligman extended his research from rats to people and found that people learned to be helpless too. So people are not born grumpy and helpless. These self-defeating traits are learned. Sadly, parents who learn helplessness train their children to do the same. And when people learn helplessness, they increase their chances of despair and depression, and they decrease their ability to grow from adversity.[25]

Seligman found that helplessness was associated with how people explained their experiences. People who had learned to be helpless viewed negative events as permanent rather than temporary. They held this view even when there was clear evidence that the negative event was temporary. So if they flunked a math test, this meant they have never been good at math and never will be. They generalize a single negative math test experience to all events, leading helplessness to become pervasive. They also learn to personalize their flaws to explain negative outcomes rather than consider the impact of external circumstances beyond their control. Of course, people need to accept responsibility for their mistakes. However, learned helplessness goes way beyond personal responsibility to blaming ourselves for everything by concluding, "I've always been a failure."[26]

While the pessimist—one who lacks hope—views failure as permanent, pervasive, and personal, the optimist has the view that good outcomes result from hard work, collaboration, and learning. So the really good news is that people can learn to replace helplessness with optimism. Hope can be learned. Our thoughts are not fixed. They are malleable. Just as people learn to be helpless, they can learn to be optimistic, once they view negative events as temporary, limited, and not unique to them.[27] For example, optimists who have not been able to grow an organization are deeply disappointed, but they learn from mistakes so they can improve performance next year (negative events are temporary). Optimists do not believe that past failure precludes future performance (negative events are limited). Economic downturns happen to everyone (negative events are impersonal).

There are additional benefits to optimism. Angela Duckworth uncovered that optimists persevered more than pessimists. Perseverance also correlates with a "growth mindset," a belief that the ability to learn can be developed with effort. The empirical evidence is certainly hopeful that optimism, grit, and a growth mindset—components of the 4Gs—all make clear that people can change.[28]

Gaining Optimism by Developing Character

"Leadership is a potent combination of character and strategy. But if you must be without one, be without strategy," said General Norman Schwarzkopf.[29] Retired Rear Admiral Bob Wright tested this quotation during a panel discussion of the directors of character education at West Point, the Naval Academy, the Air Force Academy, and one of the authors. The directors reported that 30 years ago, the band of expected military behavior was extremely tight, defined by virtue, while society had a much wider band of permissible behaviors. Today, expected military behavior is still defined by virtue just as it was 30 years ago. However, society's band of expected behavior has never been wider. This shift in moral standards certainly affects all organizations, not just the service academies.

Here's the good news. Decades of research on virtue-based leadership clearly demonstrate that a motivated person can develop character one virtue at a time. The service academies report that their greatest progress has been helping leaders become more aware of how the virtues positively affect their ability to lead and perform. Learning and practicing virtue also make cadets better people. While people cannot be pulled across the moral finish line against their will, the service academies have clear evidence that intrinsically motivated people learn to lead from a basis of virtue.

Military leaders also have clear evidence that when military laws or codes of conduct are violated, arrogance and pride are generally the root causes. This is why the directors of character education become concerned when too much status and deferential treatment goes to a leader's head. Power can lead us to take ourselves too seriously and to expect special treatment. American leaders and presidents have warned us about the hazards of pride. Ben Franklin said, "A man wrapped up in himself makes a very small bundle."[30] Similarly, Abraham Lincoln warned, "What kills a skunk is the publicity it gives itself."[31]

When leaders lack humility, their associates are reluctant to share what they know and what they can do. This is why arrogant leaders, no matter how competent, negatively affect performance. Arrogance is not just annoying. It is also dangerous. When you put devastating weapons into the hands of arrogant 25-year-olds, the risk is truly frightening.[32]

The military is not unique. Hospitals that hire residents, businesses that hire engineers and accountants, and schools that hire teachers will source candidates that will likely be far clearer about confidence and competence than practicing character with humility. An effective antidote to arrogance is gratitude. Just as we learn to practice arrogance, we can learn to be more gracious.

Gratitude

As one of the 4Gs we discussed earlier, gratitude is an important leadership competency. We discuss gratitude more fully here because having gratitude is one of the by-products of developing the virtue of hope.

In a world where people promote a "personal brand" as the basis for a successful life, practicing gratitude can feel like something chumps do. Rather than build our brand, practicing virtue engages an internal battle between personal pride and humility. Whether the winner will be our brand or our character will depend on which trait—pride or humility—we choose to embrace. Since we are all flawed, virtue is best practiced by wearing a "humility sweater," and humility is a by-product of practicing gratitude. After all, *gratitude* is not a word used to describe something we have achieved on our own. The root word of gratitude is *grace* or *gift*. Gratitude can be thought of as a gift that we have been given but did not necessarily earn. If we are lucky to have great parents, it is worth remembering that we had nothing to do with picking them.

Gratitude has been the historic focus of world religions and moral philosophers for centuries. In the first century BC, Cicero wrote, "Gratitude is not only the greatest of the virtues, but the parent of all the others."[33] While the wisdom of gratitude reaches back to ancient times, the systematic study of gratitude's impact on performance, relationships, and ability to overcome setbacks started in about 2000. Now that we have bolted social science research onto ancient wisdom, we have proof that practicing gratitude improves our health, increases our energy level, develops optimism and empathy, and strengthens our ability to respond to difficult experiences. This is true even when researchers take into account contributions like age, health, and income.

We also have insights from neuroscience that cultivating gratitude results in positive feelings that are almost instant. Perhaps feeling grateful performs the function of moral barometer, moral motive, and moral reinforcement. As a barometer, gratitude signals that we are beneficiaries of another person's moral actions. As a motive, gratitude encourages us to be gracious, which improves our relationships with others. As source of reinforcement, gratitude encourages moral action in a culture.[34]

Grateful people accept that they have fallen short on many of their personal achievements but they still manage to be grateful for small acts of decency and for the opportunity to serve others. Because we can count on life providing us with some failures, limitations, and imperfections, believing that we control everything that happens to us increases our susceptibility to becoming an ingrate. We have a choice: practice being ungrateful or practice being grateful.

So is there no downside to gratitude? Well, yes, there is, depending on how you practice gratitude. To be truly grateful means that we focus on others, not ourselves. We blow it when our focus is on how "we" feel and on "our" happiness. If we are going to practice gratitude well, we must sympathize with the virtues and efforts of others. This provides us with insights about their strengths and value. These insights are only attainable if the expression of gratitude is about the other person and not us.[35]

Here are several proven ways we can practice gratitude: create a journal, conduct a visit, write a letter, and organize a gratitude session. First, a *gratitude journal*. Typically, our problem isn't a lack of good fortune. The problem is simply not taking time to appreciate people and experiences that make our life richer. A gratitude journal is a concrete way to ensure that expressing gratitude isn't left to chance. Here's how: each day for 21 days, write down three things that happened to you for which you are grateful. Why write it down? Writing activates our neurons to change the way we think. Why 21 days? This is the least amount of time that it takes to create a habit—in this case, gratitude. Because nothing lasts forever, the impact of a gratitude journal can wane after about three months unless you continue to actively practice gratitude.[36]

Second, conduct a *gratitude visit*. Think about a person who has made a huge difference in your life, who is still alive, and whom you have not thanked properly. Write a one-page expression of gratitude to this person that is clear and specific, explaining how she changed your life (for example, doors she opened, how she made you a better person, how you learned about virtue from her conduct). Ask to meet with her face-to-face without telling her why. And then read your testament out loud.[37]

A variation of a gratitude visit is a *gratitude final*. Here is how it works in an executive MBA ethics course that applies virtues professionally and personally. On the last day of the course, students are asked to invite family, friends, and colleagues who made it possible for them to earn their degree to come to class. Wives thank husbands, colleagues thank bosses, and children thank parents. Everyone who attends is either smiling or crying. One mother thanked her middle school son who would open her computer and place a glass of water on her desk each day when she needed to do her homework. The mother spoke proudly about her son's compassion, her son smiled, and her husband cried.

Third, write a *gratitude letter*. Although a gratitude visit is powerful, here's an alternative if you are an introvert and not ready to share that much emotion up close and personally. Write a gratitude letter. The letter follows the same guidelines as the gratitude visit, except that you send a letter to the person you appreciate, rather than read it aloud.

A gratitude letter also has wider applications. You can write a letter to a spouse, a child, or to a friend.[38]

Fourth, conduct a *gratitude session*. Our research reveals that gratitude sessions are among the most powerful team builders groups can consider. When gratitude is expressed well by focusing on the other and not on ourselves, relationships are deepened rather than taken for granted. As a result, it should come as no surprise that we have clear evidence that gratitude sessions increase engagement significantly.

The process is simple. The seven virtues are listed down a column (see Table 7.1). The name of each member of a team is listed after each of the virtues. Each team member is asked to identify the one virtue he believes is his colleague's greatest strength by placing an X in the box of one of the virtues. Then, teammates share stories that illustrate why that person's virtue strength contributes to the team and organizational performance.

VIRTUE	TEAM MEMBER 1 (NAME:)	TEAM MEMBER 2 (NAME:)
Trust		
Compassion		
Courage		
Justice		
Wisdom		
Temperance		
Hope		

TABLE 7.1 Gratitude Session Worksheet

We have completed this exercise with over a hundred teams, and the common response is that people were unaware of how favorable an impact they make. We cannot possibly understand what we have done well unless people let us know. And this is best achieved when people share stories that name and amplify when we were the best versions of ourselves.

HOPE VERSUS DESPAIR

Sisyphus used cunning commerce to acquire wealth and power. He lied, cheated, and killed . . . and thoroughly enjoyed his work! He stole his brother's throne, seduced his niece, and betrayed Zeus. Finally, the Greek gods had about all they could take of Sisyphus's hubris. He was condemned to push a boulder up a steep hill, only to watch it roll back down again and again. Sisyphus's fate was an eternity of futility.

While Sisyphus may have brought his fate upon himself, you may have found yourself in a similar situation, even though you may not have done anything wrong. Maybe you have lost hope while being a member of an organization that pushes boulders up hills. You may have worked for a financial institution whose leaders lost sight of the fact that their purpose was financial stability rather than turmoil. Perhaps you are part of a school more focused on teacher job security than student learning. You may be part of a healthcare institution where caregivers come first and patients are second. You might be part of a news or public relations organization focused more on "talking points" than on clear and reliable information. Maybe you are part of a government more focused on reelection and partisanship than improving the lives of citizens.

To avoid an ancient tradition of humans' driving organizations off cliffs, businesses must offer value at a fair price, schools must educate all students, healthcare organizations must help prevent disease as well as heal, governments must govern justly, news agencies must report thoughtfully, and religious institutions must deepen our spirit.

If we are to have a reasonable hope to encourage good behavior, then we need to invest in character development, not just compliance with a set of rules. While resources to invest in virtue-based leadership are relatively modest, compliance is expensive. Without the balance of virtue, an exclusive focus on ethics defined as compliance will create a culture where the goal is simply to follow and enforce rules. Compliance focuses on the basement—the bare minimum that makes mediocrity—not on the ceiling, which is where we are at our best.

Virtue is not about rules. It is a compass. The classical virtues provide ancient moorings to navigate turbulent contemporary times. The challenge in creating a virtue-based culture is encouraging people to internalize virtue. When this happens, people create an emotional connection to each other, which reduces antisocial behavior. This isn't to suggest for a minute that people who internalize virtue will always act virtuously. Clearly, we all have plenty of evidence to the contrary. Virtue-based cultures are not composed of people who are necessarily more moral than others, but they do learn to reduce selfish behavior.

Both compliance and character aim to encourage more of some behaviors and less of other behaviors. So, it is vitally important to understand what, in fact, does lead to behavior change—something that is easy to talk about and very, very hard to achieve.

We tend to miss the mark on two fronts when it comes to behavior change. First, we underestimate how malleable we are. This means that we do not have to be a victim to either our DNA or to our circumstances. Social science research makes it clear that we can replace anger and cynicism with responsibility and resiliency. Second, we underestimate how much of our conduct is influenced by the cultures of which we are part. It is far easier to be virtuous when our culture is actively practicing to do so. Here is the really good news. Among the most hopeful results of our research is that virtue doesn't need to be "sold." Virtue is the way people want to live anyway. What they are looking for is a culture that grants and encourages virtuous conduct.

So how do you shape a culture? It starts with leadership. This is why teams so often mirror the conduct of their leaders. Virtue-based leaders provide a buffer against toxic aspects of a culture, which reduces risk. Virtue-based leaders rely on trusting and caring relationships that make a statistically significant difference in engagement and teamwork. The leaders we want to follow practice virtue. Virtue-based leaders create a trusting and caring culture that is now ready to change. Put this way, we need to preserve the practice of virtue before it is realistic that people will be open to changing business practices.

Belonging to a team capable of adapting to VUCA requires sacrifice. Importantly, the benefits we receive for our sacrifice to build a resilient team exceeds what it costs us. We do not need to be a soldier, athlete, astronaut, or someone like Nelson Mandela to do this. We are far better served to motivate engagement and teamwork with an emphasis on our shared humanity—our desire to strive for virtue. The virtues teach us to focus on what unites us, rather than what divides us. Maya Angelou wrote, "I note the obvious differences between each sort and type, but we are more alike, my friends, than we are unalike."[39]

HOPE TOOL KIT

Remember that hope is not Disneyland. Hope is realism about the circumstances we confront. Hope focuses on what we can control while we are living by our convictions. Two elements of hope that are in our control are *practicing optimism* and *gratitude*.

1. Practicing Optimism

Optimism is related to grit and to the growth mindset because when we think a better future is possible, we don't quit easily. Next time things don't go your way, focus on how you can grow from a negative experience by reflecting on three questions:

- *Was the negative event you experienced temporary?*
- *Was the negative event limited and not enduring?*
- *Was the negative event a common experience not unique to you?*

Situations that are temporary, limited, and common give us hope we can grow from setbacks to create a better future.

2. Practicing Gratitude

The benefits of practicing gratitude become clear when we compare how life goes when we practice being an ingrate!

Here are proven ways to practice gratitude:

- *Make a gratitude journal.* Write three things down for which you are grateful for 21 consecutive days.
- *Conduct a gratitude visit.* Identify someone who has had a profound impact on your life, who is still alive, and whom you haven't thanked properly. Write a one-page testament detailing what this person has done for you. Ask him to meet with you without telling him what it is about. Read the testament out loud in front of him.
- *Write a gratitude letter.* Write a letter of appreciation to a spouse, child, friend, or teammate.
- *Conduct a gratitude session.* Identify the virtue strengths of each member of your team. Share stories about how this virtue strength has made the team and organization better.
- *Make a gratitude wall.* Find a wall in a public area on which people can place sticky notes to write about people and experiences for which they are grateful.

CHAPTER 8

Integrity—A Growth Market

Innovative cultures start with innovative virtues.

Decide what you stand for. And then stand for it all the time.
—CLAYTON M. CHRISTENSEN[1]

With this book, we hope to make two contributions to the topics of innovation and growth. One contribution may be unique—linking virtues and economic value. And the other is at least distinct—cutting through the clutter of innovation information by recommending five fundamental growth habits: (1) develop virtue-based habits, (2) make the customer the boss, (3) bet on leaders and teams over ideas, (4) apply innovative organizational structures, and, (5) practice creative discipline. These five innovative habits are evidence-based, supported by field research gleaned from focused visits to organizations such as MIT, Google, Intuit, and others including WalmartLabs. Not Walmart, but WalmartLabs. Let's start there.

Can you name the three largest organizations on planet Earth? They are, in order: (1) the People's Republic Army of China, (2) the U.S. Department of Defense, and (3) Walmart. Like the Chinese army and the U.S. Defense Department, Walmart has significant military skill using its logistical expertise to protect people. When government-sponsored relief services could not reach people stranded by Hurricane Katrina,

Walmart delivered key supplies, such as water, food, computers, and toilet tissue, to the citizens of New Orleans. When the then CEO was asked why Walmart helped and what he thought the company's critics would say, he responded, "We have never claimed to be flawless. But on the other hand, we have always demanded that we as a company do care."[2]

Planet Earth's largest private employer provides jobs for over 2 million people. If Walmart were its own country, its GDP would be greater than that of Austria or Sweden. Its footprint is so huge that the square footage of all its parking spaces is about the size of Tampa, Florida.[3] Predictably, anything this big will generate controversy. At times, store openings have been greeted with protests from unions and environmentalists, rather than with a celebration from the community. Walmart has, in fact, raised hourly wages for its workforce, though not high enough in the minds of many. On the other hand, about a quarter of those who start out making an hourly wage earn promotions to positions that pay between $50,000 and $170,000 annually.[4]

When Walmart decided to initiate a sustainability strategy, it hired the former president of the Sierra Club. Walmart's environmental impact strategy includes using fewer fertilizers to grow food and decreasing the amount of packaging that ends up in landfills. At the same time, Walmart is nevertheless criticized for its impact on urban sprawl and for falling short on how its massive purchasing power could reduce global emissions even further.[5]

What can we all learn from the organization that has grown in size beyond any for-profit venture in world history? Walmart's incredible growth has centered on ways to be innovative around a singular goal, "everyday low prices," which have been made possible by brilliant logistics and economies of scale. For over 50 years, the model worked. Then this 50-year run bumped up against another low-price model created by an upstart online retailer known as Amazon.com. To some degree, Amazon.com's growth came at Walmart's expense. However, a company that has nearly a half trillion in sales is hardly on the ropes. In 2010, Walmart's board understood fully the need to integrate mobile devices and the Internet into its retailing model. So the challenging question was how to go about reinventing a proven growth model.[6] The answer to this question called for all the virtues, especially courage, wisdom, and hope.

One option was to task individual stores to develop remote shopping capability funded by their own capital investments. However, the challenge was that organizations that have excelled at serving existing customers and managing costs rarely have had the skill or experience to start new ventures. Maybe the answer was assembling a dream team of individuals who were experienced in starting new ventures to operate out of Walmart's headquarters. However, the challenge in that case was that dominant cultures usually want to pound an upstart into the existing business model. As Albert Einstein cautioned, "No problem can be solved by the same consciousness that caused it in the first place."[7]

So Walmart wisely decided to create an internal accelerator stocked with innovative talent and located away from headquarters. So the question was, where? The answer: in Silicon Valley. Thus, just down the street from YouTube, a WalmartLabs sign hangs on an unremarkable office building. In the lobby, an arrow points in the direction of Bentonville, Arkansas—1,849 miles away. The building's interior looks more like Google than Arkansas. Walmart trusted small teams of young people wearing sandals, jeans, and shorts to work intensely on e-commerce projects applied to retail. Occasionally, people break for lattes, muffins, and Ping-Pong.[8]

Walmart acquired and hired an e-commerce team located in Silicon Valley because it is fertile ground for reinventing a business. Tech companies with promising applications for retail were bought. Leadership teams with expertise in both e-commerce and retail were hired. Over a five-year period, the project grew from 100 engineers to 1,800 engineers, competing with companies like Apple for the best computer science talent the company could find.

Walmart has its share of admirers and detractors, but most important, this giant retailer has what every organization craves—lots and lots of customers. Every day, 260 million customers voluntarily visit one of Walmart's 11,500 stores located in 28 nations. A sign in Silicon Valley makes clear the scale of its customer reach, "Changing the way people shop. 1,000,000,000 at a time."[9]

Creating and Strengthening an Innovative Culture

Despite all its success, even the planet's largest private sector enterprise—Walmart—struggles continually to grow and reinvent itself. Big organizations like predictable performance and smooth earnings. Most large organizations excel at operational excellence, and they rely more on acquisitions to grow. Launching a new venture inside an existing enterprise offers challenges different from those faced by a startup. Creating a new venture from scratch is a different challenge still. Big or small, new or existing, the primary point is this: creating and strengthening an innovative culture is incredibly difficult to do. Here are some reasons why and some strategies for getting around some of these common problems.

1. Place a Higher Value on Change Than on Stability

Creating an innovative culture starts by accepting something that is hard to accept—VUCA is the world in which we live, and on the other side of VUCA is even more VUCA. This means we have to give up the idea that at some point, life will return to the way it was.

Turbulent times reward innovators and punish those who resist change, making the option to change not much of an option at all.

2. Use Whole Brains, Not Half-Wits

Organizations default to left-brain skills like process, measurement, and execution. All of those skills are important to be sure, especially when it comes to operational excellence. However, sustained innovation that drives profitable growth requires right-brain skills of empathy for the people the organization serves and a culture of teamwork and collaboration. Empathy and teamwork quickly bump us into virtue.

Can you imagine empathy and teamwork flourishing in a culture that was ruthless rather than caring, distrustful rather than trusting, cowardly rather than courageous, and despairing rather than hopeful?

3. Do Not Limit Innovation to Mean New Products

If the definition of innovation is limited to new products or new medical devices, then a stadium full of spectators will passively watch a small number of innovators. Innovation must also be thought of as including new processes or business models (how the enterprise generates revenues and allocates capital). These kinds of innovations are birthed by interdisciplinary teams that involve everyone.

4. Culture Is the Game

Lou Gerstner, former CEO of IBM, put the importance of culture this way:

> I came to see, in my time at IBM, that culture isn't just one aspect of the game—it is the game. In the end, an organization is nothing more than the collective capacity of its people to create value. Vision, strategy, marketing, financial management—any management system, in fact—can set you on the right path and carry you for a while. But no enterprise—whether in business, government, education, health care, or any area of human endeavor—will succeed over the long haul if those elements aren't part of its DNA. Culture is not one of those soft matters to be dealt with when the real business is done. Culture is a complement to the formal, established rules of doing business. An understanding of and commitment to the organization's mission will guide employees when confronted by the unexpected for which no rules exist.[10]

The last phrase is worth repeating: "guide employees when confronted by the unexpected for which no rules exist." Learning to grow in a VUCA world does not come with a clear set of rules. A virtue-based culture provides vital guideposts for managing turbulent conditions. It is the culture that creates a strong brand that people know they can trust. Put negatively, a great brand cannot be built on a toxic culture.

Put positively, just as there is goodwill on a balance sheet, and just as an organization's brand has value, a reputation for being a "good" organization has enormous economic value. While we cannot control marketplace turbulence, we can preserve what has always worked—practice virtue. In this way, a reputation for integrity, which is the outcome of virtuous practice, provides the stability we need to take the risk necessary to grow.

Overcoming Barriers to Innovation

While the common barriers to innovation, described above, illustrate why organizations struggle to grow, the fundamental challenge is lack of engagement. Here is why. Innovation and growth are hard work guaranteed to offer no shortage of dead ends, disappointments, and failures. Only the highly engaged willingly take on this arduous task.

And the person who has significant impact on engagement is the boss. As we saw, about 70 percent of the variance in engagement scores is attributed to the direct supervisor.[11] This is why it is vital for bosses to understand how they can increase engagement. Gallup's research has revealed that followers across 16 nations seek four qualities from their leaders: trust, compassion, stability, and hope. Since leaders are paid to create value, it is easy for leaders to miss that three of the four things that followers want from their leaders are virtues.[12]

Here's where things get tricky. While trust, care, and hope are in the control of the leader, stability in a VUCA world is not. Organizations can offer job security only when revenues exceeds expenses. In other words, the best employment security blanket is strong performance in the marketplace, which requires ongoing innovation and growth. We can't control the external market. However, we can control our practice of innovation habits. So we are going to detail five innovative habits that can be learned and practiced that are foundational to organizational growth.

Innovation Habit 1. Encourage a Virtue-Based Culture

Eric Teller, the head of Google's research and development, has said that technological advances that change our lives, such as smartphones, happen every 5 to 7 years. However, it takes people 12 to 15 years to adapt to change. This *adaptation gap* is why people feel stressed out, disoriented, and anxious. Teller concludes that if we could enhance our adaptability even a little bit, it would make a huge difference. Teller argues for smart leadership and quick learners. We agree. And when it comes to smart and quick, nothing packs more innovation punch than seven 25-century-old words—trust, compassion, courage, justice, wisdom, temperance, and hope.

Rules and regulations help protect us against harm. A virtue-based culture does double duty. It protects an organization against harm, and it encourages people to cooperate and care about each other, which is essential to sustainable innovation. A virtue-based culture creates a sense of belonging and trust that makes organizations faster to innovate and less expensive to run. Learning, creativity, and innovation certainly are not going to be cultivated with distrust, infighting, cowardice, injustice, and a lack of wisdom and temperance, all polished off with a depressing dose of despair.

This is why our case for a virtue-based culture is not based on sentimentalism or hopeless idealism. The business case for a virtue-based culture is to mitigate the fear that is inherent in taking risks and failing. The value of virtue is to replace angst about an uncertain future with courage and hope to invent a better future. The good news is that, as with virtue, innovation is an easy sell—people want permission to create. This is especially true of talented people, who, we should remember, have lots of options. When creative people are blocked from making a difference, they move on.

There is no exception to the rule when it comes to relying on the virtue trust as the foundation of a sustainable innovative culture. If an organization is unable or unwilling to earn, deepen, and restore trust, then innovation beyond one-offs is just a wish dream.

The task of leadership is to mitigate distrust and increase trust, and this must be done over and over again. Innovation is a social process, fueled by trust to combat fear. Teams that *trust* each other and are trusted by others more easily confront and conquer the uncertainty that is inherent in innovation.

Innovation starts with *compassion*. Innovation depends on being deeply connected to customers and patients. We increase the probability of innovation when empathy is present for customers and our teammates. Empathy depends on our having a deep understanding before we act. So empathy teaches us to fall in love with the problem that confronts a customer, patient, or teammate before we come up with a solution.

Innovation requires *courage* to take a step into the unknown. Growth depends on elements of courage such as grit, resiliency, and vulnerability.

Innovation requires *justice*. When we strive for the ideal heart valve, it is because we want to be sure that it is good enough for everyone's husband, wife, son, or daughter.

Innovation is lifted by *wisdom*. Wisdom creates a "what-if" culture, rather than a "no" culture. Wisdom involves learning about ourselves through self-awareness, which is harder than we think. We never fully see ourselves as others see us. We often learn the most about ourselves from experiences we don't want—those that come through adversity and pressure. Sometimes, we are not sure what we stand for until we are tested.

Innovation requires *temperance*. Innovation does not happen between 4 and 5 p.m. on Friday. Remember that temperance means time, and innovation takes loads of time. Applying temperance to innovation requires granting people time to innovate.

Innovation clearly depends on *hope*. We are well served to clarify what motivates us to hope for a better future, as challenging as this is. The sweet spot is leveraging our greatest strengths and greatest motivations in the service of others. Our motivation increases even further based on who we work with, not just by what we do.

Innovation Habit 2. The Customer Is the Boss

Innovation is best built inside a *customer-centric culture*. This is a culture where everyone is striving to understand the customers' "pain points" and to help fix them. Uncovering a pain point is one thing. Delivering on a promised value proposition is another. Let's take the Cleveland Clinic as an example. Few medical centers match the Cleveland Clinic's reputation for clinical outcomes. Yet, in the mid-2000s, its patient satisfaction scores were average.

To address this issue, CEO Dr. Toby Cosgrove, approached a physician who had previously left the Clinic partly because his father had a terrible experience as a Clinic patient. Dr. Cosgrove wanted that physician, Dr. James Merlino, to serve as the chief patient experience officer and to make the whole patient experience nothing short of extraordinary. Merlino accepted the role, believing that the Clinic was serious about improving the patient experience by creating an empathic culture that was very different from what his father had experienced.

Merlino started by creating patient advisory councils to get at the "voice of the patient." He started collecting information about patients' complaints, asking, "What did we do wrong?" and he shared that information with the Clinic's clinical staff. Until data on the patient experience were shared widely, the clinical staff had been unaware of how mediocre the patient experience was. The first attempts to improve the patient experience included better food and TVs, greeters at the door, and redesigned gowns that protected a patient's dignity. However, though these changes were all well intentioned, they didn't move the patient satisfaction needle. Merlino and the Clinic dug deeper, this time relying even more on a voice of the customer (VoC) approach. For example, a nursing unit with low patient experience scores was analyzed intensively. Patients described being scared, confused, and anxious. They wanted reassurance that the Clinic caregivers understood what it was like to be a patient.

The patients wanted clear communication about the plan of care and to be kept updated. The interviews revealed that patients used two important proxies to rate their patient experience. First, if the rooms were dirty, the patients concluded that clinical care was poor: "If there is inattention to my room, there must be inattention to my care." Second, if caregivers were unhappy, the patients figured they had made the clinician angry or the clinician was concealing distressing medical information.

The need for coordination became obvious when Merlino asked a patient to keep a journal of everyone who cared for her during a five-day stay. She saw 8 doctors, 60 nurses, and many others (phlebotomists and other allied health practitioners), and this didn't take into account billing, marketing, and parking. The Clinic thought that the doctor-patient relationship was preeminent and that as long as that was optimized, patients would have a satisfactory experience. However, patients viewed all employees—not just doctors and nurses—as caregivers, and they believed that all caregivers should coordinate their efforts. For example, if the attending physician dismissed the dietary services worker who was delivering the patient's meal because the physician was entering the room to make rounds, this was perceived by the patient as poor teamwork. And the poor teamwork created concern that caused the patient to perceive her care poorly.

The challenge was knocking down silos, or "stovepipes," so that social workers, nurses, and physicians could communicate effectively with each other and the patient. To this end, *huddle meetings* were implemented to review patient procedures, which forced caregivers to communicate with each other.

Nursing rounds were required, so that staff members saw patients every hour and were charged to ask five questions:

1. Do you need anything?
2. Do you have any pain?
3. Do you need to be moved?
4. Do you need your personal belongings moved closer to you?
5. Do you need to go to the bathroom?

Did the results of these efforts make a difference? Nursing units that always asked and responded to these questions ranked in the top 10 percent in patient satisfaction nationally. In contrast, nursing units that never conducted hourly rounds guided by these questions ranked in the bottom 1 percent in patient experience among all hospitals. These data led to hourly rounds becoming standard practice at the Clinic.

Then a really big step was taken to change the culture. A half-day program to focus on the "patients first" commitment was made mandatory for all Clinic employees—40,000+ employees at that time. At these sessions, teams reviewed the patient experience from their first hearing about the Clinic, to coming in the front door, to after being discharged. In these teams, a janitor might be part of a group with a cardiologist and a nurse. Each member of the team was asked to describe his impact on the patient experience and how he could do it better. The staff members learned to address patient concerns by introducing themselves and their roles, listening, answering questions, and thanking the patient.

Since there were plenty of skeptics about mandatory half-day meetings, this wasn't easy to pull off. Some physicians and nurses pushed to opt out of the sessions on the premise of busy schedules and the threat of decreased productivity. Cosgrove made it clear that exceptions would undermine the primary goal that everyone realize that he or she was a caregiver doing what was best for the patient. While the return on investment (ROI) of having 40,000+ employees each take a half-day for these meetings was fuzzy, it was also difficult to measure the impact of not executing the program. The Clinic isn't yet prepared to claim victory. The effort is ongoing. However, in 2013, it was in the top 10 percent in patient satisfaction among roughly 4,600 hospitals.[13]

Innovation Habit 3. Bet on Leaders and Teams over Ideas

We can think about investing in innovation as a horse race—the jockey is the management, the horse is the technology, and the race is the size of the market. David Morgenthaler, the dean of venture capital, attributed about 60 percent of his financial failures to a rotten jockey falling off a great horse. This means that the problem was the management team, not the idea. Sometimes, a great jockey gets more out of a horse than anyone thought possible. The problem, then, was a second-rate technology or idea, rather than the management team. A brilliant jockey and a brilliant horse can easily win a small county fair race. The problem here is the small market, not the management team or idea. A run for the roses in a big race like the Kentucky Derby (big market) requires an excellent jockey (team) and horse (idea).[14]

Here is a concrete example of what it would mean to invest in leaders and teams over ideas. Intuit, producer of Quicken and TurboTax, is located just down the street from Google in Mountain View, California. Intuit has a single mission: "to improve customer financial lives so profoundly they could never go back to another way."[15] This mission requires that at Intuit, innovation is everyone's job. Everyone is an entrepreneur tasked to improve customers' lives. Intuit relies on cross-functional teams to uncover "deep customer empathy." They work hard to fall in love with a customer's problem rather than the solution. They eventually land on a solution through rapidly generating prototypes and experiments.

Bottom-up innovation happens by granting people time to innovate on a project of interest with people they want to work with. When teams have demonstrated they are onto a critical customer pain point, then the senior management gets involved. Before senior leaders make additional investments, they take into account who is on the team, more than the idea. Let's repeat this. The team is more important than the idea because the idea will and should change as it is studied.

The second way innovation happens at Intuit is top down. Senior leaders propose "big challenges" for their 8,000 entrepreneurs to take on. Again, the process of engaging in "deep customer empathy" is followed to ensure that the correct pain point is identified. Once ideas show merit, senior leaders merge teams and provide funding to accelerate commercialization. The process isn't flawless. In both bottom-up and top-down approaches, senior leaders have received feedback that they needed to learn to coach more and judge less. So senior leaders went through training to learn how to coach better.[16]

Innovation Habit 4. Adopt Innovative Structures

Often the first step to innovation involves knocking down department silos and creating interdisciplinary teams. As organizations grow, bureaucracy gums up the works. While innovation often happens horizontally, organizations are structured vertically. Unless these hierarchical structures are changed to support an interdisciplinary approach, innovation is extremely difficult to execute.

Procter & Gamble (P&G) offers an example of how to knock down silos with a business partner to drive profitable growth. Like most companies, P&G relied on account managers to drive sales. The entire company rested on the account manager's ability to convince the grocery store manager to allocate shelf space for P&G products. Sales and profits were at risk if the account manager and grocery store manager were at odds, or if either person was unskilled at engaging the resources of their respective firms.

When A. G. Lafley was still CEO of P&G, we drew the diagram shown in Figure 8.1 to confirm that this picture illustrated P&G's past versus its new and improved account management approach.

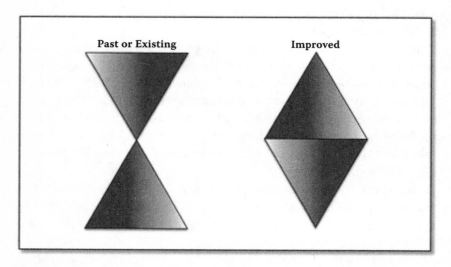

FIGURE 8.1   The Past Versus a New and Improved Account Management Approach

On the left is a typical account management method. At the point of the two triangles rests the relationship between the P&G account manager and the grocery store manager. An army of people stand behind each person.

The figure on the right represents the innovative approach to account management that P&G embraced. An interdisciplinary team from P&G collaborated with an interdisciplinary team from the grocery store. P&G finance, sales, engineering, and manufacturing departments collaborated with the grocery store's functional experts and department managers. The best partnerships created joint scorecards designed to drive business growth in a mutually beneficial way. Lafley reported that changing P&G's account management model contributed more to its growth than any other change at that point in the tenure of his career as CEO until the time of our conversation.[17]

Innovation Habit 5. Apply Disciplined Creativity

To manage short-term profitability, organizations have an impressive left-brain tool kit of strategic planning, capital budgeting, project management, pay for performance, production scheduling, cost accounting, profit analysis, and financial controls, to name only a few. But what tools are available to encourage creative deviation? After initial brainstorming, which is a strategy with significant limitations, the toolbox for creativity is often empty.

Organizations need predictable growth; "one-off" acts of creative genius are insufficient. The innovation process is risky, and failure often results. "Fail fast and fail cheap" is more than a tag line. It is a way to mitigate risk at the very starting point of innovation—"the fuzzy front end." George Day created a roadmap entitled "Real, Win, and Worth" that teaches us whether we should have hope in an idea.[18] Table 8.1 is our adaptation of this roadmap. Let's consider each step in the real, win, and worth process.

IS IT REAL?	CAN WE WIN?	IS IT WORTH IT?
What markets are open or have loopholes or opportunities? Who are the target customers?	Do we have the tangible assets needed to execute the value proposition—that is, the technical knowledge, capital, marketing, finance, legal, and so on?	Are the risks worth the reward?
What are the customers' pain points? a. Pain point 1: Describe it in detail. b. Pain point 2: Describe it in detail. c. Pain point 3: Describe it in detail.	Do we have the operational excellence to deliver the value proposition—that is, the project managers, interdisciplinary team, and so on?	If we do not have innovative talent, would the project help to build it? Should we develop the talent before starting the project?
What are the customers' competing alternatives? List these.	Do we have the intangible assets to win—that is, the champion, culture, character, sense of team, and so on?	Will senior leaders or investors support the idea? How do we make sure of their support?
For customers who have these pain points and competing alternatives, why is our value proposition the best? Reason to switch? Incentives to switch?	Do we have the partners and advisors to win?	Is the project sustainable from the people, planet, and profit perspectives?

TABLE 8.1   Real, Win, and Worth Process Roadmap

Source: Adapted from George Day, "Is It Real? Can We Win? Is It Worth Doing? Managing Risk and Reward in an Innovation Portfolio," https://hbr.org/2007/12/is -it-real-can-we-win-is-it-worth-doing-managing-risk-and-reward-in-an-innovation -portfolio.

Is It Real?

By now, you know that innovation starts with the customer, not the technology or the idea. We met a U.S. citizen when we were lecturing at Vlerick in St. Petersburg, Russia. He created several Russian businesses, the first of which was a simple mail service. Letters sent overseas from Russia could take weeks and months—this was a clear pain point. So he convinced ordinary citizens to give him their overseas mail, which he took by ferry to Finland. He used the Finnish postal service to mail Russian envelopes and packages around the world.[19]

Russians knew their mail service was inept, but they hadn't considered how Finnish freedom could triumph over their bureaucracy.

If we listen carefully, the customers will tell us their pain points. Then it is up to the innovators to create a value proposition that delivers the mail better than all the competing alternatives.

Can We Win?

Once we validate our value proposition through VoC interviews, then we need to evaluate whether we have the talent, resources, and culture to execute our proposition. Evaluating talent (technical expertise) and resources (capital and equipment) is relatively easy. It is culture that is often overlooked, even though we have shown that culture is more powerful than strategy.

Organizations create a class structure that celebrates or lifts up one function over others. Engineering cultures lift up technically trained people; sales cultures lift up rainmakers; higher education and healthcare cultures lift up professors and doctors. Each group speaks the language of their discipline, and that separates them from others. However, innovation is more likely to occur among those with more direct customer, supplier, and operational contact than they have at headquarters. Organization charts full of experts with the same background presuppose how work will get done, creating a climate that is more likely to preserve the status quo than encourage innovation. Here's an example of how innovation can be enhanced by knocking down silos.

Scott Technology made fire equipment. In this case, it was easy to identify the customer because fire chiefs drive the decision about what fire equipment to use. Scott leaders met with fire chiefs to ask about equipment that helped put out fires and learned that an infrared light attached to firefighters' helmets could locate someone lying on the floor in a smoked-filled room. However, due to the position of the light on the helmet, firefighters frequently removed their helmets to shine the light under beds or around corners. This practice endangered the firefighters. Scott's interdisciplinary team of engineers, finance, operations, human resources, and marketing staff went to work, and they designed a light with a Velcro strip and extension wire that attached to the firefighter's body rather than to the helmet. This innovation mobilized the light without its needing to be removed from the firefighter's helmet or mask.

Along with the fire chiefs, Scott's team learned together and co-designed the way to manufacture and market this product at a profit. In one year, Scott Technology captured two-thirds of a market in which they had no prior business due to the work of an interdisciplinary team collaborating with a customer to solve a problem.[20]

Is It Worth It?

What makes life interesting is stepping into the unknown. Taking risks. Yet, behavioral economics makes it clear that most of us fear loss more than we hope for gain. This fundamental tension in wanting to create, yet fearing loss has to be navigated if an organization is to innovate and grow. In addition, most organizational cultures are wired to manage price, cost, and volume, attributes that do not involve lots of risk. These traditional levers work well in a stable environment but not as well in a VUCA world.

A point that is often lost when it comes to innovation is this: people innovate because they want to, not because they have to. This is why innovation has to be cultivated and cannot be commanded. It must start with an internal drive or desire.

One reason that cultivating innovation is hard is that most people have more experience solving known problems by applying known solutions than taking on challenges that lack solutions. The difference between an operational culture and an innovation culture is quite stark. Operations is about "predict and control" while innovation is about "create and grow." The chart in Table 8.2 details some of the differences between operational cultures and growth cultures.

OPERATIONAL CULTURES VALUE AND FOCUS ON:	INNOVATIVE CULTURES VALUE AND FOCUS ON:
Inside-out thinking	Outside-in thinking
Variance reduction	Deviance seeking
Cost reductions	Creativity
Crop production feel	Greenhouse feel
Control and compliance	Commitment and new ideas
Metrics	Empathy for customers
Deficits	Strengths

TABLE 8.2 Operational Versus Growth Cultures

Clearly organizations need both types of cultures, though often organizations excel at one culture at the expense of the other. High-growth organizations can suffer from poor operations. Operationally excellent organizations can struggle with top-line growth. It is as though we are talking about two sports that have some similarities but that are fundamentally different. Consider tennis and racquetball. While they both use rackets, one serves overhand and the other underhand. One keeps a stiff wrist, and the other flicks the wrist. A few athletes can play both sports well, but not many. Ideally, organizations would perform the way the exceptional athlete performs: able to play at both the growth sport and the operational sport.

Operational and innovative mindsets collide when revenue and margin budgets are compared to actual performance. Operational cultures want to control and predict in ways that innovators often cannot deliver because innovation is not easy to control or predict. Since predicting top line and margin is a pretty squishy science, it is vitally important to sort out acceptable loss. What can be defined with clarity is how much the new venture will cost. Venture capital investors or internal C-suite leaders can define acceptable loss in collaboration with the leadership team by answering three questions:

1. *Does the leadership team want it?* You need a leadership team intrinsically motivated to pursue innovation. Investment risk is mitigated by teams that give and are grateful for the opportunity to innovate fortified by a steely grit and a growth mindset to continually improve their innovation.
2. *Does the leadership team have the resources to execute?* If not, can they figure out how to make do with what investors can offer?
3. *Does the leadership team understand the level of loss that investors or C suite leaders can afford?* If not, then create a loss level that investors or the C suite can afford.

If you are a member of the leadership team striving to innovate, you cannot delegate these risks to others. You need to own the idea and the risks, not just the potential benefits. You cannot expect venture capitalists or your employer's C suite to help you unless you help them. Be very clear, not just about the upside but also in how you plan to be diligent about managing loss. If you are a funder, you will get

231

better results acting as a coach and partner, rather than as a cop and boss.[21]

Here is the critical point: if the project turns out to be a commercial success, then we all cheer. At best, innovation succeeds in 10 percent to 30 percent of the cases. However, innovator and interdisciplinary learning can be a success 100 percent of the time. People and teams can grow only if given the opportunity to "fail fast." Applying this "real-win-worth" paradigm is an effective way to develop innovators who are needed in every organization at a loss that is affordable.

Why the Five Innovative Habits Are Important

People and culture are the most important part of innovation and also the most expensive. Total compensation, the cost of people, is the most expensive line item on most income statements. Organizational success depends on engaged people who are able to turn the cost of their salary into cash as quickly as possible.

Trusted teams fail their way to success, but they do so quickly and inexpensively. This is achieved by encouraging a virtue-based culture, making the customer the boss, by betting on leaders and teams over ideas, by applying innovative organizational structures, and by practicing creative discipline. These five innovative habits are enhanced by adopting virtue as common language to define excellence.

The Importance of a Common Language

Whether we apply virtue in a boardroom or on a production floor, to former offenders with limited education or to physicians who are highly educated, to Americans or Asians, or in Switzerland or in South Korea, the differences melt away the closer we get to someone's core. When it comes to virtue, we are separated by the flimsiest filament. The remarkable part isn't the nuanced differences in how people interpret the virtues. The remarkable part is the universal respect that people have for the seven virtues.

When practiced, these seven virtues strike something deep in us. This is why the power of a common language should not be underestimated. When the language of virtue enters routine conversations, then the culture is on its way to being created. Our research and experience demonstrate that adopting the common language of virtue is the foundation on which an ethical culture is built.

Just as accounting is the language of business, virtue is the language of character. Don't take our word for it. Try it. Ask a group of people to prepare a 20-minute presentation to discuss one of the seven virtues. Ask them to come prepared with their answer to three questions. For example, you could start with the virtue trust by asking people to share their answers to these three questions:

1. What is trust?
2. Why is trust relevant and useful to our work?
3. How could we get more of it?

People self-discover quickly the power of these words in their professional and personal life. Typically, they readily connect how their life is impacted by questions 1 and 2. They usually haven't given as much thought to how they could increase a virtue like trust in their life. It is the habitual side—the temperance side of the equation—that is not always as clear.

We learn about the relevance and usefulness of the virtues in conversations with teammates. Here are additional questions that can be used to define the culture when it is at its best by applying a common language of excellence:

- *Trust:* Confidence in One Another
  When has trust made us faster and more agile?
  How can we restore trust?
  At our best, how do we earn and deepen trust?
- *Compassion:* An Understanding of Another's Challenges
  How does compassion support our business goals?
  How does compassion increase engagement?
  When have acts of compassion improved our business results?
- *Courage:* Strength in the Face of Adversity
  When have you witnessed courage in our company?
  Who is effective in encouraging people to be courageous?
  How can we help people to be more courageous?
- *Justice:* A Concern for Fairness
  As a company, when did we go out of our way to help a coworker?

How can we further empower our people so they are more engaged in setting their own performance criteria?

When have we been our best in serving the needs of each of our stakeholders?

- *Wisdom:* Having Good, Sound Judgment

  What have been our wisest decisions?

  When faced with our most difficult decisions, when did we choose the best course and have the strength to endure?

  How can we be more intentional about integrating wisdom into decision making?

- *Temperance:* Having Self-Restraint

  How can we balance two competing rights, such as concern for the company and concern for the individual, or compassion and justice?

  How can we help people practice self-control?

  When have we been our best at encouraging life-work balance?

- *Hope:* A Positive, Optimistic Expectation of Future Events

  What are the parts of working for our company for which you are grateful?

  What do we do well, and how could we do more of it?

  When was our culture at its best?

A more succinct list of questions that can help assess how well leaders practice virtue is to ask five questions:

1. How well are we teaching character in our company?
2. How might character development benefit our company?
3. What is being done to encourage or discourage character development in our company?
4. How does character development reduce risk?
5. How does character development promote growth?

Now, to quote Aristotle: "We are what we repeatedly do. Excellence, then, is not an act, but a habit." Excellence involves lifting up people when they are the best versions of themselves so they can do more of that.[22]

CHAPTER 9

Classical Solutions to Contemporary Challenges

Get the next generation VUCA ready.

> *It has become appallingly obvious that our tech-*
> *nology has exceeded our humanity.*
> ALBERT EINSTEIN[1]

The task of making career decisions is wickedly complicated for this generation of college students because there are so many variables out of their control. Today's graduates are expected to have three to five career changes and 10 to 15 jobs throughout their lifetime.[2] The U.S. Department of Labor predicts that about 65 percent of children will have jobs that don't yet exist.[3] Who knows what high school students will be doing by the time they graduate from college, never mind at the end of their career? This is why advising students to pick one career is questionable because the pace at which jobs are created and destroyed is accelerating.

If this pace of change isn't complicated enough, then add into the mix how high school and college students don't know themselves well enough to select careers that give their life purpose. They might find that some careers that once excited them turn out to be a disappointment. They might find that other careers they never considered turn out to be the best jobs they ever had. This limited self-awareness and insight about career options is not a new problem. In 1914, Harvard

President Abbott Lawrence Lowell shared his thoughts on making career decisions with students whose experience was limited:

> People who make a rapid success in their first venture in life are not numerous, and some of them actually are injured if they do. Young people must choose careers before they have tried them. They must estimate their qualities, with which they are still only partly familiar; and must guess how well they fit for an occupation of which they have had no personal experience. Does success mean the mere satisfaction of desires or ambitions, whatever they may be? If a person's desire is to gratify immediate cravings for pleasure with as little exertion as possible, and is successful, can this type of life be a success? Certainly not. The mere satisfaction of desire then is not success unless the object desired is worthy. The world is full of people who have attained what they wanted and are neither happy nor satisfied. Mere competence, or even excellence, in a chosen field of endeavor is an insufficient basis for success, for they do not take into account questions of worth, value and merit. True success does not consist in doing what we set forth to do, what we had hoped to do, nor even in doing what we have struggled to do; but in doing something that is worth doing.[4]

Commencement speakers don't use Lowell's word "worthy" much anymore, though graduates can count on hearing advice to "follow their passion," although when the word *passion* is used, no one mentions that the word means "suffer." This is a pity since showing graduates the link between relieving someone's suffering and purpose would be instructive. Pursuit of a purpose that involves something bigger than individual achievement would help graduates push through the inevitable adversity, disappointment, and pain awaiting them.

Every generation of young people struggles to find their way in the world to learn how life can be lived well. So here's the question: do 20-year-olds from one generation differ from 20-year-olds from previous generations on what it means to live life well? This was the point of an impressively long-term 70-year study that continues to be conducted by the Harvard Study of Adult Development. Since 1938, 724 men have been interviewed, given medical exams, and visited in their homes annually from college to death.

The study has been expanded to include their 2,000 wives and children. Some earned a degree from Harvard, and then most went on to serve in World War II. Some were from Boston's poorest neighborhoods and intentionally selected because of their social and economic disadvantages. Each year, both groups were asked about their work, their home lives, and their health. Some worked in factories, others became doctors, and one even became president of the United States. Some climbed the economic ladder with great success, while others tumbled down. Some were physically fit, and others became alcoholics.

So when members of the Greatest Generation were 20, did they differ from today's 20-year-olds in what they thought would lead to a happy life? The similarities between the past and current generations of 20-year-olds is striking. Like teenagers today, when the young people in the Greatest Generation were in their twenties, they reported that happiness was a function of fame and fortune. However, as they aged, their perspective on happiness changed. The happiest learned that trusting and caring relationships were more important than material success. They learned to loosen the grip of peer pressure, and they managed to improve their ability to regulate their emotions. The least happy, the unhealthiest, and those who died early were the loneliest. This was also true of people in toxic relationships, such as high-conflict marriages with limited affection. In contrast, a loving marriage helped people to bounce back from hard times. Even rocky marriages that sometimes lacked affection contributed to people living life well, as long as they knew their spouse would have their back in a pinch. Incredibly, trusting and caring relationships predicted good health better than cholesterol levels.[5]

You might react to this information with a big duh. Everyone knows family and friendship are more valuable than fame and fortune. If most people know this, then why is it hard to live our life based on this insight? One reason is that our relationships with many of our regular family, friends, and coworkers are not easy to manage. We are imperfect and complicated mortals who are full of contradictions, shortcomings, ambitions, hopes, and fears. When we bump into other imperfect, complicated mortals all day long, some bring out the very best in us, and others bring out our worst self.

People are complicated, and meaningful relationships take incredible effort. Our worst relationships can stoke us full of anger for years. It is incredibly hard to forgive others. It can be easier to hold onto anger and remain perennially ticked off. The trouble is, even if we are right to feel a deep injustice toward someone who offended us deeply, we can become forever doomed to be our own jailer. As Buddha cautioned, "Holding onto anger is like drinking poison hoping the other person will die."

Another reason that relationships become strained is the alchemy of feeling aggrieved or entitled. People certainly sympathize with someone who is feeling like a victim when that person's life has been one brutal blow after another. Imagine a middle schooler being told by both of her divorced parents that neither wants her to live in his or her home. As this student said to her teacher, "That's messed up when your own parents don't want you." The kid's right. That's messed up. We can quickly acknowledge that a lousy hand like this is very hard to play and win. Yet, once the cruelty of it all is acknowledged, now what? Feeling aggrieved doesn't help turn things around. This is why people who impress us the most are able to convert their disadvantages into advantages with grace and grit.

Life also doesn't go well for people who feel entitled. Confidence is built on sand when a child is raised under privileged conditions, dipped in plenty of self-esteem, and reinforced with orange slices and eighth-place trophies. Fragile psyches carefully cultivated by unearned praise shatter in the presence of significant life challenges. Entitlement can turn an advantaged life into a disadvantage. What impresses us most about those who have been privileged is that they live by the motto "To those that much is given, much is expected."

We certainly are more attracted to people who choose happiness, defined as worthiness, over those who feel aggrieved or entitled. Of course, this requires that we take a whack at the question, what is happiness? A good way to answer this question is to bolt social science research onto virtues proposed by Confucius, Aristotle, and others. This is exactly what Martin Seligman and Chris Peterson did. Their research is carefully detailed in an impressive 800-page tome entitled *Character Strengths and Virtues*.[6] This exhaustive, cross-cultural study focused on character that defines what it means to live life well. Here are the CliffsNotes.

Their research uncovered six virtues valued in their own right (not just as a means to another end) in almost every culture: (1) wisdom and knowledge, (2) courage, (3) love and humanity (compassion), (4) justice, (5) temperance, and (6) spirituality (trust) and transcendence (hope). Seligman and Peterson's six virtues are the same as the seven classical virtues, though we are explicit about separating trust and hope, which fit under their virtue labeled as "spirituality and transcendence." They offer a helpful distinction between each of these virtues, all of which can be learned and compared to talents that are inherited, at least to some degree. A virtue can be developed through effort by any of us. In other words, while athletic or musical ability is affected in part by our genetics, compassion can be cultivated by all of us. However, there is a catch, and it's a big one. The kind of purpose that results in happiness can be had only with significant effort and struggle.

Their research revealed that happiness had three progressive dimensions: pleasure, the good life, and the meaningful life. Pleasure is how happiness might be defined by many people. A wonderful thing to be sure, though the pursuit of pleasures has almost no enduring impact on life satisfaction. In experiments where people do something fun and then do something for others, they report that fun comes and goes, while altruism endures.

The second level of happiness is what Mihaly Csikszentmihalyi termed "flow" to define an investment in creative work. Time almost seems to stop when we have a flow experience. The experience is so intense that we block out everything else that is going on around us. The satisfaction from a flow experience happens more in hindsight than in the moment. Seligman adds altruism to Csikszentmihalyi's notion of flow.[7] This means that we leverage our greatest strengths in the service of others. An example would include Doctors Without Borders applying medical and scientific expertise to patients who otherwise would never have access to quality care. A physician becomes so absorbed in treating cleft palates in a poor, mountainous region of the Dominican Republic that he forgets about his own happiness.

The third and highest level of happiness is meaning or flourishing, what the Greeks called *eudaimonia—eu* ("good") and *daimon* ("spirit"). Aristotle's definition of happiness was the "full use of your powers along lines of excellence." While Aristotle concluded that eudaimonia was life's preeminent purpose, he also acknowledged the importance of external pleasures such as health, wealth, and beauty.

Not surprisingly, there are critics of this perspective too. For example, the Stoics made virtue necessary for eudaimonia, but they denied the necessity of external goods.[8] We certainly respect the position of the Stoics, though we mere mortals wouldn't mind if a bit of pleasure were sprinkled onto our flow and purpose.

Character and Competition

Living life well is certainly worthy of our best efforts. As a practical matter, we also need to learn how to compete. Ideally, we learn to compete in a way that is guided by character. Athletics are full of lessons focused on character and competition. Coaches might tell athletes that the final score isn't what counts; what counts is character. The only way to be a real champion is to get back up after you get knocked down. There is no "I" in team. You get the idea. There is nothing novel about phrases that claim that sports teach athletes how to win in life, not just on the field.

Even though coaches and sportswriters routinely pound the words *character* and *athletics* into the same sentence, the words *virtue* and *sports* rarely appear together. The exception to this rule is Baldwin Wallace University, a private liberal arts school, where one out of every three first-year students is a student athlete. Two of the authors teach at the university, where in partnership with the university's athletic program, student athletes and their coaches put the virtues into practice.

Since 2010, student athletes nominated for their leadership potential have enrolled in a virtue seminar applied to sports. Students learn to practice virtue in the locker room, at practice, during games, and in the classroom. The coaches participate as well, including men's and women's basketball, track, tennis, lacrosse, and soccer, as well as women's volleyball and men's baseball, football, and wrestling. Student athletes were surveyed one, two, and again three years after they had completed the seminar to learn what, if anything, had been the impact of practicing virtue on the team's culture. Of the 60 athletes who completed a survey, 98 percent agreed or strongly agreed that "virtues increase my engagement in my work" and "learning and practicing the virtues improves teamwork." Here are additional survey results completed by student athletes:

- "I am willing to take risks, and I try to make adjustments to improve myself."
  100 percent agreed or strongly agreed.
- "I believe learning and practicing the virtues increases my engagement in my work."
  98 percent agreed or strongly agreed.
- "I am motivated to seek advice from people who bring out the best in me."
  100 percent agreed or strongly agreed.
- "I believe learning and practicing the virtues improves teamwork."
  98 percent agreed or strongly agreed.
- "You can always change basic things about the kind of person you are."
  70 percent agreed or strongly agreed.
- "I believe practicing the virtues improved our team's ability to compete."
  78 percent agreed or strongly agreed.

When asked how the virtues affected team culture, frequent comments included these:

- "We started to play for each other, as opposed to everyone playing for themselves."
- "The virtues brought our team closer together, which has led to more wins."
- "Practicing the virtues, by default, and you become a better person."

At the same time that athletes were being surveyed, coaches were interviewed to learn why they adopted the virtues as an athletic department and what's been the impact. After six years of practicing the virtues, over 20 coaches agreed with comments such as these:

- "The virtues keep us more stable in an unstable world."
- "We didn't expect to be challenged as coaches; the virtues helped us become better coaches, spouses, and parents."
- "The impact on students who take the class is massive. . . . At a wedding, alums were there and using the virtues in their professional lives."

241

- "The impact of the virtues is hard to quantify, but the impact is real. The virtues accelerate maturity."

The limitation of the study is that it captured a snapshot in time. Yet the comments made by the athletes and coaches are remarkably similar. Similar to our findings at Parker Hannifin, both athletes and coaches have reported a clear correlation between virtue with engagement and teamwork. Does this mean more wins and fewer losses? Perhaps. Clearly, other variables affect athletic performance—the ability to recruit superior talent, coaching strategy, level of competition, and so on. What all the coaches did report was that if your team isn't fully engaged, then you can't win. You could consider the impact of virtue this way—a character-based culture is necessary, but not sufficient, to win. And there is no doubt that coaches want to win. Nevertheless, even though winning is important, every coach reported that what counted most is how well they developed the character of their athletes while they played and after their playing days were over. Coaches emphasized that the purpose of their job was to build virtuous athletes.

Virtue and Career

After students graduate from college, how do they find work? When students meet Mark Shapiro and learn that he is a sports executive, you can imagine many ask: "How do I get your job?" Shapiro was president of the Cleveland Indians, the professional baseball team he served for an incredible 24 years. In 2015, Shapiro became president of the Toronto Blue Jays. He studied history at Princeton, not business. He played football in college, not baseball.

He left a California high-paying, high-status job in commercial real estate for a low-paying, low-status job in Cleveland. At the time he joined the Cleveland Indians, the team was not only the worst baseball franchise but they were also the worst sports franchise in all of America. Shapiro's decision was a head scratcher to his Princeton friends until they understood his reasons. First, the leaders who recruited Shapiro were committed to his personal and professional growth. Second, Shapiro's values aligned with these leaders' values. So Shapiro's advice to college students is this. Take very seriously with whom you are going to work, not just what you are going to do. Pay attention to whether the culture will bring out the best version of yourself.[9]

Virtue and Culture

When it comes to university cultures that are intentionally developing virtue-based graduates, few organizations match the effort of military service academies. According to the directors of character education at West Point, the Naval Academy, and the Air Force Academy, today's cadets are as competent as they have ever been. These remarkable young men and women are extraordinarily competent, as evidenced by their academic records, physical fitness, and individual achievements.

When it comes to character, the distribution is roughly 10/80/10. This means 10 percent of the cadets are not only highly competent but also as virtuous as the service academies have ever seen. About 10 percent on the other side of the distribution curve can't get to the place to lead from a position of virtue. As a result, they flame out while in the academy or shortly after their first assignment. The majority in the middle—the 80 percent—want to lead from virtue, but they don't have any idea what this means because they were never exposed to the virtues at any time during their formal education. So the challenge for the service academies is to create a virtue-based culture for the 80 percent of their cadets who want to be virtuous but don't know how.[10]

If this virtue-based leadership math of 10/80/10 is about right for the service academies, it certainly isn't likely to be much different for other organizations. Since the service academies readily acknowledge how hard it is to instill virtue-based leadership, consider the risk to any organization when there is no intentional strategy to help people lead from a position of virtue. While the service academies use the word *virtue* to define character-based leadership, business or healthcare is more likely to use the word *values* than *virtues*. For now, let's stick with the word *values*.

Plenty of organizations will tout a culture of "ethical values." They also promote their strong brand. Now here's where the alarms should go off. An organization doesn't have a chance of creating a strong employee, customer, or patient brand on a weak culture with muted values or values that stay on the wall. When values are only skin deep, employees, patients, and customers feel no attachment to the organization. All of them become flight risks.

When interviewing, the tricky part is how recent college graduates figure out whether they fit the culture and not just the job. This gets harder still when, during an interview, they start a conversation about culture, only to be told by interviewers, "We're different." No sense fighting this confirmation bias; go with it. Adam Grant reported on a study that revealed that people think their culture is more distinct than it really is. Here are some questions that recent graduates can ask about the culture to gain insights about the organization's "values."

What Is the Boss Like?

Is the boss someone like the rest of us whom you observe doing things, like cleaning a mess around the coffee pot, or is she someone who makes it clear that she is the boss and you are not? Try to tease out the degree to which the leader is a thoughtful boss who intentionally battles the negative impact that power can have on who we become. In contrast, a narcissist embraces all the trappings of power.

Does Everyone Have a Chance?

Are there stories about people who started at the bottom and made it to the top? If so, perhaps the merit of your ideas matters more than your job title. Ideally, this is a culture where everyone is encouraged to speak up and innovate. Or are people at the bottom denied promotions despite high achievement?

What Happens When People Are Let Go?

Sadly, layoffs are not a unique organizational story. What might be unusual is how the organization handles layoffs. Perhaps the company's leaders say to those who have lost their jobs, "You didn't do anything wrong. We apologize that our inability to grow cost you a job. We acknowledge the negative impact a job loss has on you and your family. We will strive to atone by offering a fair severance package that includes outplacement services to help you find another position. Beyond that, you remain our friend, and we will do everything we can to open our professional network to help you find another position."

What Happens When People Make Mistakes?

In some organizations, people who make a big mistake are fired. In contrast, Grant shares a story told about IBM. An employee who had made a huge mistake walked into the office of Tom Watson, the CEO and founder of IBM, expecting to be fired. Watson replied, "Why would I fire you? I just spent $10 million on your education."

What Happens When the Powerful Get Caught Doing an Unethical Act?

No organization is immune from the powerful getting special treatment. Yet, one way to test whether ethics are treated seriously is to ask whether a senior leader has ever been let go due to unethical conduct.

How Gritty Is the Organization?

Ask about a story when the organization went through a tough time. Consider whether the story emphasized giving, grit, growth mindset, and gratitude (the 4Gs) or lifted up incidents of people being bitter, aggrieved, or entitled. Keep in mind that outrageous stories about vice can grab our attention more than selfless stories about virtue. There's no sense in looking for a perfect culture, and you won't be short on stories about people at their worst. You are looking for a culture that at least "aims at the good."[11]

Virtue and Professional Development

Educated and employed. Now that is a terrific combination. Once a recent graduate finds work, then what? This book has detailed how high performers focus on what they can control and how practicing virtue involves living by conviction rather than circumstance. So with these thoughts in mind, here are seven self-control booster shots that recently employed graduates can practice.

1. Identify a Purpose

Victor Strecher asks us to imagine our reaction to a miracle drug that would add years to our life, reduce the risk of heart attacks and strokes, cut our risk of Alzheimer's disease in half, improve our ability to sleep well, double our odds of avoiding substance abuse, decrease inflammation, and increase good cholesterol? If you were a leader in the company that sold the drug, you would make millions. If you were the inventor of the drug, you would win the Nobel Prize. This miracle drug exists, though your doctor can't give you a prescription. The product is free, but it will cost you loads of thought and effort. The drug is having purpose.[12]

A purpose is often revealed to us by our being curious and experimenting to help us figure out our interests. As we explore our interests, we also need to be mindful that employers will not hire us just for what we want to do. They hire us to solve a pain point better than any competing alternative they can find.

2. We Are More Malleable Than We Often Think

"There is nothing in a caterpillar that tells you it's going to be a butterfly," said Buckminster Fuller.[13] We are far more malleable and resilient than is widely understood. When it comes to virtue, data from the service academies and our own data make clear that we can develop virtue through deliberate practice and effort.

3. Seek Support and Earn Support

Whom we work with will be at least as important, and sometimes more important, than what we do. When what counts most is the content of a person's character rather than his or her bloodline, then the best and brightest are selected to work on the world's most important problems. Now the world would be more fair and just if the station you were born into was not your ultimate fate. Since social connections are not going to be spread evenly across people anytime soon, we need to teach people how to ask for help.

The Prepare, Probe, and Propose Framework

Start by looking for people whose career and character intrigue you. List three to five people whom you know, like, and trust to ask for help. You can apply the "prepare, probe, and propose"[14] framework below to get clear on how you can reach out to a person you respect:

Prepare: Before you ask for help, do your homework. Learn as much as possible about the person you want to meet *before* you request a meeting. It requires homework to get very clear on what you want to learn from someone.

Probe: Request a half-hour to a one-hour meeting by clarifying why you have reached out to this person and what you want to learn. Whatever time she offers you, be sure to honor that time commitment. When you meet with the person, now it's time to probe. While you have questions prepared in advance, also look for what she most enjoys about her work and what frustrates her. Send a thank-you note after the meeting that details what you learned. You might be surprised how infrequently thank-you notes are sent. A thoughtful thank-you note leaves a favorable impression and happens to be the right thing to do.

Propose: Too often, we ask for something before we are prepared to do so and before we probe. Steps 1 and 2 might teach us that there isn't anything to propose. We should then quit while we are ahead and move on. If we can align a person's interests with ours, then go for it. This might include asking for another meeting to explore further an area of mutual interest. It might involve a request to introduce you to others who have additional insights. And, if things went really well, it might mean following up on an opportunity he presented to you.

Now, life isn't just about seeking support; it also involves giving support. Adam Grant's research makes clear that creating a habit of looking for ways to help others ultimately helps us. Perhaps we might not know enough to help another person, especially someone more experienced than we are. If we don't know what they want, it is pretty easy to solve this riddle. Ask!

Community Involvement

Another way to give is to find a community problem that you care about and offer your time and talent, even if the treasure you have to offer is limited. For example, nonprofit boards often need strategic and financial leadership.

The developmental opportunities available in civic engagement can often exceed what might be available to a person just starting her career. Build your social connections and leadership experience by contributing to the common good.

4. Leverage Strengths and Manage Weaknesses

Name and amplify your strengths. Look for ways to rely on your strengths more often. Of course, we all have to do things we don't enjoy. Yet, the more we understand and use our strengths, the more our performance improves. By all means, take weaknesses into account. In fact, build a habit of converting weaknesses and failures into growth. Just keep in mind that high performance is built on strength, not weakness.

5. Develop Healthy Habits

Aristotle said that moral virtue is acquired by repetition. Healthy habits involve our ability to self-regulate. The benefits of self-regulation include a favorable impact on academic achievement, income, job status, and even happier marriages.

In contrast, low self-regulation increases the chance that people will have legal problems, higher levels of heart disease, obesity, depression, and substance abuse. It certainly comes as no surprise that self-regulation that cultivates persistence affects life and career outcomes. What we underestimate is how much persistence matters.[15]

6. Practice Humility

One thing we can take to the bank is the certainty that we are going to mess up. This is why it is best to practice virtue with humility and to be grateful for the times we get it right. We learn when we are humble and not when we are arrogant. This is why it is important to understand the relationship between self-esteem and confidence. If we get the order wrong—that is, pumping up self-esteem without overcoming adversity—we just put ourselves on the road to arrogance or entitlement.

If we get the order right, then self-esteem and resiliency are by-products of having overcome adversity. Self-esteem is the effect, not the cause, of resiliency. A healthy dose of self-esteem doesn't mean that we stop thinking about ourselves. It does mean we think about ourselves less.

7. Develop an Innovation Mindset and Skill Set

Knowing how to start, grow, and reinvent organizations is a critical VUCA skill set. Remember that it is entrepreneurs and innovators who thrive in uncertain conditions. Now we can't invent and grow things by ourselves. We need help. Few of us come up with an idea that will change the world. But we can seek out people who have been innovative and learn how they got that way.

We can learn to innovate by starting with people, rather than ideas. The benefit of learning from innovation coaches is made clear by the experience at MIT. Their studies have revealed that entrepreneurs who have been coached well are seven times more likely to secure funds and three times more likely to grow their business.[16] Once we understand that innovation is a team sport, requiring good coaching and good teammates, then innovation is within our reach.

Virtue and Parenting

As our college graduates mature, perhaps they hit the trifecta—they are educated, employed, and married. Now they plan to start a family. Young parents might be interested in how to teach their children to be virtuous.

The central point of parenting is to ask, "What kind of child are we trying to raise?" One answer can be happiness defined by purpose, flow, and pleasure. Or, for reasons that are easy to understand, some parents answer this question by making their priority a successful child. Sounds pretty good. This is why some parents manage their kid's time, supervise conflicts with other kids and teachers, and push their kids to earn good grades. This means that good grades beget a good college that helps land a good job.

In some ways, parents follow the good grades to good college track because college admissions officers admit students more on individual achievement than concern for others or the common good. Even when admissions departments take character into account, the focus shifts back to academic achievement after the student is enrolled. Higher education seems to have lost its 25-century-old legacy of placing the virtues at the core of what it meant to be an educated person. A virtue sighting would be exceedingly rare in most university cocurricular activities and curricula. It certainly would be unusual for a professor or administrator to accept responsibility to help students cultivate virtue. Until the practice of virtue becomes the norm inside and outside the classroom, the hope of cultivating student character will go unrealized.[17]

Since most high schools and colleges fall short of integrating character and virtue into what they teach, it should certainly come as no surprise that students are unaware of what virtue is, why they should care, and how virtue could be developed to lead a good life. Part of teaching character is helping students at least to cope and ideally thrive in uncertain conditions. But this isn't the conventional way that education is set up. The primary focus is on certainty rather than uncertainty. Students are given a defined roadmap of courses they need in order to complete a major and earn a degree. For the most part, their coursework teaches them to study known answers to known questions. Students come to college uninformed and leave informed.

While students don't learn how to deal with turbulence, they might learn about the importance of self-esteem and self-awareness. Sounds good. Help the children feel good about themselves and learn who they are. However, when "self-awareness" fixates on psychological traits and preferences, what can be lost is adaptation and growth. Clearly, there is benefit in understanding personal traits and preferences, although true self-discovery requires more than an exclusive attention to who we are because when we stop here, we stunt the growth of who we can become. People can be quite clear that they are extraverts without paying attention to how to become more empathic. People can get stuck in an unhealthy rut, screening relationships by whether others are like them rather than how they can adjust to others.

When people practice wisdom and temperance, they shape their character independent of traits and preferences. People can practice being more compassionate while remaining introverts. People can become more courageous, even if they lean toward cautiousness. Through practicing virtue, people train themselves to behave better, at least in that moment. The more people cultivate virtue, the more they continue to grow and change. Rather than fixate on personal preferences, people learn to practice virtue in the mundane moments of everyday life in how they relate to family members, friends, and teammates. They spend less time embracing traits and talents, and they devote more effort to getting over themselves.

These are some of the reasons why raising a child is so bloody hard. In fact, parenting is arguably the most difficult job of all. Since there is so much that a parent cannot control, it is worth focusing on what can be controlled. Perhaps the most important point of all is to make children understand that there is nothing they need to do to earn our love, and there is nothing they will do that will ever lose our love. They can take our unconditional love to the bank.

We can also make clear that the purpose of school is not to come back as the smartest, most athletic, or most musical student of them all. In fact, they are not expected to come home the most successful at anything. What they can do is practice bravery, compassion, and growth each day they are shipped off to school. They can do this by answering three questions daily:

1. How brave were you?
2. How kind were you?
3. What did you learn from your failures?[18]

Children are the same as adults when it comes to the science of high performance. Focus on what you can control, which reduces anxiety and increases performance. Children can practice their answers to these three questions daily. They cannot control whether they will become valedictorians. In addition, decades of attachment theory research has made it clear that children raised with a secure base are more likely to be resilient and bold in taking on tough challenges. So the interesting paradox is this: parents control what they can—unconditional regard. Children control what they can—their effort and developing their character. Success is now a more likely by-product.

Trusted Bulldogs with Friends Win in the End

The generations following the baby boomers are often criticized for being coddled and lacking the mental toughness and grit that it takes to compete. Perhaps the critics are a bit harsh. After all, the baby boomers are not labeled as the Greatest Generation. This honor was granted to their parents. Perhaps members of the World War II generation concluded that it was boomers who lacked the toughness and grit to compete. The generations that have followed the boomers survived the greatest financial crisis since the Great Depression, more than a decade of war following the terrorist attacks on September 11, and the need to scramble for employment throughout this century in ways that boomers didn't have to do in the 1960s.

Perhaps every generation struggles to understand the difference between tough and rough. Being tough and resilient doesn't mean numbing all feelings and concern for others. Toughness isn't about not being quiet, not listening, and not compromising. These are attributes of an insecure person, not a tough person. We don't need roughness that disconnects rather than connects with others. In fact, when roughness is the norm, engagement goes down rather than up.

Perhaps this is why these seven words—the virtues—strike something deep in all of us, whether we are soldiers, athletes, physicians, engineers, accountants, students, kids and their parents, or former offenders. These seven words offer common ground for North and South Americans, Asians, Africans, and Europeans, all of whom understand the value of practicing virtue despite obvious cultural differences.

Over 3,000 years ago, Heraclitus, the Greek philosopher, described a person's life this way: "Character is destiny." It's a choice. And once the choice to pursue virtue is made, often the hard part isn't figuring out how we should conduct ourselves. The really hard and rewarding part is accepting a lifetime's worth of struggle to do what we already know is right.

We need tough bulldogs who make friends because they can be trusted and will not quit in the face of adversity. They strive to enhance and protect others. This is why in a turbulent world, trusted bulldogs with friends win in the end.

Epilogue and Takeaways

It is interesting that we need to prove that a culture characterized by trust, fairness, courage, and hope would somehow outperform cultures characterized by distrust, injustice, cowardice, and despair.

When Virtue Is Absent

Turnabout is fair play. Rather than put virtue on trial, let's put vice on trial. Consider what happens to our relationships when virtues are missing:

- Without **trust,** relationships with our customers, our patients, and our colleagues deteriorate. Mistrust slows down decisions, decreases quality, and costs more.
- Without **compassion,** we fail to relate to others, fail to gain insights from another person's perspective, or fail to consider how our decisions affect others. In the absence of compassion, we

alienate people. Self-serving conduct results in narrow goals and distances others, undermining teamwork.

- Without **courage,** we will not stand up to poor decisions. We back down in the face of adversity. We choose the easy wrong rather than the hard right. We lack the persistence needed to innovate.
- Without **justice,** we fail to make a difference. We do not use the diversity of others' expertise, experience, insights, and skills, so the quality of our decisions and the speed of our execution suffer. Our relations deteriorate and commitments decline when people feel they are treated unfairly.
- Without **wisdom,** we make flawed decisions, especially in a turbulent world. We fail to empower and engage a higher percentage of people. We blame others for poor performance and create a culture of fear and disengagement. People stop caring and hunker down. As apathy goes up, so does risk.
- Without **temperance,** we take unnecessary risks, we rush to judge, we fail to gather relevant facts, and our actions lack consistency. Minus the discipline to follow our convictions, our credibility suffers.
- Without **hope,** we cannot be open-minded or consider the views of others. We cannot learn from others or reflect critically on our failures, so we don't improve.

While this deficit-based approach helps people understand what happens when virtue is missing in action, virtue-based leadership is appreciative. Virtue-based leadership is about who we are when we are at our best. We are all flawed to be sure, though our aspiration is to be the best version of ourselves.[1]

This might lead you to ask whether virtue can be taught. This is actually the wrong question. Every day, we teach virtue to our colleagues, our families, and our friends more by our actions than by our words. So the question isn't, "Can we teach virtue?" Rather, the real question is, "How can we teach virtue better?"

Swing back to the value of virtue. To capture the essence of *Exception to the Rule*, here are a dozen takeaways to conclude the text.

A Dozen Key Insights

1. Is Culture More Powerful Than Strategy?

Challenge: Without devaluing the importance of strategy, we have asked this question to thousands of people, and few dispute that culture is more powerful than strategy.

Nugget: While plenty of resources are allocated to strategy in most organizations, precious few, if any, resources are allocated to culture. Culture is not the responsibility of the human resources department in an organization, though their role might be quite helpful.

Since most leaders readily acknowledge that culture is more powerful than strategy, leaders need to own the responsibility to be "keepers of the culture." Culture is a *leading performance indicator* that is best understood by stories. Strategy is a *lagging performance indicator* that is best understood by numbers.

Our advice is to start with culture and then move to strategy. For example, start a meeting with what you are doing well. Metrics are often green, yellow, and red. Start with green numbers by asking, "What's the story behind our success?" Inevitably, the answer will involve the virtues and stories about recovery from setbacks while remaining resilient in the face of adversity.

2. Soft Methods Get Hard Results: The Performance Virtues of the 4Gs

Challenge: No margin, no mission. Every profit and nonprofit organization has to make more money than it spends. So it is not without reason that leaders want a "financial results-oriented culture."

Nugget: Paradoxically, we get better results not by fixating on results but by focusing on our effort and seeking guidance. Soft methods, such as engagement, are enhanced by the performance virtues: the 4Gs, or giver, growth mindset, grit, and gratitude. These soft methods drive hard results such as financial performance. The 4Gs focus more on what we can control and less on what we cannot control (market forces).

255

3. *Exception to the Rule* Unites People on a Global Basis

Challenge: Organizations need both *e pluribus* ("out of many") and *unum* ("one"). Teams not only need to respect diversity and differences but they also need to build teams based on what unites us—our similarities.

Nugget: This is among the most intriguing aspects of this 15-years-long journey applying the virtues in multiple nations. The virtues are remarkably universal and admired. Virtues provide a forum for defining what unites—rather than divides—people. Rather than focus on people at their worst, virtues lift up people at their best. They are "appreciative," to capture one of the now popular concepts of positive psychology. Over 1,000 leader and team evaluations, follow-on coaching sessions, and continuous assessments validate that virtue builds teamwork. Virtues work universally according to leaders and teams from Asia, Europe, Africa, and the Americas.

4. Stories Inspire, and Facts Convince

Challenge: "What gets measured gets done" is a good catchphrase to convince someone to add a metric to a project. Numbers certainly have their place, though Einstein cautioned, "Not everything that can be counted counts, and not everything that counts can be counted." Math and metrics are precise. There is only one answer to the question, how much is 5 times 8? The answer is 40. But what if you are asked, "What is your response to fear?"

Nugget: Virtue is best understood by stories. When you've achieved your best results, ask what did you do right and how can you do more of that. The answer to high performance is readily founded in virtue. After all, can you imagine high performance being achieved by distrust, cowardice, injustice, and despair?

5. Virtues Put Values into Action

Challenge: Plenty of organizations want to be guided by values. An inspiring retreat in the woods can generate a wonderful list of values. Despite a leadership team's best intentions, values displayed beautifully in the lobby too often don't come off the wall. Virtues must not only be espoused. They must be lived.

Nugget: It's not a virtue until we act. Values state what we believe; virtues put our beliefs into action. The approach we are calling *Exception to the Rule* advocates starting with goals that leaders and teams already want to pursue and with regular meetings already scheduled. No one is looking to pile more work onto an already full plate. Practicing virtue as part of your normal business operations makes virtue a habit.

6. Leverage Strengths, and Manage Weaknesses

Challenge: Most psychological research has focused on how to make miserable people less miserable. Far less research has focused on making people thrive and excel based on practicing virtue.[2] Management research generally grants far more attention to addressing deficits than to defining virtue by excellence in human conduct.

Most medical research also focuses on understanding and treating deficits in the forms of illness and disease. Far less attention is given to ensuring good health or wellness. As an example, physicians are trained to be *deficit-based thinkers,* as they develop their *differential diagnoses* to understand the cause of the patient's symptoms. Deficit-based thinking often eclipses doctors' perspectives of appreciating the strengths of their colleagues and patients.

It has been said that doctors are traditionally trained to be gladiators or "heroic lone healers.[3] They learn to trust their own reflexes and knowledge over that of others. As a result, healthcare organizations can enhance performance by taking into account how a strength-based team approach can mitigate risk and contribute to growth.

Nugget: Strength-based leaders engage people at a significantly higher rate than deficit-based leaders. Gallup Poll data has revealed that 40 percent of employees are disengaged when leaders ignore them. Disengagement declines to 20 percent when leaders focus on weaknesses, and only 1 percent are disengaged when leaders focus on strengths.[4] We don't advocate ignoring weaknesses.

We recommend relying on strengths more and fixating on weaknesses less. Better yet, offset your weaknesses with your teammates' strengths. Developing well-rounded teams is far more realistic than developing well-rounded individuals.

7. Get People Ready for the VUCA World

Challenge: The brutal truth is that the marketplace is increasingly full of disruption. Turbulence rewards excellence and is harsh on mediocrity. Turbulence rewards innovation and punishes change resisters. Innovative leadership and teamwork have become nondiscretionary.

Nugget: An MIT study demonstrated that leadership and teamwork explained about 70 percent of the reason that new ventures succeeded or failed and that strategy explained only about 30 percent of successes or failures.[5] We can't control marketplace turbulence. We can control how we select and develop leaders and teams.

8. Prevent Recklessness, Not Risk Taking

Challenge: In 1977, the Foreign Corrupt Practices Act (FCPA) was passed, though it was largely ignored by prosecutors. In 2016, $2.43 billion in corporate fines and penalties were collected by the Department of Justice and the Securities and Exchange Commission for violations of the FCPA. Above and beyond fines, it is hard to quantify the cost of leadership distraction from day-to-day business activity defending against a Department of Justice investigation.[6]

It is not without reason that more regulations can lead companies to put in place more controls and more rules. Yet, an overreliance on rules creates a risk-averse culture at the very time that organizations need to take intelligent risks so they can grow. In addition, some rules merely create a check-box mentality that promotes the illusion of reducing risk without really doing so. While the rule of law is essential, too much compliance tightens controls and, at times, may have the unintended consequence of reducing trust. Innovation and growth depend on loosening controls and increasing trust.

Nugget: Our data demonstrate that effective leaders believe that virtue preserves an enterprise's reputation and protects its financial strength. When leaders support the development of virtue within the lives of their people—at work, at home, and in their communities—engagement increases. Our data demonstrate that people want permission to be virtuous. Rules don't inspire us. Aspirational virtues do. Informed people know rules; wise people know the exception to rules.

9. What Does Success Look Like? Engagement

Challenge: An engaged workforce is an incredible competitive advantage. Yet, as we have seen, only about 30 percent of a typical workforce is fully engaged, 50 percent is modestly engaged, and 20 percent is disengaged. If only 30 percent of a workforce is engaged, it is difficult to compete. Engagement and commitment are not something that good pay will fix.

Decades of research in knowledge-based work demonstrate that pay can be a source of dissatisfaction, not satisfaction. Searching for the right incentives for the wrong people is a doomed proposition.

Nugget: Pay matters, to be sure, and it is best to pay people enough so that they think about the work and stop thinking about the money. Motivation isn't bought. Motivation is cultivated by a compelling purpose, an opportunity for mastery, and empowerment to be self-directed.[7] This is why volunteers who are committed to a purpose bigger than themselves outperform mercenary conscripts who are looking out for themselves.

10. Pursue Progress, Not Perfection

Challenge: Character is not about idealism or pretending that we are better than we are. Every day, we are reminded that organizations and people are not always virtuous. The opposite is also true: we can often observe the presence of virtue. Every day, we can see people being cold toward one another. Antithetically, we also can find people caring for each other.

Nugget: Virtue is about human nature, not the laws of physics. We practice virtue. We don't master virtue. We can all become better than we used to be. We are all flawed people striving to be better people.

11. Character Is Learned

Challenge: Fixed-mindset leaders and teams believe that people either have character or they don't. They believe that character is a function of chemistry, the parents you picked, or the neighborhood where you were raised.

Nugget: The most exciting, optimistic, and powerful idea of *Exception to the Rule* is this: character is learned, practiced, and cultivated. Virtue is developed best when we feel responsible for our own growth. We are more motivated and perform best when we leverage our strengths and manage our weaknesses. And we develop faster still when we are part of a caring and cooperative culture.

12. Virtue Presents an Opportunity for Growth

Challenge: The frustrating news is that research on high performance and virtue is not widely known, and it is certainly not widely practiced in either the profit or nonprofit sectors. It starts with virtue as the common language. Without this language, we too often default to moral mediocrity rather than moral excellence.

Nugget: The good news is that we have clear evidence that virtue increases engagement, teamwork, and leadership growth. Virtue means excellence in human conduct. Virtue is what we look like when we are at our very best. This is why having character is every bit as important as learning to become an engineer, accountant, physician, attorney, nurse, teacher, artist, or scientist. We need leaders and teams who are not just competent in their craft, but who also practice character. Character is foundational to effective leadership and teamwork.

Simply put: character matters.

ENDNOTES

INTRODUCTION

1. Attributed to Thomas Merton, Trappist monk of the Abbey of Gethsemani, but Merton scholars cannot document the quotation.
2. G. A. Fava and N. Sonino, "Psychosomatic Medicine," *International Journal of Clinical Practice*, vol. 64, no. 8, July 2010.
3. Jack Hoban, personal interview with Peter Rea, April 15, 2017.
4. Oliver Wendell Holmes Jr., www.brainyquote.com/quotes/authors/o/oliver_wendell_holmes_sr.html.
5. W. Edwards Deming, www.brainyquote.com/quotes/authors/w/w_edwards_deming.html.
6. Grant Simmer, Philippe Presti, and Greg McGarlane (America's Cup Racing Team), personal interview with Peter Rea, March 2016.
7. *Aerospace Medicine Grand Rounds*, November 2016, http://pmch.utmb.edu/residency/grand-rounds.
8. Rishi Sikka, Julianne M. Morath, and Lucian Leape, "Editorial: The Quadruple Aim: Care, Health, Cost, and Meaning in Work," *BMJ Quality and Safety Online*, 2015, pp. 1–3, Doi: 10.1136/bmjqs-2015-004160.
9. Mark Twain, www.brainyquote.com/quotes/quotes/m/marktwain109624.html.
10. Douglas McGregor, *The Human Side of Enterprise*, McGraw-Hill, New York, 1960.
11. Ibid.
12. Gallup, *2013 State of the American Workplace Report: Employee Engagement Insights for U.S. Business Leaders*, September 22, 2014, www.gallup.com/services/176708/state-american-workplace.aspx.
13. John Gardner, "The Road to Self-Renewal," http://faculty-gsb.stanford.edu/aaker/pages/documents/johngardner-roadtoself-renewal2.pdf.

14. Stacey English and Susannah Hammond, Thomas Reuters, Annual Cost of Compliance Survey, https://risk.thomsonreuters.com/content/dam/openweb/documents/pdf/risk/report/cost-compliance-2016.pdf.

15. www.ibtimes.com/dodd-frank-rules-nearly-9000-pages-its-less-one -third-finished-726774.

16. NPR, "Behind the Shortage of Special Ed Teachers: Long Hours, Crushing Paperwork," www.npr.org/sections/ed/2015/11/09/436588372/behind-the-shortage-of-special-ed-teachers-long-hours-crushing -paperwork.

17. Randal Beck and Jim Harter, "Managers Account for 70% of Variance in Employee Engagement," www.gallup.com/businessjournal/182792/managers-account-variance-employee-engagement.aspx.

18. Susan Sorenson, "How Employee Engagement Drives Growth," www .gallup.com/businessjournal/163130/employee-engagement-drives -growth.aspx.

19. Michael Porter and Elizabeth Teisberg, *Redefining Health Care: Creating Value-Based Competition on Results*, Harvard Business School Publishing, Boston, May 25, 2006.

20. Daniel Kahneman, *Thinking, Fast and Slow,* Farrar, Straus and Giroux, New York, 2011, 295.

21. Mahatma Gandhi, www.goodreads.com/quotes/760902-we-but-mirror -the-world-all-the-tendencies-present-in.

22. Ralph Waldo Emerson, www.goodreads.com/quotes/11079-what-you-do -speaks-so-loudly-that-i-cannot-hear.

23. STJ Enterprises, http://stjent.pinnaclecart.com/index. php?p=product&id=439.

24. Voltaire, in *Candide*, June 8, 2009, http://files.libertyfund.org/pll/quotes /207.html.

25. https://en.wikipedia.org/wiki/Athena.

CHAPTER 1

1. Krista Tippett, *Becoming Wise: An Inquiry into the Mystery and Art of Living*, Penguin Random House, New York, 2016, 9.

2. Chevalier Louis de Jaucourt, "Hospitality," *The Encyclopedia of Diderot & d'Alembert Collaborative Translation Project*, translated by Sophie Bourgault, Michigan Publishing, University of Michigan Library, Ann Arbor, 2013. http://hdl.handle.net/2027/spo.did2222.0002.761.

3. Jeff Bertram, Northeast Ohio Reintegration Center, personal interview with Peter Rea, March 2015.

4. Jacqueline Emigh, "How Much Does Ohio Spend on Prisons?" Newsmax, http://www.newsmax.com/FastFeatures/prison-spending -ohio/2015/12/09/id/705221/.

5. David Jones, Director of Character Education, personal interview with Peter Rea, November 2012.
6. Ibid.
7. Victor (anonymous name for security purposes), personal interview with Peter Rea, February 2013.
8. Ibid.
9. John P. Kotter and James L. Heskett, *Corporate Culture and Performance*, Simon & Schuster, New York, 2011, 78.
10. Ibid.
11. Ronald Moomaw, Flight Surgeon and Psychiatrist, Johnson Space Center, personal interview with Peter Rea, December 2016.
12. Ibid.
13. Amy Adkins, "Employee Engagement in U.S. Stagnant in 2015," http://www.gallup.com/poll/188144/employee-engagement-stagnant-2015.aspx.

CHAPTER 2

1. Jody Gittell, *High Performance Healthcare: Use of the Power of Relationships to Achieve Quality, Efficiency, and Resilience*, McGraw-Hill, New York, 2009, 23.
2. Ibid.
3. Cleveland Clinic, Dr. William E. Lower, "What Is a Patient," *Cleveland Clinic*, 1921, http://my.clevelandclinic.org/star-imaging/patients/what-is-a-patient.
4. Ibid.
5. Denis Diderot, http://thinkexist.com/quotes/denis_diderot/.
6. John Hagel, John Seely Brown, and Tamara Samoylova, "Unlocking the Passion of the Explorer," *A Report in the 2013 Shift Index Series*, September 17, 2013, https://dupress.deloitte.com/dup-us-en/topics/talent/unlocking-the-passion-of-the-explorer.html.
7. Ibid.
8. Stephen Post and Jill Neimark, *Why Good Things Happen to Good People*, Broadway Books, New York, 2007, 14–18. Hereafter, cited as Post.
9. Adam Grant, *Give and Take: Why Helping Others Drives Our Success*, Penguin Books, New York, 2014.
10. Ibid., 29.
11. Ibid., 126.
12. Beth Kavelaris, Senior Vice President, Director of Culture & Integration, Robert W. Baird & Company, personal interview with Peter Rea, February 2013.
13. Brian Powers, "Doing the Voice of the Customer," Baldwin Wallace

College Lecture, Berea, OH, October 2008. Hereafter, cited as Powers, VOC.

14. *Beaches*, film directed by Garry Marshall, Buena Vista Pictures, Burbank, CA, 1988.

15. Powers, VOC.

16. William Aulet, "Entrepreneurship Development Program," MIT Management Executive Education, January 2015.

17. Charles Duhigg, "What Google Learned from Its Quest to Build the Perfect Team," *New York Times Magazine*, February 25, 2016, http://www.nytimes.com/2016/02/28/magazine/what-google-learned-from-its-quest-to-build-the-perfect-team.html. Hereafter, cited as Duhigg.

18. Ibid.

19. Ibid.

20. Paul Bloom, *Just Babies: The Origins of Good and Evil*, Crown, New York, 2013, 22.

21. Jeffrey H. Dyer, Hal B. Gregersen, and Clayton M. Christensen, "The Innovator's DNA," https://hbr.org/2009/12/the-innovators-dna.

22. David Brooks, "The Moral Bucket List," *New York Times*, April 11, 2015, http://www.nytimes.com/2015/04/12/opinion/sunday/david-brooks-the-moral-bucket-list.html.

23. Vivian Giang, "The 'Two Pizza Rule' Is Jeff Bezos' Secret to Productive Meetings," *Business Insider*, October 29, 2013, http://www.business insider.com/jeff-bezos-two-pizza-rule-for-productive-meetings-2013–10.

24. Janet Choi, "The Science Behind Why Jeff Bezos's Two-Pizza Team Rule Works," *I Done This Blog*, last modified September 24, 2014, http://blog.idonethis.com/two-pizza-team.

25. P. Klimek, R. Hanel, and S. Thurner, "Parkinson's Law Quantified: Three Investigations of Bureaucratic Inefficiency," https://arxiv.org/abs/0808.1684.

26. G. P. Pisano, R. M. J. Bohmer, and A. C. Edmondson, "Organizational Differences in Rates of Learning: Evidence from the Adoption of Minimally Invasive Cardiac Surgery," *Management Science*, vol. 47, no. 6, 2001, 752–768.

27. S. Wheelan, C. N. Burchill, and F. Tilin, "The Link Between Teamwork and Patients' Outcomes in Intensive Care Units," *American Journal of Critical Care*, vol. 12, no. 6, November 2003, 527–534.

28. P. B. O'Donovan, M. Schenk, K. Lim, N. Obuchowski, and J. K. Stoller, "Evaluation of the Reliability of Computed Tomographic Criteria Used in the Diagnosis of Round Atelectasis," *Journal of Thoracic Imaging*, vol. 12, no. 1, January 1997, 54–58.

29. Post, p. 269.

30. Paul Bloom, *Just Babies: The Origins of Good and Evil*, Crown, New York, 2013, 30.

31. Jean M. Twenge and Keith Campbell, *The Narrcissim Epidemic*, Atria Books, New York, 2010, 126.
32. Susan A. Wheelan, Christian N. Burchill, and Felice Tilin, "The Link Between Teamwork and Patients' Outcomes in Intensive Care Units." http://ajcc.aacnjournals.org/content/12/6/527.full.pdf+html.
33. Martin E. P. Seligman, *Flourish: A Visionary New Understanding of Happiness and Well-Being*, Atria Books, New York, 2012, 20.
34. Duhigg.
35. Adapted from Amy Edmondson, "The Competitive Imperative of Learning," Harvard Business Review, July-August 2013.

CHAPTER 3

1. Winston Churchill, BrainyQuote.com, Xplore, Inc., 2016, https://www.brainyquote.com/quotes/quotes/w/winstonchu124653.html.
2. "Malala, at Youth Takeover Event, Says 'Weakness, Fear, Hopelessness Died' After Assassination Attempt, Giving Rise to Strength, Power, Courage," United Nations, July 12, 2013, http://www.un.org/press/en/2013/dev3009.doc.htm.
3. "Blowing the whistle on bad behavior takes more than guts," Michigan News, University of Michigan, April 29, 2013.
4. Eugene O'Kelly, *Chasing Daylight: How My Forthcoming Death Transformed My Life*, McGraw-Hill, New York, 2008, 1.
5. "Fortune 500 Extinction," January 6, 2012, http://csinvesting.org/2012/01/06/fortune-500-extinction/.
6. Harold Wilson, "Speech to the Consultative Assembly of the Council of Europe, Strasbourg, France, January 23, 1967, reported in *New York Times,* January 24, 1967, 12.
7. Michael Lewis, *The Undoing Project: A Friendship That Changed Our Minds*, W.W. Norton, New York, 2016. See https://www.amazon.com/Undoing-Project-Friendship-Changed-Minds/dp/0393254593.
8. Edward B. Roberts, Fiona Murray, and J. Daniel Kim, *Entrepreneurship and Innovation at MIT: Continuing Global Growth and Impact*, Massachusetts Institute of Technology, Cambridge, December 2015, http://web.mit.edu/innovate/entrepreneurship2015.pdf.
9. William Aulet, "Entrepreneurship Development Program," MIT Management Executive Education, January 2015.
10. Brené Bown, "The Power of Vulnerability," TED Talk, Houston, June 2010, https://www.ted.com/talks/brene_brown_on_vulnerability.
11. Theodore Roosevelt, "Citizenship in a Republic" speech at Sorbonne, Paris, France, April 23, 1910, http://www.theodore-roosevelt.com/trsorbonnespeech.html.
12. Thomas Gilovich and Victoria Husted Medvec, "The Experience of

Regret: What, When, and Why," *Psychological Review*, vol. 102, no. 2, April 1995, http://dx.doi.org/10.1037/0033–295X.102.2.379.

13. Charles Kiefer, personal interview with Peter Rea, March 2015. Hereafter, cited as Kiefer.

14. Sydney Finkelstein, *Why Smart Executives Fail: And What You Can Learn from Their Mistakes*, Portfolio, New York, 2004.

15. Walt Kelly. BrainyQuote.com, Xplore Inc., 2016, https://www.brainy quote.com/quotes/quotes/w/waltkelly114887.html.

16. Carmen Medina, "The Heart of Innovation: Building Trust and Encouraging Risk," CIG Summit, Baldwin-Wallace College, Berea, OH, April 12, 2012.

17. Ibid.

18. *Life of Brian*, film directed by Terry Jones, London: HandMade Films, DVD, 2004.

19. Donald R. Cressey, *Other People's Money: Study in the Social Psychology of Embezzlement*, Patterson Smith, Montclair, NJ: 1973, 30.

20. Mary C. Gentile, *Giving Voice to Values: How to Speak Your Mind When You Know What's Right*, Yale University Press, New Haven, CT, 2012, 26. Hereafter, cited as Gentile.

21. Panel Discussion on Character Applied to Business and Military, Character Education Partnership Conference, Washington, D.C., November 1, 2014.

22. Gentile, 94.

23. Daniel Kahneman, *Thinking, Fast and Slow*, Farrar, Straus and Giroux, New York, 2013, 295.

24. Virtue Seminars for Parker Hannifin Controllers, Cleveland, London, Frankfurt, Shanghai, 2015.

25. Gentile, 60.

26. Adapted from Jack Hoban's Ethical Warrior Program, New Jersey, 2013.

27. Hugh Tredennick, ed., *Aristotle*, http://www.goodreads.com/quotes /1229147-virtue-lies-in-our-power-and-similarly-so-does-vice.

28. Angela Duckworth, "Grit: The Power of Passion and Perseverance," TED Talk Education, April 2013, https://www.ted.com/talks/angela_lee _duckworth_grit_the_power_of_passion_and_perseverance/transcript ?language=en.

29. John Hagel, @jhagel, January 2, 2016, https://twitter.com/jhagel/status /683295782347276292.

30. George Bonnano, *The Other Side of Sadness: What the New Science of Bereavement Tells Us About Life After Loss*, Basic Books, New York, 2010, 13.

31. Ibid., 34–35.

32. Ibid., 183.

33. Martin E. P. Seligman, *Learned Optimism: How to Change Your Mind and Your Life*, New York: Vintage Books, 2006, 64–70.
34. Lawrence G. Calhoun and Richard G. Tedeschi, *Posttraumatic Growth in Clinical Practice*, Routledge, London, 2012, 19.
35. Kiefer.

CHAPTER 4

1. Robert McAfee Brown, *Unexpected News: Reading the Bible with Third World Eyes*, Westminster John Knox Press, Louisville, 1984, 19.
2. Chuck Joyner, *Advanced Concepts in Defensive Tactics: A Survival Guide for Law Enforcement*, Boca Raton: CRC Press, Boca Raton, FL, 2010, 18.
3. Personal, firsthand experience by Peter Rea in Jack E. Hoban's Seminar, *The Ethical Warrior Program*, New Jersey, September 2013.
4. Ibid.
5. Langdon Gilkey, *Shantung Compound: The Story of Men and Women Under Pressure*, Harper & Row, New York, 1966, 135.
6. Atul Gawande, *Being Mortal: Medicine and What Matters in the End*, Picador, London, 2015, 103.
7. Joseph Badaracco presentation, Mark Collier Enduring Question Lecture Series, Baldwin Wallace College, October 17, 2010.
8. Michael Miller, "Enron's Ethics Code Reads Like Fiction," *Columbus Business First*, April 1, 2002, http://www.bizjournals.com/columbus/stories/2002/04/01/editorial3.html.
9. Jerry Useem, "What Was Volkswagen Thinking?" *Atlantic*, January/February 2016, http://www.theatlantic.com/magazine/archive/2016/01/what-was-volkswagen-thinking/419127/.
10. Abraham Lincoln, BrainyQuote.com, Xplore, Inc., 2016, https://www.brainyquote.com/quotes/quotes/a/abrahamlin101343.html.
11. Michael Lewis, "Don't Eat Fortune's Cookie," Princeton University's 2012 Baccalaureate Remarks, Princeton University, June 3, 2012, *News at Princeton*, https://www.princeton.edu/main/news/archive/S33/87/54K53/.
12. David Dubois, "How to Increase Leaders' Moral Authority," *INSEAD*, November 19, 2015, http://knowledge.insead.edu/leadership-organisations/how-to-increase-leaders-moral-authority-4372.
13. *The Big Short*, directed by Adam McKay, 2015; Beverly Hills, CA: Plan B Entertainment, DVD, 2016.
14. Michael Porter and Mark Kramer, "Creating Shared Value," *Harvard Business Review*, January 2011.
15. David Kiron, Doug Palmer, Anh Nguyen Phillips, and Robert Berkman, "Social Business: Shifting out of First Gear," *Deloitte University Press*,

August 2013, https://dupress.deloitte.com/dup-us-en/topics/emerging
-technologies/the-burdens-of-the-past.html#endnote-sup-7.

16. John Hagel, Deloitte Shift Index, Success or Struggle: ROA as a True
Measure of Business Performance, https://www2.deloitte.com/us/en/
pages/center-for-the-edge/articles/shift-index-return-on-assets-business
-performance.html.

17. Adapted from Kim Cameron and John Smart, "Maintaining
Effectiveness Amid Downsizing and Decline in Institutions of Higher
Education," *Research in Higher Education*, vol. 39, no. 1, 1998, http://
biblioteca.esec.pt/cdi/ebooks/docs/Maintainning_effect.pdf.

18. Ibid.

19. Gallup, *"Strengths-Based Leadership,* Gallup's Leadership Research,"
http://strengths.gallup.com/110251/gallups-leadership-research.aspx.

20. Angela Duckworth, Kim Cameron, Ia Ko, and Peter Rea, "Taking a
Positive Approach to Create Leadership and Organizational Excellence,"
Society for Industrial and Organizational Psychology Meetings,
Philadelphia, April 2015.

21. Peter Rea, Alan Kolp, Wendy Ritz, and Michelle D. Steward, "Corporate
Ethics Can't Be Reduced to Compliance," *Harvard Business Review*,
April 29, 2016, https://hbr.org/2016/04/corporate-ethics-cant-be
-reduced-to-compliance.

22. 2016 Edelman Trust Barometer, Annual Global Study, http://www
.edelman.com/insights/intellectual-property/2016-edelman-trust
-barometer/.

23. Ibid.

24. 2016 Edelman Trust Barometer: Executive Summary, https://www
.scribd.com/doc/295815519/2016-Edelman-Trust-Barometer-Executive
-Summary.

25. Porter and Kramer, "Creating Shared Value."

26. Ibid.

27. Greater Cleveland Regional Transit Authority, "RTA Adds 60 New CNG
Buses to Its Fleet," *RTA Website*, May 19, 2015, http://www.riderta.com/
news/may-19-rta-adds-90-new-cng-buses-fleet.

28. Chic-fil-A leaders, personal interviews with Peter Rea, March 2016.

29. Ibid.

30. Ibid.

31. Ibid.

32. Paul Tillich, *Dynamics of Faith*, HarperOne, San Franciso, 2009, 1–3.
Hereafter, cited as Tillich.

33. Patti Neighmond, "People Who Feel They Have a Purpose in Life Live
Longer," *Health News from NPR*, July 28, 2014, http://www.npr.org
/sections/health-shots/2014/07/28/334447274/people-who-feel-they
-have-a-purpose-in-life-live-longer.

34. Tillich, 105–106
35. Viktor E. Frankl, *Man's Search for Meaning,* Beacon Press, Boston, 2006, 88. Hereafter, cited as Frankl.
36. Ibid.
37. Jim Collins, "Ideas for Tomorrow: Jim Collins," Cleveland Clinic's Ideas for Tomorrow speaker series program, Cleveland, December 8, 2015.
38. "Chariot Allegory," *Wikipedia*, last modified December 15, 2016, https://en.wikipedia.org/wiki/Chariot_Allegory.
39. Ibid.
40. Ibid.
41. Ibid.
42. Jonathan Haidt, *The Happiness Hypothesis: Finding Modern Truth in Ancient Wisdom*, Basic Books, New York, 2006, 11.
43. Benjamin Franklin. BrainyQuote.com, Xplore, Inc., https://www.brainyquote.com/quotes/quotes/b/benjaminfr132478.html, accessed December 21, 2016.
44. Dominic Gover, "Nelson Mandela: Four Acts of Forgiveness That Showed South Africa Path Away from Apartheid," *International Business Times*, December 6, 2013, http://www.ibtimes.co.uk/nelson-mandela-forgiveness-south-africa-apartheid-528153.
45. Frankl, 99.
46. Collaboration with Mike McCullough, University of Miami, to create benefit finding exercise, 2014.
47. T. S. Eliot, "The Dry Salvages," in *The Four Quartets*, 1st ed. (1943), later published by Houghton Mifflin Harcourt, Boston, 1971.
48. Jean M. Twenge, *The Narcissism Epidemic: Living in the Age of Entitlement*, Atria Books, New York, 2010, 11.
49. Andrea L. Merrill, MD, Ashish K. Jha, MD, MPH, and Justin B. Dimick, MD, "Clinical Effect of Surgical Volume," *New England Journal of Medicine*, April 7, 2016, DOI: 10.1056/NEJMclde1513948.
50. Jack E. Hoban, *The Ethical Warrior: Values, Morals and Ethics for Life, Work and Service*, RGI Media and Publications, Spring Lake, NJ, 2012, 27.

CHAPTER 5

1. "&Beyond," Phinda Private Game Reserve, http://www.andbeyond.com/south-africa.htm.
2. Meredith Palmer, &Beyond naturalist, personal interview with Peter Rea, Phinda, South Africa, October 2015.
3. Ibid.
4. Ibid.
5. Jim Collins, "Building Companies to Last," *Inc. Special Issue: The State*

of Small Business, 1995, http://www.jimcollins.com/article_topics/
articles/building-companies.html.

6. F. Scott Fitzgerald, "The Crack-Up," *Esquire*, February-April 1936, http://
www.esquire.com/news-politics/a4310/the-crack-up/#ixzz1Fvs5lu8w.

7. Aristotle, "Nichomachean Ethics," in *The Basic Works of Aristotle*,
Random House, New York, 1941, 1026.

8. Robert Halley Wyllie, *The Role of the Virtue of Prudence in the Ethics of
St. Thomas Aquinas*, University of Natal Press, Cape Town, 1965, 6.

9. Stephen S. Hall, *Wisdom: From Philosophy to Neuroscience*, Vintage
Books, New York, 2011, 77.

10. Remez Sasson, *The Amazing Quotes of Lao Tzu*, October 2012, http://
www.successconsciousness.com/free_ebooks/lao_tzu_quotes.pdf.

11. Tal Ben-Shahar, "Introduction to Positive Psychology," http://whole
beinginstitute.com/course-overview/positive-psychology-intro/.

12. Charlie Munger, *Poor Charlie's Almanack: The Wit and Wisdom of
Charles T. Munger*, Donning, Virginia Beach, VA, 2005, 46–49.

13. "Employee Engagement in US Stagnant in 2015," http://www.gallup
.com/poll/188144/employee-engagement-stagnant-2015.aspx.

14. "The Strengths of Leadership," *Gallup Business Journal*, February 26,
2009, http://businessjournal.gallup.com/content/113956/Strengths
-Leadership.aspx.

15. Tomas Chamorro-Premuzic, "Does Money Really Affect Motivation?
A Review of the Research," *Harvard Business Review*, April 10, 2013,
https://hbr.org/2013/04/does-money-really-affect-motiv.

16. Susan Sorenson, "How Employee Engagement Drives Growth," *Gallup
Business Journal*, June 20, 2013, http://www.gallup.com/businessjournal
/163130/employee-engagement-drives-growth.aspx.

17. Brian Brim and Jim Asplund, "Driving Engagement by Focusing on
Strength," *Gallup Business Journal*, November 12, 2009, http://www
.gallup.com/businessjournal/124214/driving-engagement-focusing
-strengths.aspx.

18. Alexia Elejalde-Ruiz, "Hiring Bias Study: Résumés with Black, White,
Hispanic Names Treated the Same," *Chicago Tribune*, May 4, 2016,
http://www.chicagotribune.com/business/ct-bias-hiring-0504-biz
-20160503-story.html.

19. Kristin Clarke, "In Hiring, Beware Your Unconscious Bias," http://
www.associationcareerhq.org/recruitment-strategies/beware-your
-unconscious-bias.

20. "Similar-To-Me Effect in the Workplace," *Psych 424 Blog*, Pennsylvania
State University, https://sites.psu.edu/aspsy/2015/04/17/similar-to-me
-effect-in-the-workplace/.

21. Life at Google, *Google Video on Unconscious Bias: Making the*

Unconscious Conscious, YouTube video, 3:58 minutes, published September 2014, https://www.youtube.com/watch?v=NW5s_-Nl3JE.

22. Ibid.

23. Adam Grant, "Are you a giver or a taker? TED Talk, January 2017, https://www.youtube.com/watch?v=YyXRYgjQXX0. Hereafter, cited as Grant TED Talk.

24. Carol S. Dweck, *Mindset: New Psychology of Success*, Random House, New York, 2006, 31. Hereafter, cited as Dweck, *Mindset.*

25. Angela Duckworth, *Grit: the Power of Passion and Perseverance*, Schribner, NewYork, 2016, 233. Hereafter, cited as Duckworth, *Grit.*

26. Robert Emmons, *Gratitude Works: A 21-Day for Creating Emotional Prosperity*, Jossey-Bass, San Francisco, 2013, 20. Hereafter, cited as Emmons.

27. Grant TED Talk.

28. Angela Duckworth, "Grit: The Power and Passion and Perseverance," TED Talks Education, https://www.ted.com/talks/angela_lee _duckworth_grit_the_power_of_passion_and_perseverance.

29. Duckworth, *Grit*, 123.

30. Carol Dweck, "Carol Dweck Revisits the 'Growth Mindset,'" *Education Week*, September 22, 2015, http://www.edweek.org/ew/articles/2015/09 /23/carol-dweck-revisits-the-growth-mindset.html.

31. Ibid.

32. Emmons, 101.

33. Laszlo Bock, *Work Rules!: Insights from Inside Google That Will Transform How You Live and Lead*, Twelve, New York, 2015, 92. Hereafter, cited as Bock.

34. Rick Randolph, "Self-fulling Prophecy of Expectations," http://forging leaders.com/the-self-fulfilling-prophecy-of-expectations/.

35. Ibid.

36. Jeff Fermin, "13 Disappointing Performance Appraisals Facts You Really Need to Know," *Business 2 Community*, September 3, 2014, http:// www.business2community.com/human-resources/13-disappointing -performance-appraisals-facts-really-need-know-infographic -0996111##iT41YTuzLgziodTQ.97.

37. "Time and Motion Study," *Wikipedia*, last modified October 16, 2016, https://en.wikipedia.org/wiki/Time_and_motion_study.

38. Bock, 150.

39. Daniel H. Pink, "The Puzzle of Motivation," TED Talk, https://video .search.yahoo.com/yhs/search?fr=yhs-mozilla-002&hsimp=yhs-002 &hspart=mozilla&p=daniel+pink+ted+talk#id=1&vid=d42e7c8ad68d4b 50249fe0265e5258c6&action=click.

40. Lisa Barry, Stacia Garr, and Andy Liakopoulos, "Performance

Management Is Broken," *Deloitte University Press*, March 4, 2014, http://dupress.com/articles/hc-trends-2014-performance-management/?id=gx:el:dc:dup677:cons:awa:hct14.

41. William Aulet, "Entrepreneurship Development Program," MIT Management Executive Education, January 2015.

42. Mike Smith, "If you only had one job interview question to ask?" October 18, 2009, http://backwest.com/if-you-only-had-one-job -interview-question-to-ask-revisited/.

43. Carol Dweck, "The Power of Believing That You Can Improve," TED Talk, November 2014, https://www.ted.com/talks/carol_dweck_the _power_of_believing_that_you_can_improve.

44. Ibid.

45. Christine Gross-Loh, "How Praise Became a Consolation Prize," *Atlantic*, December 16, 2016, https://www.theatlantic.com/education/archive/2016/12/how-praise-became-a-consolation-prize/510845/.

46. T. S. Eliot, "The Dry Salvages," in *The Four Quartets*, 1st ed., (1943), later published by Houghton Mifflin Harcourt, Boston, 1971.

CHAPTER 6

1. Rorke Denver, *Calm Is Contagious*, February 20, 2015, https://www .youtube.com/watch?v=i5Clwch7meU. Hereafter, cited as Denver.

2. St. Thomas Aquinas, *Summa Theologica*, vol. 43, Blackfriars, London, 1968, 19.

3. Alfred F. Loomis, "Ah, Your Majesty, There Is No Second," *American Heritage*, vol. 9, no. 5, 1958, 4.

4. Stu Woo, "Against the Wind," *Wall Street Journal*, February 2014, https://www.wsj.com/articles/SB10001424052702303393804579312803 907849782.

5. Philippe Presti and Grant Simmer Oracle Team USA, personal inter- view with Peter Rea. May 13, 2016.

6. Denver.

7. Peter Rea, *Aerospace Medicine Grand Rounds*, NASA, December 2016.

8. Interview, Dr. Dehra Glueck, University of Washington at St. Louis Medical School, February 6, 2016.

9. Kelly McGonigal, *The Willpower Instinct*, https://www.youtube.com/ watch?v=V5BXuZL1HAg.

10. "Sikhism," http://www.bbc.co.uk/religion/religions/sikhism/.

11. Ibid.

12. Steelcase, "Think Better," *360 Magazine*, June 14, 2015, https://www .steelcase.com/insights/articles/think-better/.

13. NPR, "The Myth of Multitasking," *Talk of the Nation*, May 10, 2013, http://www.npr.org/2013/05/10/182861382/the-myth-of-multitasking.

14. Ibid.
15. Bianca Bosker, "The Binge Breaker," *The Atlantic*, November, 2016, https://www.theatlantic.com/magazine/archive/2016/11/the-binge -breaker/501122/.
16. Eun Joo Kim, Blake Pellman, and Jeansok J. Kim, "Stress Effects on the Hippocampus: A Critical Review," *Learning Memory*, September 22, 2015, DOI: 10.1101/lm.037291.114.
17. Ibid.
18. Abiola Keller, Kristin Litzelman, Lauren E. Wisk, Torsheika Maddox, Erika Rose Cheng, Paul D. Creswell, and Whitney P. Witt, "Does the Perception That Stress Affects Health Matter? The Association with Health and Mortality," *Health Psychology*, vol. 31, no. 5, December 26, 2011, http://dx.doi.org/10.1037/a0026743.
19. Ibid., 31.
20. Don Joseph Goewey, "85 Percent of What We Worry About Never Happens," *Huffington Post*, blog, August 25, 2015, http://www .huffingtonpost.com/don-joseph-goewey-/85-of-what-we-worry-about _b_8028368.html.
21. Elizabeth Gilbert, *Eat, Pray, Love: One Woman's Search for Everything Across Italy, India and Indonesia*, Riverhead Books, New York, 2007.
22. Seph Fontane Pennock, "Positive Psychology 1504: Harvard's Groundbreaking Course," *Positive Psychology*, June 16, 2015, https:// positivepsychologyprogram.com/harvard-positive-psychology-course -1504.
23. Doris Kearns Goodwin. "Lessons from Past Presidents." TED Talk, February 2008, https://www.ted.com/talks/doris_kearns_goodwin_on _learning_from_past_presidents.
24. Martin Buber, *I-Thou*, Touchstone, New York, 1996.
25. David Cooperrider, "The Concentration Effect of Strengths," *David Cooperrider and Associates blog*, April 22, 2012, http://www.david cooperrider.com/2012/04/22/the-concentration-effect-of-strengths/.
26. Robert Wright, *The Moral Animal: Why We Are The Way We Are: The New Science of Evolutionary Psychology*, Vintage Books, New York, 1994, 23.
27. Anders Ericcson and Robert Pool, *Peak Performance: Secrets from the New Science of Expertise*, Houghton Mifflin Harcourt, New York, 2016.
28. Wright, pp. 97–98.
29. Dan Ariely, interview with Adam Grant, "The Honest Truth About Dishonesty," *knowledge@wharton*, http://knowledge.wharton.upenn.edu /article/dan-ariely-dishonestys-slippery-slope/.
30. "Best Practices in Medical Education," Grand Rounds, Cleveland Clinic.

CHAPTER 7

1. Martin Luther King, Jr., BrainyQuote.com, https://www.brainyquote
   .com/quotes/quotes/m/martinluth297522.html.
2. "Hope," *Concise Oxford English Dictionary*, 11th ed., Oxford University,
   Oxford, 2005.
3. District Six Museum staff members, personal interviews with Peter Rea,
   Cape Town, South Africa, July 2016.
4. Christo Brand and friends, Robben Island Tour, personal interview with
   Peter Rea, Robben Island, South Africa, July 2016.
5. Ibid.
6. Iziko South African Museum, Cape Town, South Africa, July 2016.
7. Jalaluddin Rumi, http://www.goodreads.com/quotes/103315-the-wound
   -is-the-place-where-the-light-enters-you.
8. Bessel Van Der Kolk, "Trauma and Resilience Land in Our Bodies," *On
   Being*, July 25, 2016, https://onbeing.org/programs/trauma-resilience
   -land-bodies-bessel-van-der-kolk/.
9. Sebastian Junger, *Tribe: On Homecoming and Belonging*, Hachette, New
   York, 2016, 63. Hereafter, cited as Junger.
10. Ibid., 67.
11. Richard Tedeschi and Lawrence Calhoun, Posttraumatic Stress
    Research Group, University of North Carolina, Charlotte, https://ptgi
    .uncc.edu/ptg-research-group/.
12. Junger, 10.
13. Ibid., 22.
14. Dietrich Bonhoeffer, *Life Together: A Discussion of Christian Fellowship*,
    trans. John W. Doberstein, HarperCollins, San Francisco, 1954, 26.
15. William F. Lynch, *Images of Hope: Imagination as Healer of the
    Helpless*, University of Notre Dame Press, Notre Dame, IN, 1965, 32.
16. Dante Alighieri, *The Divine Comedy*, The Carlyle-Okey-Wicksteed
    Translation, Modern Library, New York, 1950, 22.
17. Victor E. Frankl, *Man's Search for Meaning*, Perseus, New York, 2000), 16.
18. Ibid., 6.
19. Ibid., 59.
20. Marvin R. Weisbord, *Organizational Diagnosis: A Workbook of Theory
    and Practice*, Basic Books, New York, 1978, 170.
21. Marvin R. Weisbord, "Why Organization Development Hasn't Worked
    (So Far) in Medical Centers.," *Health Care Management Review*, Spring
    1976, http://journals.lww.com/hcmrjournal/Abstract/1976/00120/
    Why_Organization_Development_Hasn_t_Worked__So.5.aspx.
22. D. Wheeler and J. K. Stoller, "Teamwork, Teambuilding, and Leadership
    in Respiratory and Health Care," *Canadian Journal of Respiratory
    Therapy*, Spring 2011, https://portals.clevelandclinic.org/Portals/65/
    documents/other/TeamworkTeambuildinginRespiratory.pdf.

23. James K. Stoller, "Developing Physician-Leaders: A Call to Action," *Journal of General Internal Medicine*, May 20, 2009, 10.1007/ s11606–009–1007–8.

24. Gimli, *The Lord of the Rings: The Two Towers*, film directed by Peter Jackson, 2002; USA: New Line Cinema, 2002.

25. Martin E. Seligman, "Learned Helplessness," *Annual Review of Medicine*, vol. 23, February 1972, 407–412, http://www.annualreviews .org/doi/abs/10.1146/annurev.me.23.020172.002203.

26. Ibid.

27. Martin E. P. Seligman, "Building Resilience," *Harvard Business Review*, April 2011, https://hbr.org/2011/04/building-resilience.

28. Angela Duckworth, *Grit: The Power of Passion and Perseverance*, Schribner, New York, 2016, 168.

29. John C. Maxwell, ed., NIV, *The Maxwell Leadership Bible*, Thomas Maxwell, Scotland, 2014, 207.

30. Benjamin Franklin, BrainyQuote.com, Xplore, Inc., 2016, https://www .brainyquote.com/quotes/quotes/b/benjaminfr105927.html.

31. Abraham Lincoln, BrainyQuote.com, Xplore, Inc., 2016, https://www .brainyquote.com/quotes/quotes/a/abrahamlin103270.html.

32. Panel Discussion on Character Applied to Business and Military, Character Education Partnership Conference, Washington, D.C., November 1, 2014.

33. Marcus Tullius Cicero, BrainyQuote.com, Xplore Inc, 2016. https:// www.brainyquote.com/quotes/quotes/m/marcustull122152.html.

34. Robert Emmons and Michael McCullough, *The Psychology of Gratitude*, Oxford University Press, Oxford, 2004, 112.

35. Heidi Grant Halvorson, "Stop Making Gratitude All About You," *Harvard Business Review*, June 29, 2016, https://hbr.org/2016/06/stop -making-gratitude-all-about-you.

36. Emmons, *Thanks!*, Jossey-Bass, San Francisco, 2013, 52.

37. Martin E. P. Seligman, *Flourish: A Visionary Understanding of Happiness and Well-Being*, Free Press, New York, 2011, 41–42.

38. Robert Emmons, *Gratitude Works: A 21-Day Program for Creating Emotional Prosperity*, Jossey-Bass, San Francisco, 2013, 51.

39. Maya Angelou, AZquotes.com, http://www.azquotes.com/quote/797890 (accessed December 21, 2016).

CHAPTER 8

1. "Clayton Christensen's 'How Will You Measure Your Life?'," *Harvard Business School*, May 9, 2012, http://hbswk.hbs.edu/item/clayton -christensens-how-will-you-measure-your-life.

2. Michael Barbaro and Justin Gillis, "Wal-Mart at Forefront of Hurricane

Relief," *Washington Post,* September 6, 2005, http://www.washington post.com/wp-dyn/content/article/2005/09/05/AR2005090501598.html.

3. Ujala Sehgal, "16 Facts About Walmart That Will Blow Your Mind," *Business Insider,* October 2010, http://www.businessinsider.com/16 -walmart-facts.

4. "Working at Walmart," http://corporate.walmart.com/our-story /working-at-walmart.

5. Marc Gunther, "Walmart Is Slapping Itself on the Back for Sustainability, but It Still Has a Way to Go," *Guardian*, November 18, 2015, https://www.theguardian.com/sustainable-business/2015/nov /18/walmart-climate-change-carbon-emissions-renewabe-energy -environment.

6. Clare Cain Miller and Stephanie Clifford, "To Catch Up, Walmart Moves to Amazon Turf," *New York Times,* October 19, 2013, http:// www.nytimes.com/2013/10/20/technology/to-catch-up-walmart-moves -to-amazon-turf.html?mcubz=0.

7. Albert Einstein, BrainyQuote.com, Xplore, Inc., 2016, https://swww .brainyquote.com/quotes/quotes/a/alberteins130982.html.

8. Jessica Leber, "Walmarts New High-tech Labs: You're not in Arkansas Anymore, MIT Technology Review, https://www.technologyreview .com/s/429589/walmarts-new-high-tech-labs-youre-not-in-arkansas -anymore/.

9. Walmart Labs, https://www.crunchbase.com/organization/walmart -ecommerce#/entity.

10. Louis Gerstner, *Who Says Elephants Can't Dance,* Harper Business, New York, 2002, 36.

11. "What Followers Want From Leaders," *Gallup Business Journal,* January 8, 2009, http://www.gallup.com/businessjournal/113542/what -followers-want-from-leaders.aspx.

12. Tom Rath, *Strengths Based Leadership: Great Leaders, Teams, and Why People Follow,* Gallup Press, New York, 2008.

13. James I. Merlino and Ananth Raman, "Health Care's Service Fanatics," *Harvard Business Review*, May 2013, https://hbr.org/2013/05/health -cares-service-fanatics.

14. David T. Morgenthaler, Speech to Baldwin Wallace College, *Cleveland Plain Dealer*, March 2006, http://www.cleveland.com/quiet-crisis/2006 /03/david_t_morgenthalers_speech_t.html.

15. Intuit, "Corporate Profile," http://www.intuit.com/company/profile/.

16. Hugh Molotsi, Intuit Tour) personal interview with Peter Rea, March 2015.

17. A. G. Lafley, P&G CEO, personal interview with Alan Kolp and Peter Rea, July 2006.

18. George Day, "Is it Real? Can We Win? Is it Worth Doing?: Managing Risk and Reward in an Innovation Portfolio," *Harvard Business Review*, December 2007, https://hbr.org/2007/12/is-it-real-can-we-win-is-it -worth-doing-managing-risk-and-reward-in-an-innovation-portfolio.
19. Artashes Gazarian, Lithuanian consultant, personal interview with Alan Kolp and Peter Rea, March 2007.
20. Mark Kirk, "Leadership Competence, Character and Power," Baldwin Wallace College, Berea, OH, October 28, 2002.
21. Charlie Keifer, MIT, personal interview with Peter Rea at Cleveland, OH, May 2015.
22. Peter Rea, Alan Kolp, Wendy Ritz, and Michelle D. Steward, "Corporate Ethics Can't Be Reduced to Compliance," *Harvard Business Review*, April 29, 2016, https://hbr.org/2016/04/corporate-ethics-cant-be -reduced-to-compliance.

CHAPTER 9

1. Ken Makovsky, "Is Technology Exceeding Humanity?," *Forbes*, May 7, 2012, https://www.forbes.com/sites/kenmakovsky/2012/05/07/is -technology-exceeding-humanity/#535454416ea3.
2. *Number of Jobs Held, Labor Market Activity, and Earnings Growth Among the Youngest Baby Boomers Results from a Longitudinal Survey*, Bureau of Labor Statistics, U.S. Department of Labor, March 31, 2015, https://www.bls.gov/news.release/pdf/nlsoy.pdf.
3. Ira Wolfe, "65 Percent of Today's Students Will Be Employed in Jobs That Don't Exist Yet," *Success Performance Solutions*, August 26, 2013, https://www.successperformancesolutions.com/65-percent-of-todays -students-will-be-employed-in-jobs-that-dont-exist-yet/.
4. Peter J. Gomes, *The Good Life: Truths That Last in Times of Need*, HarperCollins, San Francisco, 2002, 125.
5. Robert Waldinger, "What Makes a Good Life? Lessons from the Longest Study on Happiness," TED Talk, November 2015, https://www.ted.com/ talks/robert_waldinger_what_makes_a_good_life_lessons_from_the _longest_study_on_happiness.
6. Christopher Peterson and Martin Seligman, *Character Strengths and Virtues: A Handbook and Classification*, Oxford University Press, Oxford, 2004.
7. Ibid., 325–335.
8. Martin E. P. Seligman, *Flourish: a Visionary Understanding of Happiness and Well-Being*, Free Press, New York, 2011, 24–25.
9. Mark Shapiro, President, Cleveland Indians, personal interview with Alan Kolp and Peter Rea, November, 2007.

10. Panel Discussion on Character Applied to Business and Military, Character Education Partnership Conference, Washington, D.C., November 1, 2014.

11. Ibid.

12. Victor J. Strecher, *Life on Purpose: How Living for What Matters Most Changes Everything*, HarperOne, New York, 2016, 18.

13. R. Buckminster Fuller, BrainyQuote.com, Xplore, Inc., 2016, https://www.brainyquote.com/quotes/quotes/r/rbuckmins100112.html.

14. Ronald Shapiro, Consultant, personal interview with Alan Kolp and Peter Rea, November, 2010.

15. Laurence Stenberg, *Age of Opportunity: Lessons from the New Science of Adolescence*, Houghton Mifflin Harcourt, Boston, 2014, 120.

16. William Aulet, "Entrepreneurship Development Program," MIT Management Executive Education, January 2015. http://executive.mit.edu/openenrollment/program/entrepreneurship_development_program/#.WGK8BVxRnIU.

17. Lory Hough, "How Teachers Can Make Caring More Common," *Usable Knowledge*, Harvard Graduate School of Education, September 8, 2014, https://www.gse.harvard.edu/news/uk/14/09/how-teachers-can-make-caring-more-common.

18. Regina Brett, "No Kid-ding: Ask Children the Right Questions," *Cleveland Jewish News*, August 30, 2016, http://www.clevelandjewishnews.com/columnists/regina_brett/no-kid-ding-ask-children-the-right-questions/article_bc52f8ca-6ed1-11e6-b05d-2fddfaa736b2.html.

EPILOGUE

1. Mary Crossan, Daina Mazutis, Mark Reno, and Peter Rea, *Handbook of Virtue Ethics in Business and Management*, Springer Science+Business Media, Dordrecht, Netherlands, 2015.

2. Kim Cameron, David Bright, and Arran Caza, "Exploring the Relationships Between Organizational Virtuousness and Performance," *American Behavioral Scientist*, 2004, 47: 766–790.

3. Thomas H. Lee, "Turning Doctors into Leaders," *Harvard Business Review*, April 2010, https://hbr.org/2010/04/turning-doctors-into-leaders.

4. "Driving Engagement by Focusing on Strengths," Gallup Poll, http://www.gallup.com/businessjournal/124214/driving-engagement-focusing-strengths.aspx.

5. William Aulet, "Entrepreneurship Development Program," MIT Management Executive Program, January 2015.

6. Jones Day, "FCPA 2016 Year in Review," January 2017, http://www
   .jonesday.com/files/Publication/49d526be-7232–4c55-bdcc-2e9be916
   65ab/Presentation/PublicationAttachment/f4f19e2f-8008–408f-9d61
   –41fec28146aa/FCPA%202016%20Year%20in%20Review.pdf.
7. Daniel Pink, *Drive: the Surprising Truth About What Motivates Us*,
   Riverhead, New York, 2011.

INDEX

accountability:
  leader's intent and, 37
  metrics and, 139
  team success and, 61, 68–69
acquisitions, 110, 203, 218
action, 162, 176–177, 182–185
adaptation gap, 220
adversity:
  overcoming, 248
  reaction to, 200, 205
  self-awareness and, 222
  as universal, 199
affordable loss, 99
African National Congress (ANC), 197
age, wisdom and, 132
Allegory of the Chariot, 117–119
altruism, 23, 65, 75, 239
Amazon.com, 61, 216
America's Cup, 160–161
amygdala, 91, 123–124, 126, 165, 191
Analects (Confucius), 192
&Beyond, 129–131
Angelou, Maya, 212
apartheid, 196–198, 200
Appell, Jesse, 33
appreciative inquiry, 152
Aquinas, Thomas, 132, 159
Ariely, Dan, 188
Aristotle, 7, 20, 58, 92, 176, 234, 238, 239, 248
arrogance, 207, 248
Artie (Ethical Protector), 101–104
astronauts, performance of, 5
Athena (goddess), 20–21
athletes, performance of, 5
attention, 162, 166–175
Augustine, Saint, 18

authenticity, 200–201
awareness, 162–166
Axial Age, 134

baby boomers, 251–252
Baird, 52
balance:
  life-work, 166–175, 178–183
  through temperance, 160
Baldwin Wallace University, 240
behavior change, 212
best practices, 189–190
Bezos, Jeff, 61
bias:
  in hiring decisions, 143–144, 147
  in performance evaluations, 147–148
Bonhoeffer, Dietrich, 201
brain (*see* human brain)
Brand, Christo, 198
brands
  organizational culture and, 115, 219, 243
  personal, 207
  trust in, 28
Brooks, David, 60
Buber, Martin, 178
bureaucracy, 36, 226, 229
Burger King, 57
business model, 219
bystander education, 84–86, 91, 99
bystander intervention, 86

Calhoun, Lawrence, 200
Candide (Voltaire), 17
careers:
  decisions about, 235
  virtue applied to, 242–243

carrot-and-stick motivation, 6–10, 138, 177
Cathy, Truett, 114–115
change:
    in innovative cultures, 218
    resistance to, 13, 76, 83, 258
character:
    assessing, 144
    competence and, 141–142
    competition and, 240–242
    developing, 154, 162, 206–207, 211,
        259–260
    high performance and, 5
    in martial arts, 102
    in military, 29–30
    selflessness as test of, 122
    in sports, 242
    vs. talent, 7
    in universities, 249–250
    virtue-defined, 6, 12
Character Strengths and Virtues (Seligman
        and Peterson), 238
Chasing Daylight (O'Kelly), 75
cheating, 188
Chef George, 24–25
Chick-fil-A, 114–115
China, 32–34, 134
Christensen, Clayton M., 215
Chrostowski, Brandon, 24
Chrysler, 56
Churchill, Winston, 73
CIA, 81–83
Cicero, 208
Cleveland Clinic, 13–15, 28, 48–50, 138,
        164, 204, 222–224
Cleveland Indians, 242
coaching, 149–153, 161, 190, 225, 240, 249
codes of conduct, 107, 207
Collins, Jim, 117, 131
comfort zone, 93
commander's intent, 36
common sense, 132
communication:
    compassionate, 65–66
    in patient care, 223–224
    team size and, 61
community involvement, 114–115, 247
compassion:
    absence of, 253–254
    business case for, 48–54
    case studies in, 46–47, 49
    definition of, 45
    as increasing trust, 125
    innovation and, 221

compassion (*Cont.*):
    in organizational culture, 233
    performance-based, 148, 149
    power of, 120
    spectrum of, 44
    in teamwork, 58–63
    universality of, 64
Compassion Tool Kit, 65–66
compensation:
    job satisfaction and, 138, 259
    as organizational expense, 137, 232
competence:
    assessing, 143
    character and, 141–142
    coaching and, 149–150
    in self-determination theory, 200
    success and, 236
    (*See also* strengths)
competition, 240–242
competitive advantage:
    for America's Cup, 160
    culture as, 203
    engagement as, 259
    strategy and, 35
    virtue and, 2, 3–4, 17, 37, 105
compliance:
    vs. engagement, 7
    ethics in, 123
    vs. good character, 188, 211
    minimum expectations and, 8
    regulatory, 8–10, 91, 258
    time consumed by, 168
    workplace justice and, 112–113
Confessions, The (Saint Augustine), 18
confidentiality, 27
confirmation bias, 87, 143
conflict de-escalation, 99, 126
Confucius, 192, 238
consolidated natural gas (CNG), 114
contradictions, reconciling, 131–132
conviction vs. circumstance, 4–5
corporate social value (CSV), 114
Cosgrove, Toby, 222
courage:
    absence of, 254
    to act on ethics, 83–89, 125
    business case for, 76–77
    developing, 92, 99
    function of, 96
    hope and, 201
    innovation and, 79–81, 221
    meaning of, 75
    obstacles to, 73–74, 86, 87

courage (*Cont.*):
  in organizational culture, 233
  organizational growth and, 78
  resilience and, 94–95
  spectrum of, 72
Courage Tool Kit, 99
cowardice, 77, 92
Csikszentmihalyi, Mihaly, 239
Culinary Institute of America, 24–25
Cultural Revolution (China), 32
culture:
  acquisitions and, 203
  change and, 80
  changing, 162
  compassion in, 63
  customer-centric, 222
  employees and, 133
  ethics and, 107, 188–189
  givers vs. takers in, 144, 145
  impact on conduct, 16–17, 83, 188, 212, 260
  innovative, 218–219, 229
  just, 52–53
  leaders' control of, 202
  in military academies, 243
  operational vs. growth, 230–231
  performance-driven, 109
  staffing and, 140–142
  strategy and, 189–190, 255
  strength-based vs. deficit-based, 179–180, 189
  trust and, 23, 35–38, 191
  virtue-based, 91, 111, 219, 220–222, 232, 243–245
  whistle-blowers and, 74
customers:
  building trust of, 120
  compassion for, 50, 53, 54–57, 221
  culture centered on, 222
  identifying, 55
  as innovation starting point, 228
  jobs as dependent on, 111
  social value and, 114

Darwin, Charles, 76
Day, George, 227
death, 75
decision making:
  discretionary, 168
  free will vs. fate in, 175
  in hiring employees, 142–143
  justice and, 127
  leader's intent in, 36–37

decision making (*Cont.*):
  pause-and-plan strategy for, 126
  principle over profit in, 189
  trust and, 26
  wisdom in, 234
deficit-based thinking, 152, 257
deliberate practice, 183–185
delusion, causes of, 169
Demings, W. Edwards, 4
Deng Xiaoping, 32
Denver, Rorke, 159, 162
dignity:
  earning, 34
  maintaining, 196
  for nursing home residents, 106
  treating others with, 103–104, 126, 187
discretionary effort, 6–7, 10, 38, 42, 43, 105
discretionary time, 183
disrespect, 2–3
District 6, Cape Town, South Africa, 196–197, 199
DIY (do it yourself), 57
DN (do nothing), 57
Doctors Without Borders, 239
Dodd-Frank Wall Street Reform and Consumer Protection Act, 9
Drucker, Peter, 115, 117
"The Dry Salvages" (Eliot), 121
Duckworth, Angela, 92, 145, 206
Dweck, Carol, 146, 152, 153

Eat, Pray, Love (Gilbert), 175
ecotourism, 129–131
Edelman trust barometer, 112–113
Edwins Leadership and Restaurant Institute, 24–26
egotism:
  changing habits and, 180
  in organizational culture, 35–36, 203
  overcoming, 104, 121–124
Einstein, Albert, 217, 235, 256
Eliot, T. S., 121, 154
Ellison, Larry, 160
Emerson, Ralph Waldo, 17, 129
empathy, 50, 52, 59, 150, 218, 221
employees:
  character vs. competence in, 140–142
  in China, 33–34
  coaching of, 149–153
  compassion in, 53
  with criminal records, 25
  culture and, 133
  executives as examples for, 107

employees (*Cont.*):
  hiring, 143–147
  as investment, 137–138
  layoffs of, 109–112, 244
  motivating, 6–7, 10, 138–142, 149, 220, 257, 259
  passion in, 50
  pay of (*see* compensation)
  performance evaluations of, 147–149
  trust building and, 113
employment projections, 235
empowerment, 36, 61, 259
engagement:
  of business leadership, 113
  vs. compliance, 7
  culture and, 38
  human capital investment and, 137–138
  increasing, 140–142, 258–259
  just work environment and, 105
  in organizations, 10–12, 42–43, 220
  performance and, 6, 139, 149
  relationships and, 4, 10
Enron, 8, 107
entitlement, 238, 248
entrepreneurship, 32, 77–78, 150, 249
Erikson, Erik, 178
Ethical Protectors, 15, 101–104, 123
ethics:
  compliance and, 8–9
  essence of, 122
  vs. legality, 105, 211
  in military academies, 29
  in organizations, 3, 85, 91, 188
  vs. profitability, 109–116
  teaching, 103
  (*See also* codes of conduct)
eudaimonia, 239

failure
  approaches to, 52
  innovation and, 78, 227, 232
  learning from, 93, 248
false growth mindset, 153
Fastow, Andrew, 107
fear:
  actual impact of, 175
  brain and, 123
  coping with, 76, 163, 165, 221
  of failure, 78, 83
  of loss, 87, 174, 230
  in organizations, 52, 115, 116
  suppressing, 173
  as survival tool, 76

fight-or-flight brain response, 123–124, 165, 172
financial crisis, 8–9, 109
Fitzgerald, F. Scott, 131
five5Cs (company, challenge, competence, character, conditioning), 181–182
flextime work, 169–170
flow, 239
Foreign Corrupt Practices Act (FCPA), 258
forgiveness, 119–121, 197, 198, 238
4Gs (giving, grit, growth mindset, gratitude), 144–147, 206, 245, 255
Four O'Clock in the Morning Test, 65
Frankl, Viktor, 116–117, 119, 201–202
Franklin, Benjamin, 119, 155, 192, 207
fraud, 84–85, 88–89, 107
free will, 174–175, 176, 179
Fuller, Buckminster, 246

Gandhi, Mohandas (Mahatma), 16, 91, 168
Gardner, John, 7
Gazarian, Artashes, 95–96
Gerstner, Lou, 219
Gilbert, Elizabeth, 175
Gilkey, Langdon, 104
Gilovich, Tom, 79
Gittel, Jody, 47–48
givers (personality type), 51, 52, 144–146, 201
globalization, 167–168
Global Leadership and Learning Institute, 15
global warming, 114, 216
goal setting, 145–146, 150, 183
Good to Great (Collins), 117
Goodwin, Doris Kearns, 178
Google, 58–59, 61, 149, 171, 215, 220
Gorbachev, Mikhail, 95
government, 113, 114
Grant, Adam, 51, 145, 244, 245, 247
gratitude:
  of employees, 144–146
  function of, 207–208
  journal of, 184, 209, 213
  justice and, 111
  as learned, 154
  practice of, 209–210, 213
  wisdom and, 125
Greatest Generation, 251
Great Recession, 109
Greece, 134
grit, 92–93, 144–146, 154, 213, 245, 251

groupthink, 83, 87
growth mindset, 144, 146, 152–154, 156, 206, 213
Guru Nanak Khalsa College, 166–167

habits:
    bad vs, good, 192
    changing, 134–135, 154, 164, 176–178, 182–185
    character and, 125
    controlling, 161
    for innovation, 220–232
    technology and, 171
    temperance and, 159
    time to create, 209
    virtue as, 257
Hagel, John, 93
Haidt, Jonathan, 118
happiness, 176, 200–201, 237, 239–240
Harris, Tristan, 171
Harvard Study of Adult Development, 236–237
healthcare:
    achieving quality in, 52–53
    compassion as factor in, 48
    economics of, 13, 138
    teamwork in, 62–63, 204
    trust as factor in, 29
Heraclitus, 134, 252
Hippocrates, 45
hiring, 143–147, 244
Hoban, Jack, 103–104, 123
Holmes, Oliver Wendell, Jr., 4
hope:
    absence of, 254
    after adversity, 200
    as decision, 202
    function of, 195, 201
    gratitude as by-product of, 207
    innovation and, 222
    as learned, 205–206
    in organizational culture, 234
    realistic, 201–204, 213
    spectrum of, 194
Hope Tool Kit, 213
huddle meetings, 223–224
human brain:
    calming, 164–165
    development of, 152
    justice and, 123–124
    multitasking and, 170–171
    in pause-and-plan strategy, 126
    rationality of, 169

human capital, 137
human nature, 259
humility, 86–87, 207, 248
Humphrey, Robert, 103
Huxley, Aldous, 17
hypocrisy, 16, 17, 107–108, 125, 186–187

IBM, 219, 245
India, 166–167
Individuals with Disabilities Education Act (IDEA), 9
injustice, 119–121
innovation:
    as company culture, 218–219
    courage and, 79–82
    5 growth habits for, 215–232
    as mindset, 248–249
    passion and, 144
    rules compliance and, 9, 10, 258
    social capital and, 59–60
    trust and, 26, 221
    virtue as factor in, 5
    in VUCA world, 258
    vulnerability and, 78
Institute for Management Development (IMD), 15
integrity:
    of business leadership, 113
    organizational culture based on, 91
    reputation for, 219
    virtues as supporting, 19–20
intelligence, 135, 141
intemperance, 160
Intuit, 61, 215, 225
investing, 24, 28, 111

Jake (athlete with cancer), 97–98
Jamna Auto, 166
Jaucourt, Louis de, 24
Jauhar, Randeep, 166
Jauhar, Sadar Bhupindar Singh, 166
job interviews, 143–147, 244
jurisprudence, 105–106, 133
justice:
    absence of, 254
    definition of, 101, 107, 112
    as goal, 133
    hypocrisy and, 107–108
    as increasing trust, 125
    in innovation, 221
    in organizational culture, 234
    practice of, 117–119, 123, 126–127
    self-interest and, 104–105, 121–122

justice (*Cont.*):
  spectrum of, 100
  standards for, 126
  in workplace, 109–116
Justice Tool Kit, 125–127

Katrina, Hurricane, 215–216
key performance indicators (KPIs), 5–6, 255
King, Martin Luther, Jr., 91, 195
Klaipeda, Lithuania, 95–96

Lafley, A. G., 226–227
Lao Tzu, 134
law:
  vs. ethics, 105
  performance evaluations and, 112, 148
  workplace justice and, 112
layoffs, 109–112, 244
leaders, leadership:
  carrot-and-stick, 6–8
  challenge of, 133
  character-based, 260
  checklist for, 68
  compassion in, 48
  courage of, 77
  culture shaped by, 35–36, 212
  employee engagement and, 220
  financial, 87–90
  focus on hard vs. soft assets, 136–137
  hypocrisy and, 17, 108, 186
  to improve society, 112–113
  in military, 162–163, 207
  mistakes acknowledged by, 87
  in operational vs. innovative culture, 231
  self-governing, 11
  strategy and, 58
  strength-based, 257
  success vs. virtue in, 18
  trust and, 30, 34, 43, 113, 221
  virtue-based, 7–12, 14, 37–38, 111, 134,
    206, 220, 254
leader's intent, 36–37, 42, 43, 61
learned helplessness, 175, 205
Lee, Tom, 204
Lewis, Michael, 108
Life of Brian (film), 83
life purpose, 93, 116–117, 132–133, 202,
  235, 239, 245–246
life-work balance, 166–175, 178–183
Lincoln, Abraham, 108, 207
listening skills, 151, 198
logos (logic) vs. *mythos* (meaning), 11–12
Lombardi, Vince, 183

longevity, 116, 173
Lowell, Abbott Lawrence, 236
Lower, William E., 48, 53
Lynch, William, 201

Mandela, Nelson, 91, 119, 197–198, 212
Man's Search for Meaning (Frankl), 201
Mao Zedong, 32
martial arts, 102–103
Massachusetts Institute of Technology
  (MIT), 77–78, 150, 215, 249
matchers (personality type), 51
Mayo Clinic, 138
McDonald's, 57
McGregor, Douglas, 6–7
Medina, Carmen, 81–83
meditation, 166
Medvec, Vicky, 79
meetings:
  huddle, 223–224
  strength-based, 190–191
mentors, 150
Merlino, James, 222–223
Merton, Thomas, 1
metrics:
  function of, 190–191, 256
  inadequacy of, 106
  need for, 139
  strategy and, 255
micromanagement, 36, 37
Microsoft, 149
middle way, 160
military:
  behavior expectations of, 206
  commander's intent in, 36
  performance expectations of, 5
military academies:
  virtue-based culture in, 243
  (*See also specific institutions*)
mistakes:
  accountability for, 74–75, 87
  being judged on, 29–30
  compassion and, 63
  customer relationships and, 120
  gratitude and, 146
  learning from, 78, 81, 93
  in organizations, 245
Montaigne, Michel de, 175
moral courage, 73, 75
Morgenthaler, David, 225
multitasking, 170–171, 183
Munger, Charlie, 135–136
My Prisoner, My Friend (Brand), 198

Nanak, Guru, 166
narcissism, 64, 121–122, 180, 244
NASA, 5, 39, 163–164
Nass, Clifford, 170
net worth, 34
Nietzsche, Friedrich, 117
not-yet growth mindset, 152–153, 156
nursing homes, 106

office politics, 136
O'Kelly, Eugene, 75
operational organizations, 230–231
optimism, 94, 202, 205–206, 213
Oracle Team USA, 160
organizational silos, 60, 80, 81, 223, 226, 229
organizations:
    compassion in, 48, 51–54
    culture of (see culture)
    entrenched processes in, 80–81
    ethics in, 3, 85, 91, 188
    fraud in, 84–85, 88–89
    good vs. bad rebels in, 81–83
    growing, 215, 218–220
    hard vs. soft assets in, 136–137
    performance expectations of, 5
    profit vs. principle in, 109–116
    relational coordination in, 48
    resistance to change in, 13
    ultimate concern of, 116–117
oxytocin, 173

pain points (of customers), 54, 55, 57, 222, 229
parenting, 249–251
Parker Hannifin, 14, 15, 46–47, 114, 242
Parthenon, 19, 20
passion:
    benefits of, 50
    for career, 236
    innovation and, 144
    stress and, 173
patients:
    compassion toward, 48, 49, 53, 54, 221
    vs. customers, 55
    satisfaction of, 222–224
    trust by, 28, 29
pause-and-plan strategy, 126, 165
pay (see compensation)
performance:
    culture driven by, 109
    evaluations of, 147–149
    expectations of, 164

performance (Cont.):
    focus in, 251
    4Gs and, 144–147, 255
    leveraging strengths and, 140–142, 148
    organizational, 220
    personality type and, 51
    relational coordination and, 48
    rules as factors in, 10
    stress and, 174
    teaching high level of, 4–6
    unconscious bias and, 143–144
    virtues as factors in, 1, 256, 260
pessimism, 205–206
Peterson, Chris, 238–239
Petraeus, David, 29–30
Phinda wildlife preserve, 129–131
physicians:
    as deficit-based thinkers, 257
    leadership approaches of, 151–152
pillars-and-pediment graphics:
    Compassion, 44
    Courage, 72
    explanation of, 19–20
    Hope, 194
    Justice, 100
    Temperance, 158
    Trust, 22
    Wisdom, 128
Plato, 18, 117, 118, 133
Plato's Academy, 12
Porter, Michael, 114
post-traumatic growth (PTG), 196, 199–201
post-traumatic stress disorder (PTSD), 3, 199, 200
power:
    arrogance and, 207
    self-interest and, 108, 244
    unethical conduct and, 245
prefrontal cortex, 86, 91, 123, 124, 126, 165, 191
prepare, probe, and propose framework, 246–247
Procter & Gamble (P&G), 226–227
productivity:
    compassion and, 49, 51
    flextime work and, 169–170
    happiness and, 176
    improving, 140–142
    measuring, 139
    multitasking and, 170
    stress and, 174
    team size and, 62
professional development tips, 245–249

profitability:
  ethical principles and, 109–116
  innovation and, 227
Project Aristotle, 58–59
prudence, 132
psychosomatic conditions, 2
publicly traded companies, 111

Real, Win, and Worth Process Roadmap,
  227–232
recession, 109, 115
reciprocal altruism, 23
redcoats (greeters), 49
reflection techniques, 155–156
regret, 78–79
relational coordination, 47–48
reputation, 28–30, 85, 91, 113, 219, 258
resentment, 119–120
resilience:
  after adversity, 93–95, 121, 145, 199,
    200
  courage as foundation of, 125
  neglect vs. care and, 172
  neurological basis for, 164
  physical, 161
  underestimated, 246
respect, 103–104, 123, 126, 187
restaurant industry, 24–26
return on assets (ROA), 109–111, 114
revenge, 120
risk:
  assessment of, 80
  compassion and, 53
  courage and, 77–81, 92, 99
  innovation and, 79, 230
  rules/regulations and, 258
  trust and, 26, 28, 42
Rita (apartheid survivor), 196–197, 199
Robben Island (South Africa) prison,
  197–198
Roosevelt, Theodore, 79
rules and regulations:
  bureaucrats and, 36
  compliance and, 8–10, 91, 188
  fostering trust and, 26
  function of, 220
  in jurisprudence, 105–106
  leadership based on, 11
  overreliance on, 258
  practicing wisdom and, 139
  in right to profit, 112
  virtuous conduct and, 88–89
Rumi, Jalaluddin, 199

sadness, effects of, 94–95
Sam (apartheid survivor), 197–198
Samson Global Leadership Academy, 15
Sarbanes Oxley (SOX) legislation, 8
scapegoating, 52
Schwarzkopf, Norman, 206
Scott Technology, 229–230
scripting, 89–91
self-awareness, 146, 164, 222, 235, 250
self-determination theory, 200–201
self-employment, 50
self-esteem, 238, 248, 250
self-interest:
  justice and, 104–105
  power and, 108
  vs. selflessness, 122–123, 125
self-preservation, 52, 117, 122, 201, 203
self-regulation, 248
Seligman, Martin, 205, 238–239
Selye, Hans, 172
seven classical virtues:
  function of, 1, 211
  in hospitality trade, 25–26
  interdependence of, 19–20
  vs. seven deadly sins, 135
  in team gratitude sessions, 210
  universality of, 12, 134, 232–233, 252,
    256, 260
  (see also individual virtues)
seven deadly sins, 135
Shapiro, Mark, 242
Sikhism, 166–167
similar-to-me syndrome, 143
Sisyphus, 211
social capital, 23, 59–60, 179
social interaction, 173, 201, 237
social media, 121
social support networks, 200, 246
Socrates, 18, 186
South Africa, 129–131, 196–197
space program, 39, 163
stewardship, 115
Stoics, 240
Stony Brook University School of
  Medicine, 15
stop list, 182–183
strategy:
  leadership and, 58
  organizational culture and, 189–190,
    255
  organizational role of, 35
  virtuous culture as, 37–38
Strecher, Victor, 245

strengths, leveraging, 140–142, 183, 187, 248, 257–258, 260
stress:
  neurology and, 164–165
  positive effects of, 172–174
  responses to, 172
  technology and, 171, 220
success:
  engagement and, 259
  gratitude and, 146
  leadership vs. strategy in, 58
  role of virtue in, 18
surveys, 56–57
survivors vs. victims, 195–196, 202, 238

takers (personality type), 51, 52, 144–146, 201
Taylor, Frederick, 148
teams:
  acquisitions and, 203
  compassion and, 48, 58–63, 67–70, 221
  culture and, 212
  givers vs. takers on, 145
  gratitude sessions for, 210, 213
  in healthcare, 62–63, 204
  in innovative cultures, 218, 224–226
  interdisciplinary, 226–227, 230
  leader's intent and, 37
  leveraging strengths in, 140–142, 257
  in organizational culture, 234
  personality types on, 51–52
  size of, 61–62
  in space program, 39
  trust and, 26, 27, 34–35, 42, 59, 221
  virtue practiced by, 4, 186–191, 256
Team Tool Kit, 68–70
technology:
  advances in, 220
  as distraction, 168, 183
  Walmart initiative in, 216–217
  workplace implications of, 169–171
Tedeschi, Richard, 200
Teller, Eric, 220
temperance:
  absence of, 254
  forming good habits via, 125
  function of, 159–160, 199
  innovation and, 222
  spectrum of, 158
  3As of, 162–177
Temperance Tool Kits:
  individual, 178–185
  team, 186–191

Theory X, 6, 7
Theory Y, 7
3As (apologize, acknowledge, atone), 40, 41
3As (awareness, attention, action), 162–177
Tijuana case study, 46–47
Tillich, Paul, 116
timelines:
  personal, 178
  team, 189
time management, 168, 169–171
Time Well Spent, 171
Tippett, Krista, 23
Tool Kits:
  Compassion, 65–67
  Courage, 99
  Hope, 213
  Justice, 125–127
  Team, 68–70
  Trust and Engagement, 42–43
  Wisdom, 155–156
training:
  to change habits, 162–164
  in ethics, 188
  nature of, 135
trauma, 93–95, 199
trust:
  absence of, 253
  barometer of, 112–113
  business case for, 26–28
  case studies, 24–26, 27, 31
  earning, 39–41, 42, 125
  as foundational, 23–24
  layoffs and, 110
  organizational culture of, 34–38, 59, 233
  relational coordination and, 47
  reputation and, 28–30
  rules and, 11, 258
  of society in business, 114
  on space program teams, 39
  spectrum of, 22
  sustainable innovation and, 221
  teams and, 26, 27, 34–35, 42, 59
trust and engagement tool kit, 42–43
Tutu, Desmond, 101
Twain, Mark, 6
Tyler (wildlife naturalist), 130

ultimate concern, 116–117, 132–133 (see also life purpose)
unconscious bias, 143–144, 147–148
unethical conduct, 245

universities, 249–250 (*see also specific institutions*)
University of California, Berkeley, 108
University of Louisville Medical School, 190
University of Miami (Florida), 15
University of Pennsylvania, 15
U.S. Air Force Academy, 15, 29, 206, 243
U.S. Marine Corps, 3, 103–104
U.S. Military Academy West Point, 15, 29–30, 73, 163, 206, 243
U.S. Naval Academy, 15, 29, 243
U.S. Navy SEALs, 162–163

value creation, 114
value proposition, 57, 111, 222, 229
values, organizational, 243–245, 256–257
Vinci, Leonardo da, 60
virtue:
    absence of, 253–254
    Athenian, 21
    business practice and, 18
    as competitive advantage, 2–4, 17, 37, 105, 203
    definition of, 1, 5
    developing, 154, 177, 239, 246
    in eulogy vs. on résumé, 60
    financial crisis and, 8
    interconnection of, 19, 174
    introduction into workplace, 12–14
    organizational culture and, 91, 111, 113–114
    as performance driver, 1–2, 6, 8, 14–16, 260
    personal relationships and, 2
    as practice, 2–3, 14, 18, 29, 86, 123, 155, 174, 177, 183–185, 211–212, 248, 250, 257, 259
    rules and, 8, 258–259
    sports and, 240–242
    teaching, 16, 189, 249–251, 254
    teamwork and, 58, 69, 189–190
    in ultimate concern, 118
    vice competing with, 133
    (*See also* seven classical virtues)

voice of the customer (VoC), 54–57, 223, 229
voice of the patient, 222–223
Voltaire, 17
VUCA (volatile, undertain, complex, ambiguous) world
    coping with, 4–6, 18, 69, 258
    financial stability vs. employment stability in, 110–111, 220
    innovative cultures in, 218, 219, 248
    organizational flexibility in, 137
    performance evaluations and, 149
    risk and, 230
    stress and, 174
    teams and, 212
vulnerability, 77–78

Wake Forest University, 15
Walmart, 215–218
WalmartLabs, 61, 215, 217
Watson, Tom, 245
Weisbord, Marvin, 203–204
whistle-blowers, 74, 83–84
Wilson, Harold, 76
wisdom:
    absence of, 254
    in action, 129
    cultivating, 125, 136, 154, 155
    in decision making, 234
    definition of, 132–134
    through forgiveness, 121
    innovation and, 221–222
    in jurisprudence, 105–106
    spectrum of, 128
Wisdom Tool Kit, 155–156
work environment:
    bias in, 144
    justice in, 105, 109–112, 126–127
    revenge in, 120
WorldCom, 8
Wright, Bob, 206

yoga, 166
Yousafzai, Malala, 73

ABOUT THE AUTHORS

PETER REA is Vice President of Integrity and Ethics at Parker Hannifin Corporation. In 2012, Peter joined Parker in a newly established position with the purpose of preserving Parker's reputation and protecting its financial strength. Previously, Peter was the founding Burton D. Morgan Chair for Entrepreneurial Studies and the founding director of the Center for Innovation and Growth at Baldwin Wallace University. The center provides a practical forum for students, business leaders, and business owners to create economic and social value through innovation guided by integrity. He has lectured and consulted internationally in the areas of strategy, leadership, culture, and ethics defined as virtue.

JAMES K. STOLLER, M.D., M.S., is professor and chairman of the Education Institute at Cleveland Clinic and a pulmonary/critical care physician in the Respiratory Institute there. He holds the Jean Wall Bennett Professorship in Emphysema Research and the Samson Global Leadership Academy Endowed Chair at Cleveland Clinic. He designed and has codirected the Cleveland Clinic Leading in Health Care course and the Samson Global Leadership Academy for Healthcare Executives at Cleveland Clinic. He also directs the American Thoracic Society's Emerging Leadership Program. He has presented and consulted internationally regarding developing physician leaders at medical schools, business schools, and healthcare organizations.

ALAN KOLP is the holder of the Baldwin Wallace University Chair in Faith and Life and professor of religion. Alan was the cofounder of the Center for Innovation and Growth at Baldwin Wallace University. Before coming to Baldwin Wallace, Alan was dean and professor at Earlham College and Earlham School of Religion in Richmond, Indiana. He spent a year in Germany on a Fulbright Fellowship and has taught in England. He has been a visiting scholar at the Graduate Theological Union, University of California at Berkeley and at Kellogg College, Oxford University.